Postmodernism and Continental Philosophy

Selected Studies in Phenomenology
and Existential Philosophy 13

SPEP

Postmodernism and Continental Philosophy

Edited by
Hugh J. Silverman
and
Donn Welton

State University of New York Press

Published by
State University of New York Press, Albany

Printed in the United States of America

For information, address State University of New York Press,
State University Plaza, Albany, N.Y., 12246

Library of Congress Cataloging in Publication Data

Postmodernism and continental philosophy.

(Selected studies in phenomenology and existential
philosophy ; 13)
1. Philosophy, Modern. 2. Postmodernism.
I. Silverman, Hugh J. II. Welton, Donn.
III. Series.
B790.P67 1987 190 86-30068
ISBN 0-88706-521-X
ISBN 0-88706-522-8 (pbk.)

10 9 8 7 6 5 4 3 2

Contents

Introduction

Hugh J. Silverman

What is the relation between Postmodernism and Continental Philosophy? And why should this relation be a matter of importance now? In the North American context, a volume on such a topic would have been practically inconceivable ten years ago. Something important has taken place in the development of continental philosophy that its relation to postmodernism should now become relevant. Something important in the development of cultural criticism has taken place such that postmodernism enters into the context of continental philosophy. Indeed the question might well be asked at the present stage: is postmodernism anything other than continental philosophy, and is continental philosophy anything other than postmodernism?

To answer the latter question affirmatively and unequivocally would doubtless be extreme. However, that the question is even possible is indicative of a significant reformulation and consolidation of thinking in the 1980's. Continental philosophy has become the name for that whole orientation in thinking that appeals to certain trends in European philosophy since the late nineteenth century. Hegel, Marx, Nietzsche, Freud, Husserl, Heidegger, Sartre, Merleau-Ponty, Gadamer, Ricoeur, Foucault, Derrida, and Kristeva have become the textual context out of which continental philosophy is moulded. These figures (among others) unquestionably mark the domain characterized by continental philosophy as it is practiced in the English-speaking world.

Contrary to what one might expect, continental philosophy does not refer to whatever thinking takes place or has taken place in Europe. Indeed, many currents of thought originating from and practiced in Europe would not be considered to be within the frame of continental philosophy.

Rather, continental philosophy constitutes a general network of communication and dialogue in which common concerns, identifiable issues, and a recognizable language prevail in the practice of philosophy. This does not mean that all continental philosophers agree with one another. Not by any means. However, the basis of their disagreement can be articulated and identified. Criticism, debate, and disagreement have a context and a space in which philosophizing takes place. Sometimes one can translate these concerns into alternative modes of philosophical research. In the end, however, the real task is to advance research within the domain of continental philosophy *per se*. To the extent that translation and cross-communication is possible – all the better, but current research and new strides in the field must necessarily continue independently of their reformulation into alternative practices.

It is sometimes thought that continental philosophy has a restricted domain, that it is limited to matters of metaphysics, aesthetics, philosophical psychology, and political theory. One need only look at the tables of contents of former volumes in this series, such as *Descriptions* and *Hermeneutics and Deconstruction* (edited by Silverman and Ihde), to see the breadth of concerns from philosophy of science to philosophy of language to philosophy of literature exhibited by those working in continental philosophy – particularly in North America.

And what of postmodernism? Originally formulated in the context of architecture – even by some architects who were former proponents of modernism – postmodernism has become a broader concern in the arts and culture at large. What was modernism in literature, in painting and sculpture, in fashion, in science, and in philosophy is reread in relation to the limits of such modes of thinking. Taking modernism to its extremes, to its margins, to its frames is to rethink modernism altogether.

Modernism in philosophy goes back a long way: Bacon, Galileo, Descartes – pillars of the modernist conception of the fashionable, the new, and the innovative, – in short, all that is a break with classical and ancient tradition. Here philosophy attempted to be "scientific," to appeal to a rigorous method and not to authority. With Kant, modernism took on a new shape: it combined the rationalism of Descartes and the empiricism of Locke and Hume. Modernism in philosophy could now be defined in relation to a transcendental and an empirical aspect – particularly where the transcendental could offer a unification of the manifold of experience by rational means. An *'Ich denke'* which could prescribe what was presented to it would set the limits to apperception. With this coordination of the subjective and the objective, the groundwork for a modernist philosophy was established solidly for Western philosophy in general. What European philosophers did with this ground was to formulate a notion of subjectivity that would not only become the place of retreat but also the condition for all knowledge.

This double strategy reformed modernism in such a way that it could be consistent with the literary and artistic movements that would later carry the same name. What Hegel, Kierkegaard, and Husserl – to name three diverse examples – did with the concept of subjectivity made a theory of consciousness possible. And it was some variety of this theory that various writers such as Kafka, Joyce, Woolf, and Proust found indispensible for a proper view of the world. The proper worldview was also a complexed one: Freud, Bergson, and James all presented a theory of the pure ego, of temporal experience, and of consciousness as separate from the objective view of things. The only way for modernism to gain its ground was to abstract itself from the external world. Heisenberg and Gödel found ways to incorporate uncertainty and indeterminacy, Tarski and Russell sought to provide a theory of descriptions which would not be contaminated by natural language, and Klimt, Klee, Dufy, and Matisse escaped into a world of fantasy and design. Modernism established itself by assuring itself of a transcendental view of things, a *pensée de survol* that would be indubitable, a meta-language about which multiplicity could be understood and explained. Modernism's optimism was combined with a deadly despair. Modernism's aspirations were mixed with the horror that the very idea of faschism, namely the dominance and overcoming of the whole world, could even be attempted.

In response to and corresponding with the development of faschism in Europe, modernism also elaborated an artform that sought to express the anguish, despair, frustration, and exaggerations of human experience at that time. German expressionism – as in Beckmann, Nolde, and Munch – showed that the powers of a transcendental view of things, where all could be put in order, where rules could replace human existence, where a plan could resolve all confusion and disharmony was exceptionally dangerous and horrifying. Fritz Lang's *Metropolis* dramatizes the particular effects of such attempts to actualize a certain utopia, one whose effect was fundamentally dystopian. The Charlie Chaplin *Modern Times* film (from which Sartre *et al* devised an ironic title for their journal in 1945) depicts with humor the stultifying effects of over-technologization without thought and mechanization without humanization. The context was one of supernationalism and political blackmail in the face of extreme economic threat and unemployment.

The philosophical response of a Heidegger was to reject the transcendental overview and to replace it with an account of our being-in-the-world as a relation of beings to Being. Interpretation, understanding, and authenticity were called for. To hear the call of Being was to situate oneself in a context in which despair and related emotions could be meaningful but not oppressive. Return to thinking, return to the fields and countrypaths, return to the Greek philosophers – these were effectively Heidegger's aspirations. Meanwhile Sartre picked up on the phenomenology, but in its existentialized version. While Sartre agreed with the basic response to a transcendental view of the self, of subjectivity, of knowledge, he also found something worrisome in it. Correspondingly he offered an account of consciousness that had no content, no rules, no form, no ordering of the world. In consciousness was freedom. In consciousness was negation. In consciousness was the constitution of self as other. Not that Rimbaud did not already say *"je est un autre,"* but Sartre made philosophical sense of the claim. In the face of oppression, occupation, and human destruction everywhere, he offered an account of freedom. We are free. To be free meant to be able to choose even when it looked as though no choice were possible anywhere, where it seemed that contraint was the only possible interpretation of things. Sartre was not alone in this view. Malraux, Camus, and many others also called for political action, resistance, refusal to follow orders, to mould to the modernist view offered to them. With this refusal and theoretical account of freedom, it became possible to think of a philosophical, theoretical, and political practice based on rebellion, anti-self-reification, and ultimately choice and reaction. These were the signs of modernism in crisis.

What Merleau-Ponty offered and what the others were unable to develop effectively was a theory of embodiment. From the end of the Second World War in 1945, the modernism of the interbellum period, of despair, of anguish, of escape into fantasy or off to America, of anti-authoritarian consciousness and yet an obsession with the existentialization of consciousness as the only resource now took on new shape. Experience was not just projectively free, unconstrained, and unbounded as Sartre had been proposing. With Merleau-Ponty, it was clear that experience is embodied, lived, and imbued with signification. It was not until after Merleau-Ponty produced his first major work – the *Phenomenology of Perception* (1945) – that he realized how important a theory of language was for his account of the lived body.

His reading of Saussure and the linking up of phenomenology with semiology was the first indication of a new way of thinking about modernism. Wittgenstein was right: language is important. For a long time, the European phenomenologists could not see it, – not that Merleau-Ponty learned it from Wittgenstein any more than did Heidegger who also turned to language in the post-war period. Similarly the early American commentators on phenomenology and existentialism in the 1950s did not grasp the importance of language. For them, the existential, experiential, consciousness-based epistemology along with a theory of perception and a way to read literature intelligently were the primary interests. Even Merleau-Ponty's own accounts of a phenomenology of language were largely ignored until the 1970s. The growth of structuralism in the 1960s, however, made such negative attitudes toward language effectively impossible in the succeeding decade.

In the 1950s, signs of the breakdown of modernism could be seen in the theatre of the absurd, in the new French novel of surface presentations, in the very idea that science might not be cumulative, and in the appeal to language in philosophical thinking. Beckett, Ionesco, Genet, Robbe-Grillet, Sarraute, Simon, Duras, Butor – the list seems almost unending – were the marks of a new way of thinking about human experience. Officially "absurd," effectively "realistic", these writers sought to express the decline of modernism by offering something radically other – a sense of repetition, conformity, accumulation, meaninglessness, aimlessness, enigma, complexity, ambiguity, dramatic intensity, and perceptiveness. To be modern was fundamentally to be new, *à la mode*, excitingly different. In this sense, the 1950s were not devoid of modernism. One might even say that there was new hope in novelty. But the character of novelty had changed. As Beckett's character in *Malone Dies* reports: "I must go on, I can't go on, I will go on . . . " The end of modernism would not mean that everything stops and the world comes to an end. Yet the fear of such a cataclysmic destruction was paramount in the 1960s. By contrast, however, there was as yet no way to think apocalypse without the postmodernist incision.

The confluence of structuralism, phenomenology, marxism, and psychoanalysis in the 1960s brought about the phenomenon known as post-structuralism. In America, structuralism can be dated from the time of the famous *Structuralist Controversy* conference at Johns Hopkins in 1967. Shocking to literary scholars in the United States, the aftershocks of the controversy about structuralism did not hit philosophers until much later. Many phenomenologists were at first quite hostile. While Merleau-Ponty was close friends with Lévi-Strauss and Lacan, American phenomenologists were loath to accept the affinities between phenomenology and structuralism despite their many differences. With the *Schizo-Culture* conference at Columbia University in 1974, new light was shed on this conflict. Post-structuralism began to take shape in America. While Lacan and various Lévi-Straussians had been speakers at the 1966 Hopkins event (and Derrida, who was effectively unknown in the United States, presented his now celebrated "Structure, Sign and Play in the Human Sciences" and concerned primarily the writings of Lévi-Strauss), the principal names at the 1974 Columbia conference included Foucault, Deleuze, Guattari, Lyotard, R. D. Laing, and Arthur Danto. With the Schizo-Cuture conference, poststructuralism in America was born.

This history of landmark conferences in America has itself become an item of notice, at once a spectator sport and a colloseum. The 1976 Stony Brook conference on "The Post-Structuralist Enterprise: Reading(s) of Jacques Derrida" was the first in America to both incorporate Derrida and concentrate on his writings. Perhaps the particular confluence of some Stony Brook philosophers and literary scholars with "continental" tendencies (including Jan Kott, who had been a participant at the Johns Hopkins conference a decade earlier) made such an event possible. Here figures such as Gasché, Garver, Hillis Miller, *et al.* showed that structuralism had entered a new phase – and most importantly this new phase included a rapprochment with phenomenology on the one hand and analytic philosophy on the other. The interest in post-structuralism gradually became a preoccupation with the significance and practice of deconstruction. Here the Derridean mark had become unmistakeable. And the International Association for Philosophy and Literature (IAPL) conference on "Deconstruction and its Alternatives" in 1983 (again at Stony Brook) was one of its dominant expressions. The dimensions of the debate around deconstruction had become enormous. Advocates of Derridean readings of texts, differences between Derrida and De Man, and the impact of Heidegger on Derridean practice were juxtaposed with debates about the differences between deconstruction and Frankfurt-style critical theory, pragmatism, Althusserian marxism, and post-structuralism in general. Here the voices of Donato, Spivak, Allison, Gasché, Wood, and De Man *in absentia* were the most marked. But finally with the Loyola (Chicago) conference on "Deconstruction and Philosophy" in 1985, the question of the role of deconstruction in philosophy *per se* was thematized and given explicit consideration. Throughout the conference, Derrida's own questioning and responding to interpretations and accounts of deconstruction in philosophical study made it an important event. Finally the IAPL conference on "Postmodernism" at the University of Kansas in May 1987 brought the traditions of continental philosophy into full debate with themes in postmodernism *per se*. Not only were the figures of Jameson, Spivak, Casey, Margolis, Bernstein, and Framton brought into juxtaposition but also important issues in architectural theory, feminism, theory of language, political theory, and poetics were intensely debated within a postmodernist framework.

The present volume entitled *POSTMODERNISM AND CONTINENTAL PHILOSOPHY* can hardly be abstracted from this sequence of events on the American scene in the 1980s. Resulting directly from two conferences of the Society for Phenomenology and Existential Philosophy in 1984 and 1985, these essays must necessarily be situated in the context of other research activities taking place during that "time-frame." While none of the contributors to this volume would have been present at the 1966 Johns Hopkins or the 1974 Columbia events, only a couple participated (and not as speakers) at the 1976 Stony Brook conference on Derrida and post-structuralism. However many of the authors of essays here either attended or offered papers at the 1983 "Deconstruction and its Alternatives" conference and again in a major way at the 1987 Kansas "Postmodernism" event. Some of the contributors to this volume are seasoned continental philosophers. Lingis, O'Neill, Dillon, Gillan, Wurzer, Krell and Young are recognized figures on the North American continental philosophical scene. Although McDonald, McKenna, and Judovitz all come officially from French studies, their work is eminently philosophical. Furthermore, a range of younger scholars (including Chaffin, Olkowski, White, Taft, Vasey, Freeman, and Schrift) are already bringing eminence to newer tendencies in continental philosophical research.

Julia Kristeva opens the discussion with an essay on the role of imagination in melancholic discourse. With the exception of the 1985 SPEP meetings in which she gave this lecture, Julia Kristeva has not attended previous conferences of the Society. Nevertheless Kristeva, who teaches in the department of "Texts and Documents" at the University of Paris-VII, is a significant figure in the development of postmodernism and continental philosophy in North America. She signals the particular confluence of phenomenology, structuralism, semiotics, psychoanalysis, deconstruction, and feminism. That her writings incorporate interpretations and aspects of all of these tendencies in continental philosophy is an important feature of current directions in postmodernism as well.

The themes that prevail in this volume arise out of and mark the vanguard of research in the continental tradition as it has been practiced in North America for at least three decades. The Merleau-Pontean concern with embodiment is here linked up not only with the importance of language but also with desire. Desire as one of Lyotard's major concerns in *Discours, Figure* (1971) and *Economie libidinale* (1974) is also an indispensable feature of Deleuze's writings of the 1970s. The debate among Lingis, Dillon, and Krell arises out of a Merleau-Pontean perspective but is linked implicitly with the problem of desire in postmodernism. In short, a key problem for postmodernism – as is particularly evident in Kristeva's essay – is what to do with desire.

One way to answer the question about desire is to raise again the issue of representation. As Foucault presents it in *The Order of Things* (1966), representation as a way of thinking, as an epistemological framework, arose sometime at the end of the Renaissance and continued up to about the time of Kant's anthropology in the late eighteenth century. In this sense, Descartes would be one of the classic models for the notion of representation. Judovitz examines this possibility and shows how representation operates in the cartesian formulation. With Hegel, the problem of representation has become acute, for in the end the logic leaves no room for representation. Dialectic makes representation ultimately impossible. And with Heidegger, interpretation has replaced representation. A hermeneutics of being removes any position from which representation could take place.

In this respect, metaphysics is no longer possible in anything like a traditional sense. The end of metaphysics could quite naturally be the achievement of metaphysics. This would have been the Hegelian hope. But if metaphysics is no longer viable, what is the place of values? The Nietzschean problematic is to continually revalue all values. Yet when Heidegger reads Nietzsche, as White shows, another consideration appears. European nihilism implies the interpretation of being as nothing. For Heidegger, however, the nothing that affirms itself in the understanding of what is (i.e. beings) brings out the very space in which truth can appear. The difficulty is that with the appearance of truth comes a set of values. This is where Gillan's account of value is linked up with power, discourses of power, and the role of desire or affectivity in the articulation of power. Values are constituted in discourse, and the domination of certain discourses determine the prevalance of certain values. The insistence of certain discourses establish therefore the values that are to be preferred. The effect is that as the line from Nietzsche through Heidegger to Foucault shows, there are no ultimate values, – at best values are to be reformulated – revalued for oneself, but the limits of such revaluation are set by the limits of possible discourses at any particular time.

The concern of philosophical feminism has been that male discourse predominates, establishes values, and asserts them without regard to gender difference. Male discourse – especially in philosophy – offers patriarchical texts as the model for human sexuality, desire, and even fashion. One of the tasks of a philosophical feminism is to re-write this discursive (male) dominance through the reinterpretation and re-reading of traditional texts, traditional forms of logic, traditional presentations – even of clothing.

Within the framework of postmodernist discourse, deconstruction has come to play an important role. Christie McDonald offers a reading of the status of deconstruction in the 1980s, while Schrift traces some of its history back through Nietzsche to Derrida. O'Neill (in his own inimitable style) takes up the very context in which the essays, texts, and discourses in this volume were proffered. Here then the whole question of the professional conference, its formations and formulations are brought under scrutiny. Taking the conference itself as a text, reading it deconstructively, brings together the whole history of continental philosophy as it has been articulated in North America through a reading of the invitational and presentational structure of the conference itself.

If this array from the problem of desire and language, the limits of representation as a philosophical preference, the ends of metaphysics as a traditional philosophical commitment, the rewriting of patriarchial discourse as gender dominance, and the assessment of deconstruction itself in its present forms and practices can offer a viable account of where postmodernism links up with continental philosophy, then the project of this volume will have achieved its aim. However, to thematize the issue even more precisely, two essays – one by McKenna, the other by Wurzer – provide an account of postmodernism itself, its articulation, its verbal play, and its relation to tradition *per se.* The philosophical reading of culture will presume a theoretical formulation not only of its traditions, but also of its contemporary assessments and activities. This volume acts in aid of such an end.

Without the careful proofreading and indexing by James Hatley, help with copyediting questions by Anderson Weekes, and the effective managing of some administrative details by J Barry, this volume would have undergone more delays and tie-ups than are its due. I am grateful to the State University of New York at Stony Brook for providing support of their time and assistance, and to the Philosophy Department for making xeroxing facilities available. The helpfulness of the SUNY Press staff in Albany, notably its Director William Eastman and its Production Manager Judy Block have been invaluable in the continued development and success of these SPEP volumes.

Wien, Austria
3 August 1987

Part I.
Psychoanalytic Discourse of the Speaking Subject

1. On Melancholic Imagination

Julia Kristeva

In my book, *Histoires d'amour* (*Stories of Love*), I argue that the transferential discourse is an amorous one and that in our modern civilization the psychoanalyst's couch is the only place explicitly designated by the social pact for the complaint of a wounded lover to be articulated and the search for a possible love to be (verbally) enacted in the register of narcissism or the oedipal complex. Now precisely because it is an amorous discourse, analytic speech possesses the qualities that both give it its effectiveness and at the same time reveal the essential (but otherwise undetectable) laws governing every enunciation. Which ones?

The paradoxical artifice of the psychoanalytic situation – a couch where one reclines and speaks and a chair where the other sits and listens – blocks the motor functions and facilitates the displacement of drive energy towards speech. Because it is essentially a transferential, that is to say, amorous discourse, the analytic speech known as "free association" is not merely intellectual, but also implicitly affective. Therefore, it cannot be understood on the basis of the linguistic model which deploys verbal signs as "signifiers" and "signifieds." Analytic speech operates with signs that include at least three kinds of representation: *word presentation [Wortvorstellung]* (close to the linguistic signifier), *thing presentation [Ding- or Sachvorstellung]* (close to the linguistic signified), and *representation of affects* (unstable, fluctuating, psychic inscriptions controlled by the primary processes of "displacement" and "condensation," which I call "semiotic" as opposed to "symbolic" representations tributary to the system of language). In his *Metapsychology*, Freud firmly establishes the first two types of representations (that of words and that of things). His theory on the representation of affects is, however, more obscure. As you may know, several French psychoanalysts such as Green, Rosolato, and Aulagnier have applied their efforts in this domain. And it is there that my definition of the *semiotic*, a term which I proposed in 1973, also belongs.

On the Melancholic Imaginary

Melancholy is amorous passion's somber lining. A sorrowful pleasure, a lugubrious intoxication constitute as much the banal background from which our ideals or euphoria break away as that fleeting lucidity which fractures the hypnosis entwining two people.

Rather than seeking the meaning of despair (which is evident or metaphysical), let me admit that there is no meaning aside from despair. The child-king becomes irremediably sad before proffering his first words: it is being separated from his mother, despairingly, with no going back, that makes him decide to try to recuperate her, along with other objects, in his imagination and, later, in words. The semiology interested in the degree zero of symbolism is unfailingly led to pose itself questions concerning not only the amorous state but also its somber corollary – melancholy. Thereby to recognize, in the same movement, that if no writing exists that is not amorous, nor does an imagination exist that is not, manifestly or secretly, melancholic.

Nevertheless, melancholy is not French. Protestantism's rigor or Christian Orthodoxy's matriarchal weight show themselves to be more ready accomplices of the bereaved individual – when they do not invite him to a morose revelry. For the Catholic West, sadness is a sin and the wretched citizens of the "abode of woe" are placed by Dante in the circles of Inferno (Canto III). True though it be that French medievalism presents us with delicately perceived portrayals of sorrow, the Gallic tone, renascent and enlightened, belongs more to jest than to nihilism; Rousseau and Nerval cut here sad – and exceptional – figures.

Variable according to the religious climate, melancholy is affirmed in religious doubt. Nothing sadder than a dead God, and Dostoevsky himself was troubled by the distressing image of the dead Christ in Holbein's painting, counterposed as it is to the "truth of the resurrection." Particularly propitious to this black, melancholic humor are those epochs witnessing the collapse of religious and political ideals: the epochs of crises. An unemployed worker is, admittedly, less suicidal than a jilted woman; but in times of crisis, melancholy imposes itself, lays down its archaeology, produces its representations and its knowledge. Certainly, melancholy in writing has little to do with the clinical stupor of melancholia; I find myself here before an enigmatic chiasmus that will not cease to preoccupy me: if loss, mourning, absence set the imaginary act in motion and permanently fuel it as much as they menace and undermine it, it is also undeniable that the fetish of the work of art is erected in disavowal of this mobilizing affliction. The artist: melancholy's most intimate witness and the most ferocious combatant of the symbolic abdication enveloping him .... Until death strikes and suicide imposes its triumphant conclusion upon the void of the lost object ....

Melancholia is to designate here the clinical symptomatology of inhibition and asymbolia that an individual displays sporadically or chronically, often in alternation with the so-called manic phase of exultation. These two phenomena (dejection-exultation), in less marked forms and in more frequent alternation, constitute the depressive temperament of the neurotic. While recognizing the two phenomena to be different, Freudian theory detects in both the same impossible mourning of the maternal object. Question: Impossible because of what paternal failing; or, because of what biological fragility? Melancholia – for let me take up again the generic term after having distinguished the psychotic and neurotic symptomatologies – has the formidable privilege of situating the analyst's interrogation at the intersection of the biological and the symbolic. Parallel series? Consecutive sequences? Or aleatory intersection requiring specification? Or, again, another relation to be invented?

The Depressive: Hating or Hurt?

According to classical psychoanalytical theory (Abraham, Freud, Klein), depression, like mourning, hides an aggressivity against the lost object, thereby revealing the ambivalence on the part of the afflicted with respect to the object of his mourning. "I love him/her" (the depressive seems to say concerning a being or object lost), "but, even more I hate him/her in myself; but because I hate him/her, this other in myself is a bad ego, I am bad, I am worthless, I am destroying myself."

However, with the treatment of narcissistic personalities, modern analysts have been led to comprehend a different modality of depression (Jacobson, among others). Far from being a dissimulated assault upon another – imagined hostile because frustrating – sorrow would be the signalling of an incomplete, empty, and wounded primitive ego. Such a person does not consider himself as injured but as striken by a fundamental lack, by a congenital deficiency. His grief hides neither the guilt nor failing of a vengeance hatched in secret against the ambivalent object. Rather, his sorrow would be the most archaic expression of a narcissistic wound, unable to be symbolized or named, too precocious for any exterior agent (subject or object) to be correlated to it.

For this type of narcissistic, depressive sorrow is, in reality, his only object; more exactly, it constitutes a substitute object to which he clings, cultivating and cherishing it, for lack of any other. In this context, suicide is not a camouflaged act of war but a reuniting with sorrow and, beyond it, with that impossible love, never attained, always elsewhere; such are the promises of the void, of death . . . .

Is Mood a Language?

Sorrow is the fundamental mood characterizing depression and even if manic euphoria alternates with it in the bipolar forms of this state, grief is the principal manifestation betraying the sufferer. Sorrow leads into the enigmatic domain of affects such as anxiety, fear, or joy. Irreducible to its verbal or semiological expressions, sorrow (like every affect) is the *psychic representation of displacements of psychic energy* provoked by external or internal traumas.

Presuming that the affect is the most archaic inscription of internal and external events, how does one get from there to signs? By following one hypothesis, the infant, prompted by separation (note the necessity of a "lack" if the sign is to arise) at first produces or utilizes objects or vocalizations that are the symbolic equivalents of that lacking (H. Segal, 1957). Subsequently, and from the so-called depressive position, he tries to signify the sorrow that submerges him by producing in his own ego elements that, while alien to the exterior world, are to correspond to that lost or displaced exteriority: we are, then, no longer in the presence of equivalences but of symbols in the proper sense of the word. I add to the position of Segal that such a triumph over sorrow is rendered possible by the ego's capacity to now identify no longer with the lost object but with a third position: father, form, schema. This identification with a third position, that may be called phallic or symbolic identification, ensures the subject's entry into the universe of signs and of creation. This triumph operates on the basis of denegation (*Verneinung*) and can in some circumstances condition a position of disavowal or of mania ("No, I haven't lost anything; I evoke, I signify: through the artifice of signs and for myself, I bring into existence that which has separated itself from me.").

The father-support of this symbolic triumph is not the well-known Oedipal father but, indeed, that "imaginary father," "father of personal prehistory" that for Freud guaranteed so-called primary identification. Later, that essential moment in the symbol's formation which is constituted by the manic position lining depression can, in entirely different circumstances, such as literary creation, manifest itself by the constitution of a symbolic filiation (hence the recourse to proper names arising out of the subject's real or imaginary history, of which the subject presents himself as the inheritor or the equal).

Object-depression (implicitly aggressive), narcissistic depression (logically anterior to libidinal object relations): affectivity at grips with signs – exceeding, threatening, or modifying them. Departing from this picture, the problem that interests me here could be summarized as follows: Aesthetic – and, in particular, literary – creation, as well as religious discourse in its imaginary fictional essence, proposes a configuration of which the prosodic economy, the dramaturgy of characters and the implicit symbolism are an extremely faithful semiological representation of the subject's battle with symbolic breakdown. This literary or religious representation is not an *elaboration* in the sense of "becoming conscious" of the inter- and intrapsychic causes of moral pain. In this it differs from the psychoanalytic path that proposes for itself the dissolution of this symptom. However, this literary (and religious) representation possesses a real and imaginary efficacy that, concerned more with catharsis than elaboration, is a therapeutic method utilized in all societies throughout the ages. If psychoanalysis considers itself more effective, particularly in reinforcing the subject's ideational possibilities, it additionally owes to itself the enrichment to be gained through an added attention to sublimation solutions of our crises.

In the following, I attempt to outline two variants of these sublimation solutions – in Nerval and Dostoevsky.

"Black Sun" – Prosody – Esoterism

Gerard de Nerval (1808–1855) interweaves with "melancholy's black sun" a complicity formed of evasion and osmosis, of triumphant flight and voluptuous immersion. "El Desdichado," which translates from the Spanish as "the disinherited" or, rather, as "the despairing," confesses to being "gloomy," "bereft," and "unconsoled." But he is only the funereal double of that conqueror who has "twice traversed . . . the Acheron" and who is no other than the poet Orpheus.

Two essential methods seem to offer themselves to the protagonist enshrouded in gloom as means to displace melancholy's "black sun." On the one hand, it is a matter of the esoteric symbolism that often retakes, amplifies, or embellishes the traumatic or maturative moments or themes essential to the psychic economy, becoming, in this context, initiation themes. On the other hand, and above all, the antidepressive is the "starred lute": the poetic art that transposes the affect into an elliptic, lacunary prosody, formed by condensation and allusion. Repetitive, often monotone, this prosody imposes upon affective fluidity a grid as exacting in its deciphering (presupposed is a detailed knowledge of mythology and of esoterism) as it is supple and indefinite by its very allusiveness. Who are the Prince of Aquitaine, the "only dead star," Phoebus, *Lusignan, Biron* . . .? It is possible to know; the interpretations consolidate or diverge . . . . But, ultimately, one can read the sonnet without knowing anything of these references; letting oneself be seized solely by the phonic and rhythmic coherence that marks a boundary relative to the free associations inspired by each word or name. One understands thereby that the triumph over melancholy consists as much in the constitution of a symbolic family (ancestor, mythical personage, esoteric community) as in the construction of a symbolic object: the sonnet. This construction, due to the author, replaces the lost ideal in the same movement as it turns melancholy's lugubrious shades into lyrical song incorporating "the sighs of the Saint and the cries of Fairies." The nostalgic object – "my only star is dead" – is transformed into feminine voices incorporated within that symbolic anthropophagy that is the poem's composition, within the prosody created by the artist. It is in an analogous manner that I interpret the massive presence of proper names in Nerval's texts, particularly in his poems.

Not only do these names restitute to him a historical or mythical filiation, but they seem to have quasi-ritual, incantatory value. It is not their concrete referents that these proper names signal – with *signal* opposed here (both for the profane reader as, I would allege, for the hyperlucid Nerval) to *signify* – as much as it is a massive, unavoidable, unnameable presence. As though they were the anaphora that replaces the unique object: not the "symbolic equivalent" of the mother but the deictic "this" which, devoid of meaning, points towards the lost object from which there, at first, emanates "melancholy's black sun" before the putting into place of the artifice of linguistic signs and, last of all, their archaeology that is the provisionally victorious poem. "I cried for a long time, invoking my mother under the names given to ancient divinities" (*Manuscript of Aurelia, OC* vol. I, 423).

The melancholic's past never passes. Nor does that of the poet, that permanent historian, not so much of his real history but of the symbolic events which have led his body to signification or, indeed, which threaten to overwhelm his consciousness.

Whatever may be the allusions to free-masonry and to initiation – and perhaps parallel to them – the text evokes (as in analysis) archaic psychic experiences that few people attain in their conscious discourse.

The Writing of Suffering's Pleasures

The tormented universe of Dostoevsky (1821–1881) is, without a doubt, dominated more by epilepsy than by melancholia in the clinical sense of the term. And if Hippocrates identified the two ills – if Aristotle, in distinguishing them, compared them – current clinical reality considers them to be thoroughly separate entities.

The hypostasis of suffering imposes itself as the essential trait of the Dostoevskian anthropology. So, in *The Notebooks of the Possessed* (or of the *Devils*) (1873), suffering seems to be an "in excess," a force, a sensual pleasure. The "black mark" of Nervalian melancholy has given way to a passional torrent: to an hysterical affect – the fluid overflowing of which carries away the placid signs and quiescent compositions of "monological" literature, thereby conferring a vertiginous polyphony on the Dostoevskian text and imposing as the ultimate truth of Dostoevskian man a rebellious flesh that takes its pleasure in nonsubmission to the Word. Sensuality of suffering's pleasure that has "nothing of the coldness, nothing of the disenchantment, nothing of that which has been made fashionable by Byron," but, on the contrary, an "intemperate and insatiable thirst for pleasures," "a thirst after inextinguishable life," including pleasures of theft, of banditry, the sensual pleasure of suicide" (*The Notebooks of the Devils*). This exultation of a mood that can turn from suffering to an incommensurable jubilation is admirably described by Kirilov in the moments preceding suicide – or the epileptic fit: "There are seconds – they come five or six at a time – when you suddenly feel the presence of eternal harmony in all its fullness. It is nothing earthly. I don't mean that it is heavenly, but a man in his earthly semblance can't endure it."

It is probably such an intimacy with the affect that led Dostoevsky to his vision according to which the humanity of man resides less in the pursuit of a pleasure or a profit (an idea extending even to Freudian psychoanalysis despite the predominance finally accorded to a "beyond the pleasure principle") than in the aspiration for a voluptuous suffering. "Suffering – after all, that is the sole cause of consciousness. Although I declared to begin with that in my opinion consciousness is man's supreme misfortune, I know that man loves it and would not change it for any gratification" (*Notes from Underground*).

Let us not be precipitate in interpreting these remarks as an avowal of masochism. Is not it in *signifying* his hate, the other's destruction and, perhaps before all else, his own acts of "putting to death," that the human being survives as a symbolic animal? A violence, exorbitant yet curbed, leading to the self-annihiliation of the ego in order that the subject might arise. From a diachronic point of view, we are here at the minimal threshold of subjectivity, before an other comes to be demarcated as the object of an amorous or aggressive assault. Now, this curbing additionally allows mastery over signs: I do not attack you, I *speak* (or I write) my fear or my pain. My suffering is the lining of my word, of my civilization. One can imagine the masochistic risks of this civility. The writer is however, for his part, able to extract from this a jubilation through the manipulation that, upon this base, he knows how to inflict upon signs and things. So, too, this exaggeration of humor, this pretentious inflation of "propriety" or peculiarity, states an essential truth of the psychism in process of constitution or of decomposition, a process which takes place under the gaze of the ego ideal: under the law of an Other, already dominant albeit still not recognized in its omnipotent alterity.

For this very reason, the suffering being found in Dostoevsky recalls the paradoxical adventures of Job which had, moreover, so struck the writer: "I am reading the Book of Job from which I derive a morbid exultation: I stop reading and pace up and down in my room, an hour at a time, almost in tears . . . . The strange thing is, Anna, that this book is one of the first to have made an impression upon me . . . and, at that time, I was still almost a babe in arms" (Letter to his wife, January 10, 1875).

Job, nourishing himself upon sighs and groans (as though on bread and water) was, it will be remembered, a man who – prosperous and faithful to Yahweh – finds himself suddenly beset by various misfortunes . . . . By Yahweh or by Satan? And yet here is this "man of grief," object of scorn ("If one should address a word to you, will you endure it?" IV,2.) who is, in sum, *sad only* because he holds fast to God. That the God be pitiless and unjust to those faithful to him, and even generous to the wicked, does not lead him to break his divine contract; on the contrary, he places his life under the constant scrutiny of God. Striking avowal of the depressive's dependence with respect to his super-ego *cum* ego-ideal: "What is man that you [God] should make so much of him" (VII, 17); "turn your eyes away, leave me a little joy" (X, 21). And yet, Job does not accredit God with his true force ("Were he to pass me, I should not see him" IX, 11), and God himself will be required to recapitulate all of Creation before his depressive, to affirm his position as Legislator or as super-ego, in order for Job to recover hope. Would the sufferer be a narcissitic, a man too concerned with himself, attached to his own importance and close to taking himself for an example of transcendence's immanence? However, after having punished him, Yahweh finally favors him and places him above his detractors: "I burn with anger against you," he says to them, "for not speaking truthfully about me as my servant Job has done" (XLII, 8).

In the same manner suffering – preeminent index of humanity – is, in the texts of the Christian Dostoevsky, the mark of man's dependence and, at the same time, of his irremedial difference with respect to a divine Law. Simultaneity of bond and fault, of fidelity and transgression – such as is refound in the ethical order itself, where Dostoevskian man is an idiot through saintliness, a prophet through criminality.

Suicide and Terrorism

One will recall at least two solutions, both fatal, for Dostoevskian suffering – that ultimate veil of chaos and destruction: First, that of Kirilov, who is persuaded that God doesn't exist but who, in adhering to the divine position, wishes to raise human liberty to the height of the absolute by that exemplary act of denial and freedom which, for him, is suicide. God doesn't exist – I am God – I do not exist – I commit suicide: such would be the paradoxical logic of this negation of an absolute divinity or paternity nonetheless maintained in order that I possess myself of it.

The second solution is that of Raskolnikov, who, as in a manic defense against despair, turns his hate back not onto himself but onto another, denigrated, denied. By his gratuitous crime, consisting in killing an insignificant woman, he breaks the Christian contract ("Love your neighbor as yourself"), thus signifying that he denies his love for the original object ("Because I don't love my mother, my neighbor is unimportant to me, which permits me to eliminate him without worry") and that, departing from this implicit premise, he authorizes himself to realize his hate against an entourage and a society experienced as persecutory.

The metaphysical meaning of these behaviors is, as one knows, the nihilist rejection of the supreme Value, provoking, on the part of Dostoevesky, the believer's revolt against this erasure of the transcendental. Additionally, the psychoanalyst will see here the fascination, at the least ambiguous, of the writer before as much exquisite depression itself, as certain manic defenses against this suffering, both of which are, moreover, cultivated by the writer as the necessary and antinomic linings of his writing. That these ramparts be abject, the abandonment of all morals, the loss of the meaning of life, or the terrorism and torture so frequent in our quotidian reality; all are recalled for us incessantly. The writer, for his part, chose the adhesion to a religious orthodoxy and this "obscurantism," so violently denounced by Freud, is, all things considered, less harmful to civilization than terroristic nihilism. As too, obviously, is the painful and permanent battle to compose a work of art side by side with the innumerable pleasures comprising destruction and chaos.

Religion, or the mania born of paranoia, are they the sole counterbalances to despair? Artistic creation both integrates and consumes them; works of art leading us thereby to establish less destructive, more pleasurable relations with ourselves and with others.

Psychoanalysis – a laic discourse creating and dissolving the transferential bond, is an apprenticeship in living beyond despair. Not by a manic defense countering it, but through a receptivity to it, an endowing of it with meaning for a while before going further. In this manner, consolidating the ego, psychoanalysis allows it to assume an existence upon the basis of its very vulnerability in relation to the other.

This overview of a certain number of depression's facets could not be terminated without evoking the pharmacological advances and the modern biochemical knowledge concerning melancholia's edogenous factors. The hypothesis seems to be gaining ground according to which it is an insufficiency of (nor) adrenalin and serotonin, or of their reception, that hampers the conductability of a synapsis and *possibly* conditions the depressive state. However, in the star-shaped structure of the brain, the role of a few synapses could not be absolute. Such an insufficiency can be counteracted by other chemical phenomena and, too, by different external effects (including symbolic) upon the brain which accommodates itself to these through biological modifications. Without then renouncing the chemical role in the battle against melancholia, the analyst has – if he so chooses – at his disposal an extended range of verbalizations of this state and its overcoming, the example of which is presented in works of art. Therefore, the attention brought to bear upon religious or aesthetic discourses in relation to melancholia is not solely a means of rendering a phenomenological description of this symptom more penetrating: by the interpretation that this knowledge allows us to elaborate, by a verbalization as exact as possible of destructive affects, it can also be an essential therapeutic measure.

We are, no doubt, permanent subjects of a speech that also keeps us alive but all the same, we are subjects in process, continually losing our identies, destabilized by the fluctuations of those same relations with the other, from whom a certain homeostasis keeps us unified. In postulating this eclipse of subjectivity at the threshold of life, in understanding a hiatus in that subjectivity already unified during the most intense moments of passion, psychoanalysis does not "biologize the essence of man," as Heidegger feared. It gives, on the contrary, an exorbitant confidence in the power of the transreferential bond and in the interpretative discourse knowing as we do, by experience, that they are capable, once the eclipse and hiatus of the subject are recognized and thus named, of provisionally re-establishing the unity of the subject, for a new trial in the infinite process of our living passions . . . .

Let me go one step further. When I say that signification is itself a *significance* that encompasses three types of representation, I am not simply trying to render the concept dynamic by adding the active suffix *-ance*, nor am I trying to retrieve the medieval usage of the word. Rather, I wish to extend the sphere of linguistic representation, to include a pre- or translinguistic modality of psychic inscription that I call *semiotic* in its truest etymologic sense, rooted in the Greek *semeion*: trace, mark, distinctiveness. At the very foundation of philosophy, even before the mode of thought encloses itself within the confines of language understood as the translation of Idea, Plato, recalling the atomists, spoke of a *chora*; the psychic receptacle – archaic, mobile, unstable, prior to the One, to the father, and even to the syllable; metaphorically designated as nurturing and maternal (the *Timaeus*). The tendency to rethink a psychic modality logically and chronologically prior to the sign, to the meaning and to the subject, reminds philosophers of that Platonic source. It inscribes itself as well in the Freudian theory, seeking to distinguish different types of representation in the psychic dynamic. These types are more or less capable of being subsumed by that language of communication, but surely escape consciousness's grasp. In emphasizing and specifying more strongly than Freud the status of affective "semiotic" inscriptions, we acquire a new theoretic means of clarifying the heterogeneity of representations, including unconscious ones. Such a concern corresponds well to the clinical observation of a psychic lead to an eclipse of signification, but not deprived of some drive or sense that raises the bioenergetic signals in already intrapsychic inscriptions, no doubt fluid but still tenacious (as exhibited in narcissistic affectations and psychoses). Such a layering of the significance belonging to the analytic speech applies, of course, to all discourse as well, even if it is true that the analytic transfer manifests it in the most obvious, observable manner. A model of the significance, so stratified, permits us to understand how the logical word, supported by infralinguistic (i.e., semiotic) representations can resonate in the physical register as well. A strong model of the human specificity is thus proposed, wherein language is not separated from body, where, on the contrary, the Word can, at every moment, profoundly touch and affect the living flesh.

In this model, and in the analytic experience as I conceive it, a paradoxical subjectivity is found. First, agree that it is legitimate to speak of the subject, whenever language simultaneously unifies an identity in the instant of enunciation and confers upon it an interlocutor and a referent. The Freudian "other scene" has accustomed us to conceive of a heterogeneity essential to the human being. Insofar as we are speaking beings, we break with nature, and this doubling leaves us irradicably marked by the pre- or translinguistic, semiotic, processes which are our only access to the species memory and to the bioenergetic neuron maps. These semiotic processes (archaic inscriptions of the ties between our erogenous zones and those of others, in as much as sonorous, visual, tactile, olfactive, and rythmic traces) constitute, diachronically speaking, a presubject. Synchronically, this semiotic chorus is found in the catastrophic anguish (passion) of the melancholy psychosis. Their insistence undermines our basically fragile lucidity and fills us with forgetting, dizziness, and phantoms.

Part II.
Language and Desire

2. Substitution

Alphonso Lingis

A man can be a sign.

A sign has meaning, a referent, and a value. Intentionality would be the act, being performed by the one that issues signs and induced in the one that understands or interprets signifiers, that institutes the reference to the term *signified.* Husserl takes what Frege called the *Sinn* to be a noema, that is, a formed pattern of hyletic matter synthesized in function of an ideal identity-term, which functions not as a mental image but as a referential function designating a transcendent object. Hintikka takes the *Sinn* to specify the *Bedeutung,* the referent, by drawing a line through a number of possible worlds, linking up, by continuity or similarity, the roles something plays in each of them. The *Sinn,* he says, is a transworld heir line; what the sign identifies is the role passed down, inherited, from possible worlds to the actual world. The lack in phenomenology, to us glaring as a result of the work of structural linguistics, is any understanding that a sign is also a value. A sign functions in a system of signs, an economic system, such that every sign is taken to be equivalent to, and substitutable for, other signs. Its value is specified by the signs for which it can be exchanged. Phenomenology has completely failed to see that the meaning of a sign, the way it functions to designate its referent, is conditioned by its value within the economy of signs.

In addition, a sign signifies because it is an appeal and a demand. It is not only indicative, but vocative and imperative. The movement by which it is addressed to someone makes it be a value, have meaning, and designate a referent. Thus, sounds and visible marks made by natural causality are not signs, Husserl did say, unless one takes nature to be a text written by a Creative Word and addressed to men.

The signifier, the sound uttered by a throat or the mark made by a hand, refers to some transcendent term, but it can do so, existential philosophy declared, because the lips and throat and lungs, and the arm and shoulder and torso, can support and mobilize this sign-production. There is not first a discharge of mere sounds or visual marks by the physiological mechanism, and then a *Sinngebung* operation that refers them to further terms; the assigning to them a reference is one with the shaping and issuing of them, and this is done with the whole posture, musculature, and nervous circuitry of the organism. Husserl extended his analysis of expression down into the sensibility; perception forms or patterns the sensations that affect our sensory surfaces and takes them to, or makes them refer to, external things. Existential analysis shows that emotions and moods also recognize something moving, dangerous, or unpredictable, and an outlying field, melancholic or desolate, arrayed about us; they function to signify, to refer to that something and that field. They, too, are in this sense expressions and signifying. A libidinous impulse is not just an augmentation in psychic and physiological tension; it intends a referent beyond itself.

Similarly, a reach or a manipulation relates itself to an objective like a linguistic move functions to direct one to an object; the inner diagram – pacing, force, and style – of the reach or manipulation is a sort of *Sinn*, meaning or noema, which specifies how one refers to that objective. The existential analysis shows that the whole sensory-motile substance of a man is expressive, is a signifier; not only the grammatically coded signs and marks he issues, but all his pleasure-pain feelings, the exhilarations of his sentient substance and the anxious feelings of vulnerability, and his motor tensions and contractions of effort function as *hylê* formed and animated by a movement identifying external referents. The hand that reaches for the doorknob has, Merleau-Ponty wrote, from the start captured the form of the doorknob on its own muscular contractions – or has made of the form it gives its palm and fingers a material signifier of the referent. And for the witness of that gesture, the hollow formed in the palm and fingers functions as a materialization of the doorknob, both a reference to the external objective and a stand-in for it before it is there. For a witness to read the hand's move as referring to the doorknob and not the light switch is to see that hollow as provisionally occupying the place of the terminal referent.

What is the strange necessity of the intentional movement not only to direct itself to the signified identity term, but to put in place of that signified reality or ideality something material, something hyletic, the signifier? Hintikka vehemently criticized what he called the reifying tendency in Husserl to take the *Sinn*, the noema, to be itself a sort of object, an entity; it is, he explains, nothing but a function. Yet the visible and audible signifiers of language are real entities – Husserl would say *reel*: taken not in their here-and-now factual place in nature but in the way they are *abgeschattet* on the passivity of the mind as sensuous patterns. And when one who feels the danger coming, or the unreliability of the whole material world, crouches back or shudders anxiously, and when the one who makes the doorknob his objective inscribes its form in the hollow of his hand, he makes his grimaces and his gestures signifiers, and these are real entities, visible to the outside witness and intuitable reflectively by himself as hylé. A sign is not only a means to aim at or to constitute transcendent identity terms; it is a stand-in, a substitute for them, put in place of them.

In addition, the *Sinn*, the sense of a signifier, the *way* it refers to the referent, is determined by the constellation of other signs that are equivalent to it. One defines the functioning of a sign by specifying the other signs that would stand in for, substitute for, it. Hintikka's modal logic takes the *Sinn*, the meaning of the signifier, to be not an individual object, a noema, but a complex of relationships, a world, which specify a role for the referent; the complete *Sinn* links up that role with roles in worlds that might have been realized in the place of the actual world, and designates the referent as the identification of those similar or continuous roles. As *Sinn*, the actual world functions as a representative of possible worlds. The subsistence of a sign as a stand-in, a substitute for, a representative of other signs is what Saussure calls its value.

Thus, inasmuch as a sign has a reference, its real, sensory, or hyletic materiality figures as a stand-in, a substitute for the presence of that referent; inasmuch as it has a meaning, the referential signifier figures as a stand-in, a substitute for, a representative of other signs.

How would existence-philosophy ground this substitutive structure of signs? It would be grounded in inauthenticity. A sound a speaker issues, a mark he traces with his hand are representatives of other sounds, other marks, as the whole speaker, the whole writer is a representative of other speakers, other writers – as the one who expresses his feelings, the one who picks up tools usable by anybody, feels and acts as a representative of other diagrams of feeling and other agents. For Heidegger, the substitution is first practical. The one that deals with entities ouside himself, implements, envisages them as useful not just once, and in one singular way, but as useful for a time and for a range of manipulations; he simultaneously structures himself as one of that range of manipulatings, equivalent to and interchangeable with any other variant. Then, he envisages another as another operator of implements, equivalent to and interchangeable with himself, and perceives him as such by virtually putting himself in the other's place, comprehending the entities surrounding the other by envisaging them as they would appear to him if he were there where the other is. Thus, he could take himself, his own inner dynamic diagram, to stand for the only ideally signified life of the other. And he could take the modulations of his own stance, the signs he makes, including those syntaxically and semantically codified, as equivalent to and interchangeable with those the other makes.

Hintikka makes a rather parallel analysis. The objects and objectives we identify are constituted by identifying roles in a multiplicity of possible states of affairs or courses of events. These possible worlds are, in Hobbes's phrase, "drawn and described by ourselves." Not by each individual alone, but by the tacit collective decisions embodied in the grammar and semantics of our language. The possible worlds are not perceived or perceivable layouts and networks of relationship simply; they are also systems of beliefs, which, as Quine has argued, are behavioristically determined.

What sets into movement this substitution, this taking oneself to be equivalent to and interchangeable with another, this projecting oneself into the place of another, this taking oneself to be a value in an economy of signifiers, is, in Heidegger's vision, the flight in the face of one's ending, one's dying. Evasiveness, a will for self-deception irremediably lies at the bottom of all significant behavior, all constitution of signs, all making oneself into a sign, that is, equivalent to and interchangeable with, substitutable for, another. For, thus, one makes oneself a crest or trough on a beginningless, endless wave of life.

Inauthenticity makes possible authenticity. Once having perceived the other as another, another operator of tools like myself, by having virtually exchanged places with him, one can then perceive him as *other*, as one who has his own field of possibilities and his own task, divergent from mine. Simultaneously I am brought back to the singularity of my own situation. Casting myself over the full range of what is possible for me, unto the last limits of possibility, unto the certain eventuality of the nothingness to come for me, I designate to myself and to others all that is possible for me.

How would this authentifying differentiation, this "authentic solicitude," transform my speech, my significant behavior, inasmuch as it is a practice of putting hyletic material to mark the place of signified identity terms, objects and objectives, putting my own corporeality forth as a signifier for the ideal identity of another life – and a practice of putting forth one signified term to stand in for other signified terms, putting my implement-handling existence in the place of others?

I will develop this question by profiting from what we can learn about a man becoming significant, becoming a sign, becoming a value, a substitute for and representative of another, from contemporary psychoanalysis.

Infancy (*in-fans*) is insignificant. The sentient – or more exactly, sensuous – infantile substance is inexpressive and nonreferential; it is for itself as for the fond, fondling mother, a pleasure – and an irritation. The exposed infantile body is an erotogenic surface, zone not of sensations, signifying material, but of excitations and immediate, contact gratification. The surface of infantile sensibility, susceptibility, is not perceptive, intentional, but productive, a pure expanse of nonintentional intensities which arise on contact with the flows of maternal milk, murmur, kisses, and caresses and are consumed in discharges of pleasure. The oral and anal poles of the infantile sentience do not aim at ideally identified transcendent objects, but are couplings where contact is made more intensely. The infantile babbling does not designate anything, but consumes the pleasures of vibrating throat, buzzing lips, bubbling slobber.

The child will come to see another surface of himself. One day, while looking at the visual pattern the surface of a mirror holds before him, his parent came up from behind and told him: that is you. It was an identification the other has to make for him; for the mirror surface is not only at a distance from where he feels himself to be, alienated from his motor-affective substance, but is of a totally different nature. In identifying it as himself, he does not recognize as identical the vectors of motor and impulsive tensions and the pleasure-pain erotogenic surface over them, in which he finds himself, with this colored design; he recognizes what the others see of him, and identifies *with* that, alienates himself into it. The mirror surface functions now as the hylé in which he now too posits his ego, as the ideal identity-pole that is objective, that is, posited first by the others. He signifies himself with the signifier with which he is named in their discourse.

It is the word of the father – imperative and not indicative, informative, word, law, prohibition – that introduces, then, distance between the infant and what now becomes the object, the other, the mother. The father threatens castration, orders self-castration, that is, orders the infant to suppress his erotogenic surface under his affective-kinesthetic fondling hand. He orders the child to invest himself only in the insentient, objective surface-form he is for others. The child laughs at this threat, statistically more frequently formulated by the mother, even as she fondles him. He will come to take it seriously when he discovers, in horror and in anxiety, the castration of the mother. He will be able to detach from himself the primary-process, erotogenic surface when he finds how he can positively value the distant surface of himself the eyes of the others hold over him. He comes to realize that he is himself the absent organ, the phallus, that has been detached from that gaping wound between his mother's thighs. He understands now why all this time she has been fondling him, holding him close to herself, drooling over him. He realizes now the chance he is – chance to be the phallus the mother demands. He identifies himself with, projects himself into, the phantasmal image of her phallus he sees reflected in the mirrors of her craving eyes. And he abandons his little penis, as real surface of contact gratification. His phantasmal, ideal phallic identity is put in the place of his affective-kinesthetic erotogenic-surface corporeity materialized under masturbation.

As a phallus, he has become a sign. That is, not simply a hyletic matter indicating a public referent, but an appeal addressed to the other, a demand put on the other. For a sign is not simply an indicator for an interpreter of a referent through its meaning; it has vocative and imperative force; indeed it is informative for the others because it is addressed to them and makes demands on them, commands their attention. The erotogenic surface of lived infancy was inexpressive and insignificant; now the perceptible surface of the child, this hylé, functions to refer to, to stand in for, to represent the purely ideal phallus missing from the objective sphere, the other.

But how will the child, now become a sign, a signifier signifying phantasmal ideality, come to function as a value, that is, a substitute for another signifier? The child comes to understand that the father, who has mutiliated the mother of her penis, puts his penis in its place. The son, who interiorizes the word of the father, exteriorizes himself as a representative of the father. Assuming the name of the father, he will make his substance the representative of the father.

This will occur when the child puts his real penis in the place of the ideal phallus the others, and he himself, took him to be. That is, when he approaches the other, the mother and her representatives, not in order, as so long ago, to extend the infantile erotogenic contact-zone – but now to answer with his penis the phallic demand he has seen in her eyes, and to demand of her what the father demands and receives – the exclusive devotion from which long ago the infant found himself excluded. He substitutes his real penis for the phantasmal phallus she craved, giving her a substitute for the organ she lacks, and uses it to impregnate her with an infant she will take as her phalus. He has become a value in an economy, that is, etymologically, a household. But as one that has interiorized the law, the prohibition of the father, that has put the voice and the law of the father in the place of the primary process gratifications of his infantile body, he will in his turn order the severing of her child from the mother, claim it as his own; he fathers a family in order to castrate infancy in turn. His virile and paternal word orders a cosmos, a world everywhere detached from immediate gratification, a universe of signs.

What is different in the psychoanalytic understanding, when we compare it with what is understood from Heidegger, is that there is now no longer that evasiveness in the face of one's dying, that will for self-deception in the child's anxiety before the castration menace. The child learns to accept castration, and accepting the ending of his infantile, primary-process, erotogenic corporeity, he puts it to death himself. He can do so because he discovers himself being reborn in the sphere of ideality, as a sign.. He puts to death his insignificant infancy in order to subsist in the sphere of ideal omnitemporality, which prolongs itself not through the eternally enduring presence, but the eternally recurring incarnation of the father as sign, as word, as prohibition.

But what was so undeveloped in Heidegger now becomes impossible in psychoanalysis – the possibility of authenticity, of one that is significant as singular, one who is an unsubstitutable sign. In Heidegger, what limits the extent to which I put myself in the place of others and in charge of their tasks, and take others to be but the indefinitely-multiplying recurrencies of myself, is the mordant sense of my own mortality. It is the oncoming of death, singling me out, that destines me to my range of possibilities, my tasks, my future.

If we now project this eventuality back over the libidinal adult who has now become fully a sign, phallic representative and representative of the father, what then? The death sublated returns now, to threaten this reincarnated father, this sign the living, that is, libidinous, organism has made of itself. The death that threatens now his significant existence, as Eternal Father, resurrects his infantile, primary-process corporeity, resurrects the masturbating-infant, narcissistically closed-in surface-horizons of immediate gratification. Not really resurrects – for this infantilism had never really died, had been buried alive, and it was its cravings that all the appeals, demands, gesticulations made in the direction of the other by the castrated adult always meant to signify. For what is timeless, not eternally enduring but eternally recurring, is not the subsistence of signs, but the unconscious, the primary-process libido, infancy.

Whereas in Heidegger the movement in the authenticated existence, the one who goes further than just being another stand-in, substitute for, representative of the others, casts forth unto a future that is authentically a future, a destiny that is one's own, possibilities never before seen in humanity. In what exchanges, in what solar economy, will the erotic substance become an unsubstitutable sign, will the erotic word become prophetic?

3. Desire: Language and Body

M. C. Dillon

Proteus was the sea god who had the power to assume many shapes. Imagine another such deity abiding in the dark depths of the wet element whose form changes with each of the many names by which it is called. Plato calls it ἐπιθυμία and it shows itself as lack, the presence of an absence. Freud calls it *libido* and it shows itself as energy, an overflowing presence that is never absent. Can a proper name be found for this deity, or will it respond equally to all appellations?

Imagine this dark deity swimming through time, collecting names, gathering them to itself, retaining them in a wordrobe of physiognomies, becoming a history whose inception is as obscure as the birth of a cell in the sea. These names are rights of passage: the deity passes into us through them; through them we pass into the obscurity of our past and future. We invoke ourselves through the names of the deity. We are the creatures of pleasure and pain; we are the creators of good and evil; we are the slaves and masters of recognition. Who, then, are we that we seek our own names in the wordrobe of the deity

What is in a name? What happens to the deity when it passes through the defiles of the signifier? Let us say that the deity exists, that in some sense of the word it is real. What happens to this reality when it is represented by the signifier? At the very least, this passage is a passage into ideality. What then becomes of the reality? We cast our nets into the sea to capture the deity – every net a matrix of words with its own pattern of holes – and each one nets a different form, a different name, a different physiognomy: words catch words, and the quarry slips through their interstices. We venture into the sea and return to feed upon words.

What is in a name? The power of transformation is in a name. Call love aim-inhibited Oedipal longing and the lover is transformed into a frustrated infant. If Eros is mystified sexuality, Socrates is transformed into a repressed child molester. If desire is the will to reduce the other into a mirroring object, a reflecting surface with no interior, then we are all transformed into sadistic narcissists.

If you call out the wrong name, the person you want will not come forth. So it is with persons, but what about the deity? Can the deity be called the wrong name? If it is defiled by the signifier, will it come forth? And how?

Let us say that it is of the essence of the signifier to defile. To call the deity by a name is to corrupt its silent dignity. It is to cage the deity in one context, one more or less familiar text, and thereby to sully its wondrous transcendence. The deity responds to this name-calling by changing faces. The signifier idealizes what it signifies, and this transformation is a desecration because it violates the ipseity of the real.

Do we then call the deity with the cacophony of many names? Even when those names are antiphonal and produce an incoherent eclecticism? Or shall we say that the deity has no proper name, could not have one, that there is no real ipseity beneath the multiplicity of signifiers? Then the names of the deity refer only to each other, agreeing here, disagreeing there, with no hope of resolution, no measure of adequacy, and, ultimately, no reason for gathering themselves into an evolving argument.

But now suppose the deity has a body whose form does not change. Would that corporeal schema not ground an identity? Could we not then name desire, recognize it, and approach it with understanding as well as awe?

Hegel

I begin again where Kojève's illustrious students – Sartre, Lacan, Merleau-Ponty – have begun: with Hegel.

> . . . Self-consciousness [is] only certain of itself through the sublation and overcoming [*durch das Aufheben*] of [the] other, which presents itself to it as an independent life; it [self-consciousness] is desire [*Begierde*]. Certain of the nullity [*Nichtigkeit*] of this other, it posits this nullity *for itself* as the truth of this other, it annihilates [*vernichtet*] this independent object, and thereby grants itself the certainty of itself as *true* certainty . . . (PhG,143).[1]

Desire is self-consciousness seeking the certainty of its own self by means of negating the other. But it does not "aim at extinguishing the entire objective essence [of its object], but only at the form of [its] otherness or independence . . . " (PhG,271). The negation of the other sought in desire is, thus, not a total annihilation; this is because self-consciousness needs the other for its own self-certainty. "Self-consciousness is *in* and *for itself*, in and through being in and for itself for an other; *i.e.*, it *is* only as something recognized . . . (PhG,145).

Self-consciousness seeks to find its self-certainty, its existence, in the recognition of the other. Desire is, then, the project of self-realization through the mediation of the other's recognition. But this project of recognition must, at least initially, be carried out by means of a life and death struggle for domination. The basis for the struggle is the alienation of the self-other difference. The struggle is initially to overcome the difference of alienation by negating the otherness of the other. Thus, recognition degenerates into assimilation and ensures its own defeat, role-reversal, and repetition. Only through the negation of a negation, *i.e.*, through the *Aufhebung* of the difference (or alienation) itself, can the unhappiness of struggle ultimately be overcome.

On the question of desire, Hegel and Freud are the two major modern sources. Hegel conceives desire as an immanent structure of self-consciousness. Desire is thus autonomous with respect to biology: its reality reposes in ideality. Hegel's identification of desire with self-consciousness sets him at odds with Freud because it seems, at least, to preclude anything like an unconscious desire. Desire, as self-consciousness, is essentially reflexive, and its reflexivity is essentially mediated by consciousness of the other. Or, again, desire exists through an ego seeking its own existence in its recognition by an other.

Sartre

Sartre's account of desire is a variation on the Hegelian theme of consciousness seeking its own self-realization through appropriation of the other. Despite terminological differences, the telos of desire as conceived by Sartre and Hegel is essentially the same: self-consciousness lacks something and attempts to satisfy that need by means of another consciousness. In both cases, it is the otherness – or transcendence – of the other that creates the ambivalence that drives the dialectic. Self-realization requires mediation through a transcendent other because, without that mediation (*i.e.*, within the narcissism of a purely immanent self-self relation), self-consciousness remains nothingness aware (of) itself as such. On the other hand, the transcendence of the other poses an obstacle to self-realization because it threatens self-consciousness with an alien objectification. The basic self-other difference both enables desire to act and prevents that action from reaching culmination. At this initial level of the dialectic, the struggle for recognition between self and other cannot reach resolution for either Hegel or Sartre: to succeed in negating the otherness of the other is to annihilate that transcendence and thus fail at the project of appropriating it. Instead of resolution, there is role-reversal: master becomes slave, and the sadistic project of domination is transformed into masochistic submission.

Although their agreement on the teleology of desire places Hegel and Sartre in the same ontological context, the thematic differences in their accounts are consequential: Hegel's optimisim with regard to the destiny of resolution as the dialectical opposition moves toward synthesis is countered by Sartre's pessimistic conclusion that the opposition is inevitable and can never be resolved. They ultimately differ on the ultimacy of difference. Why?

For both Hegel and Sartre, desire is consciousness in the mode of reflexivity or self-conscioueness. But, for Sartre, "desire is consciousness because it can only *be* as a non-positional consciousness (of) itself (BN,502).[2] Desire is reflexive; it exists as a relation of consciousness to itself (*i.e.*, as a cogito), but "desire is of itself nonreflective,[*le désire est par soi-même irréflêchi*]" (BN,500; EN,453–4). Desire is reflexive, but nonreflective: that is, desire exists in the mode of the prereflective cogito, prior to the reflective positing of an ego.

Sartre conceives desire as consciousness in flight from its own lucidity toward the troubled opacity of incarnation. In desire, "the nonthetic consciousness allows itself to go over to the body, *wishes to be* the body and only body" (BN,505). Desiring consciousness seeks its own incarnation, and by means of the caress, seeks to incarnate the other, reduce the other's consciousness to flesh, and render it available for appropriation. This project, however, is doomed to failure because acts of appropriation (*i.e.*, grasping, penetrating) transform the flesh of the other into an object in which the consciousness to be appropriated no longer resides.

For Hegel, the self-realization of desire is achieved by self-consciousness at a *higher* level, the level of *reason*, where its intrinsic universality overcomes the opposition of difference. For Sartre, it is intrinsic to desire to seek mediation through a *lower* level of self-consciousness, the level of *incarnation*, where the objectification of the other necessarily results in differentiation (hence, alienation) of self and other.

Follow the Sartrean problematic a step further. "Desire," he says, "is expressed by the caress as thought is by language" (BN,507). And again: "the problem of language is exactly parallel to the problem of bodies, and the description which is valid in one case is valid in the other" (BN,487). Desire is consciousness mediating its relation to itself through the other by means of the caress. If the parallel holds, thought is consciousness mediating its relation to itself through the other by means of language. Thus, I express my desire in the caress in order to discover it in the other. The other, in both cases, is a mediator in the process of self-realization. Language and the caress both have the aim of "causing to experience." The other is to validate my experience – my thought, my desire – by mirroring it for me. My thought/desire is valid if it is reflected in the thought/desire of the other. However, the aim is necessarily frustrated in the case of language as it is in the case of desire – and for a parallel reason: "the 'meaning' of my expressions always escapes me" (BN,486) because the meaning of the expression for the other can only be the meaning the other confers on it, and that, like the consciousness of the other, is always hidden from me. The significance I find mirrored in the other is always only a significance I project upon the other's body or language. The meaning of his gesture for me is as opaque to him as the meaning of my gesture for him is opaque to me. The problem of language is exactly parallel to the problem of bodies because both language and body necessarily fail to fulfill the aim of mediating the relation of consciousness to itself. The necessity of failure resides in the opacity of the other, in the difference that cannot be overcome. The other is necessarily opaque/alien/different because all self-other relations – be they mediated through the look, bodies, or language – inevitably proceed through objectification of self or other, and this precludes the possibility of the recognition or appropriation of a self-consciousness by an other self-consciousness (which recognition remains the telos of desire).

Note that Sartre conceives language here as only externally related to thought or significance. The meaning of a word does not reside in its physiognomy, but must be assigned to it by consciousness. Language, as a worldly transcendence, is thus ontologically disjunct from the immanent sphere of consciousness, and can communicate only by magic.

> Attitudes, expressions, and words can only indicate to [the other] other attitudes, other expressions, and other words. Thus language remains

> for him a simple property of a magical object – and this magical object itself (BN,487).

The working of language has to be magical for Sartre because it is an object that does what objects cannot do in Sartre's ontology: it conveys significance. Language and the body fulfill the function of expression; that is, they mediate between consciousnesses sealed in solitary spheres of immanence. But this mediation is impossible – or magical – because it requires an object to be the bearer of meaning when, for Sartre, objects can only have the meanings freely assigned to them by consciousness. The result is that the mediating function fails. "I never know exactly if I signify what I wish to signify nor even if I *am* signifying anything" (BN,486). Hence: " . . . I do not know my language [for the other] any more than I know my body for the other" (BN,487). Because neither body nor language has intrinsic significance, both fail as mediators, and self and other remain opaque/alien/opposed to each other. Hence, desire, as the project of recognition/appropriation, is necessarily "doomed to failure" (BN,515).

Lacan

Like Sartre, Lacan begins with an Hegelian understanding of desire, but proceeds in his own direction (LDO,162–63).[3] Still, the teleology of desire remains the same: desire remains desire for recognition (LDO,189), the overcoming of a lack grounded in negation (otherness) by negating that negation; desire exists by virtue of the presence of an absence (otherness), and that absence is ultimately grounded in difference.

It is also the case with Lacan, as it was for Hegel and Sartre, that the problematic of difference works itself out through a dialectics of mediation.

> The very desire of man, [Hegel] tells us, is constituted under the sign of mediation; it is desire to make its desire recognized. It has for its object a desire, that of the other, in the sense that there is no object for man's desire which is constituted without some form of mediation – which appears in his most primitive needs: for example, even his food has to be prepared – and which is found again throughout the development of satisfaction from the moment of the master-slave conflict throughout the dialectic of labor.[4]

As noted earlier, Hegel conceives the dialectic of mediation as taking place within the immanent domain of consciousness. Sartre remains within the immanent sphere, but articulates the dialectic through the mediation of body and language. For Lacan, the prime mediator is language – although his understanding of language differs from Sartre's – and the role of the body is largely symbolic (*i.e.*, itself mediated by language). The immanence of consciousness is displaced in Lacan by the immanence of language. Whereas, for Sartre, language is an external means deployed by consciousness, for Lacan, consciousness is thoroughly permeated by language and does not exist for itself (hence does not exist absolutely) apart from language. Indeed, for Lacan, even the "unconscious is structured like a language" (SSDD, *Écrits*,298)[5] – *i.e.*, affects only manifest themselves symbolically. The affect in question here, desire, is "an effect in the subject of that condition which is imposed upon him by the existence of . . . discourse to cause his need to pass through the defiles of the signifier" (LDO,185).

Passing on to the body – specifically to the complex of relations between embodiment, language, and desire – we find that, for Lacan, "the phallus is a signifier – the signifier of signifiers in fact" (LDO,186) and, moreover, "the signifier of desire."[6] Rather than the penis, it is the phallus as signifier that mediates in the dialectic of desire between child and parent, self and other. There is a problem here: one must ask whether this naïve distinction between penis and phallus can finally be sustained in the context of Lacanian discourse – despite the fact that he, himself, trades on it.[7] " . . . The phallus," he says, "that is, the image of the penis, is negativity in its place in the specular image. It is what predestines the phallus to embody *jouissance* in the dialectic of desire" (SSDD, *Écrits*, 319). Phallus, signifier that it is, wins its status as symbol in contradistinction to penis. But here 'penis' is also already a signifier. And as signifier, falls prey to Lacan's absolute definition:

> My definition of a signifier (there is no other) is as follows: a signifier is that which represents the subject for another signifier (SSDD, *Écrits*,316).

The point – to appropriate David Krell's term – is that once the penis has been engorged, taken into the gorge of language, it is lost as flesh, and transformed into a signifier.[8] Here is a castration that Freud did not anticipate: once the penis becomes the phallus, it can no longer *be* a penis, much less function as one. And, since the phallus depends on the *aufgehoben* penis for its own significance, one begins to wonder how it can have one.

One might ask the same question about need. Once engorged, once taken into language (as it always already must have been), once defiled (*i.e.*, caused "to pass through the defiles of the signifier"), it exists as desire. It is demand that gives desire "its proper place" – that is, "the margin in which demand becomes separated from need" (SSDD, *Écrits*,311). Again, "desire is born from the split between need and demand" (LDO 189), in the *Spaltung*, in the place of the difference. But this is a place opened by language. Need has been displaced by desire. It has been put out of play: it has been *aufgehoben*, defiled, barred from *jouissance* – it cannot be satisfied, because it can no longer *be* need. But then what of desire, the signifier that needs need for its own significance? It cannot be satisfied either – which Lacan acknowledges (LDO,190) – it can only be mediated further in the discourse of analysis, in the cut [*coupure*] in false or ordinary discourse, where demand can be recognized as such (although reciprocation is barred here, too). Yet, this recognition is also mediated, defiled: as with need, so too with demand: "there is no demand that does not in some sense pass through the defiles of the signifier" (SSDD, *Écrits*,309). Hence, this defilement of recognition, this prohibition of reciprocation, is preordained – although the authentic recognition of love seems (to me, at least) to presuppose some sort of reciprocation.

Desire, once engorged, leads only to further engorgement.

Or, in other signifiers, both differences – the difference between self and other, and the difference between the subverted subject and its Other – once inscribed into existence, cannot be erased, ridden over: there is only iteration of mediation which never reaches its end, even momentarily (*i.e.*, in any of its moments).

Merleau-Ponty

The Hegelian teleology is as apparent in Merleau-Ponty's scattered account of desire as it is in the thematic treatments offered by Sartre and Lacan: the telos of desire is recognition and reciprocation of desire. And the fundamental obstacle – difference – also remains constant. However, the pessimism of Sartre and Lacan is not found in Merleau-Ponty, but neither is he an Hegelian optimist. The difference lies in difference.

Hegel's optimism is grounded in his speculative projection of higher levels of self-consciousness in which the difference generated by the particularity of subjectivities will be surpassed in the passage to universality.[9] For Merleau-Ponty, no consciousness can exist without incarnation, and because "I am always on the same side of my body" (VI,148),[10] there is a fission/dehiscence/*écart* intrinsic to flesh which ensures that incarnate consciousness will never merge in the oneness of a universal *Geist*. This ultimate reconciliation, nonetheless, endures in Merleau-Ponty's philosophy as the regulative ideal of philosophical discourse[11] – "there is no doubt that language is the presumption to a total accumulation . . . " – but "the fact remains that language could deliver up the thing itself only if it ceased to be in time and in situation. Hegel is the only one who thinks that his system contains the truth of all others . . . " (ILVS,*Signs*,81).[12] So, for Merleau-Ponty, difference is never totally overcome.

But this does not generate pessimism, as it does for Sartre and Lacan, because the difference of *écart*/divergence is different from the difference of irremediable alienation. Alienation, for Merleau-Ponty, is founded upon something more primordial. In the *Phenomenology of Perception*, it is the prepersonal world of communality, the world of the child "which he unhesitatingly believes accessible to all around him" (PP,355),[13] a world in which our perspective views are not independent but "slip into each other and are brought together finally in the thing" (PP,353). In "The Child's Relations with Others," it is the world of "syncretic sociability," with its correlative moments of "transitivism and mimesis," founded upon "the absence of a division between myself and others" (PriP,135).[14] This is a world of primordial unity which is sundered when the infant learns, through his experience with the mirror, to distinguish himself from others, and, later (at about age twelve)[15] is fragmented with the achievement of the cogito when, as Merleau-Ponty – citing Hegel – says, there "begins that struggle between consciousnesses" in which each one "seeks the death of the other" (PP,355). The point here is that alienation presupposes a prior solidarity.

> For the struggle ever to begin, and for each consciousness to be capable of suspecting the alien presences which it negates [*pour que chaque conscience puisse soupçonner les présences étrangères qu'elle nie*], all must necessarily have some common ground and be mindful of their peaceful coexistence in the world of childhood (PP,355; PP-F,408).

Difference, for Merleau-Ponty, is subtended by the common world of childhood, but aggravated by the emergence of the separate identity or ego, and reaches a crescendo with the alienated reflection of the adolescent cogito. It is then – magically coincidental with the sudden onslaught of the body's sexual maturation – that desire appears full-blown in reaction to the alienation it feeds upon and opposes in the effort to overcome difference.

Let me stress this point: for Merleau-Ponty, it is difference that is to be overcome, not the other as person. But – to anticipate the obvious objection – can this distinction be drawn? The other as person is the other as *other, i.e.*, as different. How can the difference be overcome without overcoming the person who *is* other?

First, the *via negativa*. Difference is not overcome in the retrograde nostalgia for infantile oneness: not in futile longing for a return to the womb or in an equally impossible retrieval of the era before the fateful Socratic cogito. Nor is difference to be overcome in the projection of an ascension from the body into the universal ideality of the Absolute's homecoming. Rewind or fast-forward: to go all the way is to end in emptiness, nonbeing, or death.

The very fact of embodiment precludes absolute overcoming of difference: as noted earlier, I am always on the same side of my body. But the same fact of embodiment precludes difference from becoming the absolute that it is for Sartre, Lacan, and one or two others. The other is not absolutely other because the other is flesh as I am flesh, because other and I partake in the flesh of a common world. Flesh of the world: is this glib metonymy, sleight of tongue to dissemble a dissemblance? Flesh has certainly been used that way – by Sartre and the all-too-ardent of Merleau-Ponty's followers. But Merleau-Ponty articulates the flesh sufficiently to let us see its philosophical significance.

In the early texts is found the transfer of corporeal schemata, Merleau-Ponty's refinement of Husserl's pairing,[16] which is the perceived functional identity of my own body and the other's. This common modality or shared style of motility induces the baby of fifteen months to open its mouth "when I playfully take one of its fingers between my teeth and pretend to bite it" (PP,352), "because the body image ensures the immediate correspondence of what he sees done and what he himself does" (PP,354). Here, together with Merleau-Ponty's recurrent correction of Sartre's ontological bifurcation of "double sensations" – that is, his doctrine that my finger must be touched if it is to touch, as my eyes must be visible if I am to see – are the origins of the corporeal reflexivity, the ill-named tacit cogito, that emerge in *The Visible and the Invisible* as the reversibility of flesh.[17]

Let me turn now to that text and quote a passage that will provide the foundations for the conclusions I draw on the subjects of desire,[18] language, and embodiment.

> As soon as we see other seers, . . . henceforth, through other eyes we are for ourselves fully visible; that lacuna where our eyes, our back, lie is filled, filled still by the visible, of which we are not the titulars . . . What is proper to the visible is . . . to be the surface of an inexhaustible depth: this is what makes it able to be open to visions other than our own . . . For the first time, the seeing that I am is for me really visible; for the first time, I appear to myself completely turned inside out under my own eyes. For the first time also, my movements no longer proceed unto the things to be seen, to be touched, or unto my own body occupied in seeing and touching them, but they address themselves to the body in general and for itself (whether it be my own or that of another), because for the first time, through the other body, I see that, in its coupling with the flesh of the world, the body contributes more than it receives, adding to the world that I see the treasure necessary for what the other body sees. For the first time, the body no longer couples itself up with the world, it clasps another body, applying itself to it carefully with its whole extension, forming tirelessly with its hands the strange statue which in turn gives everything it receives; the body is lost outside of the world and its goals, fascinated by the unique occupation of floating in Being with another life, of making itself the outside of its inside and the inside of its outside. And henceforth movement, touch, vision, applying themselves to the other and to themselves, return toward their source and, in the patient and silent labor of desire, begin the paradox of expression (VI,143–44).

What I see in the world is visible to and can be seen by others. The seeing that I am, my body's perceptual relations to the other objects of the world, is visible to the other. And through the reversibility of vision – that is, because his seeing is reciprocally visible to me – the seeing that I am becomes visible to me. Because we have bodies, because we are flesh, we are visible to ourselves through other eyes. If I were not incarnate, if I were a consciousness separable from my body, if my body were absolutely alien, this reversibiity would not be possible, and I would not be visible to myself through the eyes of the other. It is embodiment that allows me to find the recognition I desire in the other's eyes. But it is also my body that keeps me from coinciding with the other: from where I stand, here, I can see the recognition in his face over there. There is an ek-stasis of vision, but not a merging.

There is a similar tale to be told in the domain of touch where reversibility grants an intimacy to the caress that Sartre somehow missed. I can feel my own tangibility/substantiality/presence in her enveloping touch, and I can feel her feeling me – not because her caress incarnates me, but because we were both flesh from the start.

But note that Merleau-Ponty speaks of this as the *silent* labor of desire. That does not mean that we cannot or should not speak. It means that what we seek to express is something beyond words, transcendent to speech; something to talk about, to evoke, but never capture. It is, perhaps, more evident here than in any other case that "expression fades out before what is expressed," (PP,401), that "language goes beyond itself to what it signifies," "that signs do not simply evoke other signs for us and so on without end, and [that] language is not like a prison we are locked into . . . " (ILVS, *Signs*,81). Merleau-Ponty agrees with Lacan that vision itself and therefore also touch are "'structured as a language'" – but they are "articulation before the letter" (VI,126). The paradox of expression is that it articulates a logos it did not create, a logos which would not be a logos without that articulation.

This is not to deny the transcendental function of language, to ignore the structures of *Sinngebung* and sedimentation. It is true that "the sensible gives back to me what I lent to it" – what had been sedimented there through the meaning-giving power of signifiers – but it is also true that "this is only what I took from it in the first place" (PP,214). The symbolic value of phallus endows the penis with overdetermined significance, but it is from the penis as natural endowment that this significance came. The phallus is only symbolically capable of *jouissance*, but it enjoys that significance only by virtue of the generative power of the body's own penis.

The origin and obstacle of desire is difference, essentially the difference between self and other.[19] If self and other are conceived as insular, each imprisoned within his own sphere of immanence – either the immanence of consciousness or the immanence of language – then difference becomes absolute and all attempts at mediation ultimately fail. Even if one postulates a system of signifiers whose significances are somehow intersubjectively understood – that is, "a secondary speech which conveys thought already acquired" (PP,389) – there is no way within it that a self can experience his recognition by a genuine other, because the only meaning such an other could convey would already be among the self's acquisitions, hence could not provide what is sought in desire, namely, recognition of his "outside" or authentic encounter with transcendence, *i.e.*, the recognition of himself as he has not yet seen himself. And any language capable of authentic expression (or "originating speech"), *i.e.*, a language capable of expressing the transcendent vantage, derives that capacity by breaking the bonds of immanence and referring beyond itself to the silent world before the letter, *i.e.*, to the perceptual domain of pre-linguistic, mute significance.

Desire originates in difference and feeds upon it. It would vanish if, *per impossible*, the obstacle of difference were removed. Hence, the movement of desire, its *Trieb* or moving force, is based on the dynamics of mediation: *i.e.*, the economy of desire is a dialectical economy. And, as I have attempted to demonstrate, the mediating term is flesh: flesh of the body, flesh of the world. It is the separation of flesh into bodies that creates the difference, the reversibility of the flesh of the world that mediates it, and the *écart* or divergence of the flesh that maintains the obstacle of difference on the horizon – thereby ensuring the self-transcending growth of Eros.

Notes

1. G. W. F. Hegel, *Phänomenologie des Geistes* (Frankfurt am Main: Suhrkamp, 1973), p. 143. I am indebted to Dennis Schmidt for providing the translations appearing in my text. (Henceforth cited as *PhG*.)

2. Jean-Paul Sartre, *Being and Nothingness*, trans. Hazel Barnes (New York: Washington Square Press, 1966), p. 502. (Henceforth cited as *BN*.) *L'être et le néant* (Paris: Gallimard, 1943), p. 455. (Henceforth cited as *EN*.)

3. Anthony Wilden, "Lacan and the Discourse of the Other" in *The Language of the Self* (Baltimore, MD: Johns Hopkins University Press, 1968), pp. 162–63. (Henceforth cited as *LDO*.)

4. Jacques Lacan, "Propos sur la causalité psychique," *L'Evolution Psychiatrique*, No. 1 (1947). Reprinted in *Le Problème de la Psychogenèse des névroses et des psychoses*, ed. Henri Ey (Paris: Desclée de Brouwer, 1950) p. 45.

5. Jacques Lacan, "The subversion of the subject and the dialectic of desire in the Freudian unconscious," in *Écrits*, trans. Alan Sheridan (New York: Norton, 1977), p. 298. (Henceforth cited as *SSDD*.)

6. Jacques Lacan, Seminar, April–June 1958, p. 252. Quoted in *LDO*, pp. 187–88. See also "The signification of the phallus," *Écrits*, p. 285: " . . . The phallus is a signifier, a signifier whose function, in the intrasubjective economy of the analysis, lifts the veil perhaps from the function it performed in the mysteries. For it is the signifier intended to designate as a whole the effects of the signified, in that the signifier conditions them by its presence as a signifier."

7. "In Freudian doctrine, the phallus is not a phantasy, if by that we mean an imaginary effect. Nor is it as such an object (part-, internal, good, bad, etc.) in the sense that this term tends to accentuate the reality pertaining in a relation. It is even less the organ, penis or clitoris, that it symbolizes." [Jacques Lacan, "The signification of the phallus," *Écrits*, p. 285.]

8. "The phallus is the privileged signifier of that mark in which the role of the logos is joined with the advent of desire.

> "It can be said that this signifier is chosen because it is the most tangible element in the real of sexual copulation, and also the most symbolic in the literal (typographical) sense of the term, since it is equivalent there to the (logical) copula. It might also be said that, by virtue of its turgidity, it is the image of the vital flow as it is transmitted in generation.
>
> "All these propositions merely conceal the fact that it can play its role only when veiled, that is to say, as itself a sign of the latency with which any signifiable is struck, when it is raised [*aufgehoben*] to the function of signifier.
>
> "The phallus is the signifier of this *Aufhebung* itself, which it inaugurates (initiates) by its disappearance." [Jacques Lacan, "The Signification of the phallus," *Écrits*, pp. 287–88.]

And thus it was that the Flesh became Word.

9. "Hegel's expression: *an sich oder für uns* = there is a thought (the reflective thought) that, precisely because it would like to grasp the thing in itself immediately, falls back on the subjectivity – And which, conversely, because it is haunted by the being for us, does not grasp it and grasps only the thing 'in itself,' in signification." [Maurice Merleau-Ponty, *The Visible and the Invisible*, ed. Claude Lefort, trans. Alphonso Lingis (Evanston: Northwestern University Press, 1968), Working Note of June 4, 1959, p. 199.] What Merleau-Ponty says here of the thing holds as well for self and other: they are grasped only in the move to the universal, *i.e.*, to pure significance – which means that they are grasped only in abstraction from the concrete, *embodied* self and other.

10. Maurice Merleau-Ponty, *The Visible and the Invisible*, p. 148. (Henceforth cited as *VI*.)

11. "There is one particular cultural object which is destined to play a crucial role in the perception of other people: language. In the experience of dialogue, there is constituted between the other person and myself a common ground; my thought and his are interwoven into a single fabric, my words and those of my interlocutor are called forth by the state of the discussion, and they are inserted into a shared operation of which neither of us is the creator." [Maurice Merleau-Ponty, *Phenomenology of Perception*, trans. Colin Smith (London: Routledge and Kegan Paul, 1962), p. 354.]

12. Maurice Merleau-Ponty, "Indirect Language and the Voices of Silence" in *Signs*, trans. Richard McCleary (Evanston: Northwestern University Press), p. 81. (Henceforth cited as *ILVS.*)

13. Maurice Merleau-Ponty, *Phenomenology of Perception*, p. 355. (Henceforth cited as *PP.*) *Phénoménologie de la perception* (Paris: Gallimard, 1945), p. 407. (Henceforth cited as PP-F.)

14. Maurice Merleau-Ponty, "The Child's Relations with Others," trans. W. Cobb, in *The Primacy of Perception*, ed. James Edie (Evanston: Northwestern University Press, 1964), p. 135.

15. "At about twelve years old, says Piaget, the child achieves the *cogito* . . ." (*PP*, 355).

16. Edmund Husserl, *Cartesian Meditations*, trans. Dorion Cairns (The Hague: Nijhoff, 1960), sect. 51.

17. See M. C. Dillon, "Merleau-Ponty and the Reversibility Thesis," *Man and World*, vol. 16, 1983.

18. See M. C. Dillon, "Erotic Desire," in *Research in Phenomenology*, vol. XV, 1985.

19. There is, however, an equally important difference between self and self since reflection is essentially self-alienation, *i.e.*, self becoming other to itself.

4. Engorged Philosophy II*

David Farrell Krell

Two very different plans occupied my thoughts in preparation for the "Language and Desire" symposium. The first plan: I would take my departure from Lacan's 1972–73 seminar *Encore* and discuss the meaning of hysteria in relation to the *jouissance* of God, tracing such hysteria back to Plato's grand comedy, *Timaeus*, and then forward to Schelling's magnificent tragedies, *On the Essence of Human Freedom* (1809) and *The Ages of the World* (1810–14). Yet the very thought of compressing the history of hysteria into a twenty-five-minute presentation induced in me shortness of breath, a nervous tic, and irrepressible giggling. The second plan: I would leave all books aside and recount a fable about a man and woman who were lying together telling the truth, and about how, as they were together lying telling the truth she let it slip out that she had come to be lying on account of his *voice*, and he, after initial shock and chagrin, suddenly hearing in this confession the echo of his own desire for her, or of his desire for her own desire of him, or of herself, neither could say. Yet this second plan seemed even more intricate than the first. I therefore determined to do something straightforward and uncomplicated – and so I shall speak about Husserl, Merleau-Ponty, and Jacques Derrida.

Yet even this third plan – for there was no fourth – involves a story of its own. Several years ago I was asked to participate in a workshop on Jacques Derrida's essay "Differance" (1968). My task was to interpret what Derrida writes there about Freud. Following the trace of *desire* through Derrida's text, desire as constitutive of all signification, I was led back to the books *Voice and Phenomenon* and *Of Grammatology*, both published in 1967. There the thread of desire plunged into a complex weave of the nature of writing and the voice, the repression of writing in metaphysics, and the silencing of the voice in that phenomenon by which one hears and understands oneself while talking – the *s'entendre parler.* Derrida seemed to argue that in and for the history of metaphysics, as desire for presence, speech is privileged and writing repressed.

My initial reply to *Voice and Phenomenon,* a reply that was no doubt based on a misunderstanding, was that in our history the voice is suppressed every bit as much as writing is repressed: only in the absolute silence of pure autoenoesis – thought thinking itself – is the philosopher allowed to raise his or her voice. Similarly, for every Derridean example of repressed writing, I could think of several celebrations of writing in our tradition, from Sacred Scriptures to the Code of Hammurabi to Descartes, nestled before the hearth, meditating perhaps, but writing indubitably.

To be sure, *Of Grammatology* complicated my rather too neat separation of voice and writing when it introduced its analyses of phonetic writing, linearity, "proto-writing," and "good" and "bad" writing. "Bad" writing, as the tradition reads it, is writing in which the "corporeal integument" of signification, the signifier, obtrudes in such a way that the signified loses its transparency and becomes opaque, inky, worldly, well-nigh immoral. However, it still seemed that the identical structures of repression were, in fact, at work in the suppression of the voice, and the title of my reply, "Engorged Philosophy," meant to combat such repression. I found it arresting to associate the gorge, the profound throat, if you will, with other kinds of engorgement: of the penis, lips, clitoris, and other organs with blood; of the esophagus with chyle (those luscious clumps of food and spit); and of the breast with milk. And I became obsessed with the very words lodged in and around the throat: *la gorge,* the anterior/interior part of the neck, home of the larynx and pharynx, that is, the voice-box and the place where the nostrils, esophagus, and windpipe converge, the space of the glottis as well as the cleft known as the *rima glottidis.* Yet *la gorge* is also a cleft or hollow in the landscape. And finally, it is the cleavage and, by metonymy, the breasts of woman. The Germans say *Schlund* when they want to stress the animal cravings of the throat [*der Schlund,* from *schlingen,* to swallow or gulp] or when they wish to indicate that declivity in the forest that is so dangerous for woodcutters. They say *die Kehle* when it is a matter of the throat's getting split. Again emphasizing the animal in man, they may refer to *der Rachen,* related to both the Nordic *hrāka,* "saliva," and the Greek κράζω, to crow or caw, clearly the origins of the French *cracher,* to clear the throat and expectorate. *Der Rachen,* after Abelian-Freudian inversion, is the beautiful English word *craw*. The upshot of all this was that for a tradition bent on getting the σῆμα out of the σῶμα, signification out of its incarcerating incarnation, the word *engorgement* and the phrase *engorged philosophy* seemed designed to stick . . . in the throat.

Yet it is not simply a matter of words. It is also a matter of a particular kind of experience of the voice and throat. Sartre described one such experience in *La nausée*. There Roquentin invokes the *je pense*, yet one whose flavor is rather different from the *cogito* of Descartes's *Meditations*. Roquentin muses in this way:

> There is effervescent water in my mouth. I swallow it, it slides down my throat, it caresses me – and there it is again, reborn in my mouth; into all eternity I shall have in my mouth a tiny pool of whitish water – quite discreet – which glides across my tongue. And this pool, it too is me. And the tongue. *Et la gorge, c'est moi.*[1]

Sartre's description induces the following questions: If for the tradition there is bad writing and bad talk, are the repression of the former and banishment of the latter nothing other than a denial of the human body as such, a refusal of flesh? If so, how would Derrida's suspicion confront the thought of Maurice Merleau-Ponty? How would deconstruction encounter the phenomenology of embodiment? If the scene of writing proves to be *in* and *of* the world,[2] must not deconstruction run headlong into a phenomenology that is *at* the world and a thinking that is interlaced *with* the world?

Three questions:

1. What status do the descriptions of the voice have in Derrida's *Voice and Phenomenon*? Are they meant to be, must they be, *can* they be, "phenomenological" descriptions?
2. Can we elaborate Derrida's descriptions with the aid of Merleau-Ponty's texts in a way that would be fruitful for our reading of both?
3. Might such descriptions and the theme of engorgement serve as a matrix for a discussion of "language and desire?"

Derrida De-scribes

Derrida's inquiry into the Husserlian distinction within the sign between expression (*Ausdruck*) and indication (*Anzeichen*) comes to a head, so to speak, in the sixth chapter of *Voice and Phenomenon*, "The Voice that Preserves Silence." Let us read closely a number of its central paragraphs, those on pages 84–90 of the French edition, pages 75–80 of the English translation.[3] They are, perhaps, the central paragraphs of the book. Their subject is nothing other than voice and phenomenon. Here the *voice* comes to be heard *phenomenologically*; the latter word resounds repeatedly in these paragraphs. Derrida's initial argument – though I do it an injustice to call it an argument, as though all its terms were known – may be reduced to the following eight steps.

1. There is in Husserlian phenomenology an "unfailing complicity" between idealization and the voice.

2. Because the phenomenological voice does not enter the space of the world, it conducts expression to putative universality and infinity.

3. "The passage to infinity characteristic of the idealization of objects is one with the historical advent of the φωνή."

4. The history of φωνή is also the history of τέχνη, understood as the compulsion to technical mastery: phenomenology claims that within the realm of the *ich kann* it can posit an infinite number of times its ideal objects as identical.

5. Phenomenological ideality must be constituted, expressed, and reiterated in a medium that does not impair the presence of its object and the self-presence of its act.

6. *"The name of this element is the voice."*

7. The speaking subject hears and understands itself speaking – *s'entend parler* – in such a way that its words remain "alive," perdure in a "living present," and never lose themselves in the reaches of a lost time.

8. All nonphonic signifiers, all *written* signs, bar passage to the infinite, inasmuch as they are visible, spatial, "outside," in the world: dead.

Derrida's demonstration is itself quite intricate, highly technical. Yet it points to something pervasive in our culture. Consider the following lines from Coleridge's "Dejection: An Ode":

> Ah! from the soul itself must issue forth
> A light, a glory, a fair luminous cloud
> Enveloping the Earth –
> And from the soul itself must there be sent
> A sweet and potent voice, of its own birth,
> Of all sweet sounds the life and element![4]

And recall William James's eminently sober account of the complicity of idealization and the voice.[5] The context, in chapter ten of *The Prin-*

ciples of Psychology, is the "difficulty of apprehending Thought as a purely spiritual activity." James writes:

> In consenting and negating, and in making a mental effort, the movements seem more complex, and I find them harder to describe. The opening and closing of the glottis play a great part in these operations, and, less distinctly, the movements of the soft palate, etc., shutting off the posterior nares from the mouth. My glottis is like a sensitive valve, intercepting my breath instantaneously at every mental hesitation or felt aversion to the objects of my thought, and as quickly opening, to let the air pass through my throat and nose, the moment the repugnance is overcome. The feeling of the movement of this air is, in me, one strong ingredient of the feeling of assent.[6]

James notes the way in which strongly felt desires or aversions cause the feeling of centeredness in the head to be displaced downward to the rest of the body. Yet the head and throat retain a certain privilege: it is still the "godly" head of Plato's *Timaeus* (69d–e), with the neck serving as the "isthmus and boundary" that separates the head from the bestial body. James continues:

> In a sense, then, it may be truly said that, in one person at least, *the 'Self of selves,' when carefully examined, is found to consist mainly of the collection of these peculiar motions in the head or between the head and throat.* I do not for a moment say that this is *all* it consists of, for I fully realize how desperately hard is introspection in this field. But I feel quite sure that these cephalic motions are the portions of my innermost activity of which I am *most distinctly aware.* If the dim portions which I cannot yet define should prove to be like unto these distinct portions in me, and I like other men, *it would follow that our entire feeling of spiritual activity, or what commonly passes by that name, is really a feeling of bodily activities whose exact nature is by most men overlooked.*[7]

James himself appears to shy away from the conclusions toward which his own descriptions and analyses draw him.[8] And at all events, it may be perverse to extend the parallel between *The Principles* and *Voice and Phenomenon* any further. Therefore, I will return to my proper theme.

Derrida now proceeds to question what he calls "the phenomenological value of the voice." His series of moves may be summarized in three steps:

1. The transcendental dignity of the phonic signifier rests on a peculiar semblance, one that defines the metaphysics of truth in terms of an opposition between Being and "mere" appearance.

2. The ruling semblance – the origin of the fabulous "True World" – arises from the phenomenologically *given* convergence of expressed signification and expressing act.

3. Such convergence and such "giving" eventuate because the phenomenological body of the phonetic signifier "seems to fade away at the very moment it is produced," *phenomenologically reducing itself* to pure transparency and ideality.

An unexpressed corollary of this last point is that the famous phenomenological *epochē* or reduction (in all its transcendental and eidetic varieties) is but a bemused repetition of a particular auto-affection (or even *automatism* in Lacan's sense), a repetition that takes itself to be – because it gives itself out as – originary and founding. This, of course, makes the question of the phenomenological status of Derrida's own descriptions, and of his access to the phenomenon under discussion, a burning question: indeed, a conflagration. For Derrida has already quite unobtrusively adopted the gestures and the tone of voice – as though in impersonation – of The Phenomenologist himself: "In any event, the phenomenon of voice, the phenomenological voice, *gives* itself out in this manner" (VP,85/76). How true-to-life Derrida's impersonation is! Only the slightest demi-semiquavers of commas, indicating (if not expressing) pure apposition and equivalence, separate the two phrases: "the phenomenon of voice," comma, "the phenomenological voice," comma. Here indeed is what David Wood has called "the high-grade mimicry of transcendental arguments" in Derridean strategy.[9] In sober mimicry, Derrida continues: "When I speak, it belongs to the phenomenological essence of this operation that *I hear/understand myself* at the same time that I speak." Let us now interrogate the mime, the *mimique*.

"When I speak . . . ." Is this the *I* of Husserlian "solitary speech," the "universally operative indication" that Derrida discusses at the beginning of his chapter? Or is the *I* being written (if not spoken) in *epochē*? Do either the *I* or the *epochē* by this time have any *life* left in them?

" . . . it belongs to the phenomenological essence of this operation . . . ." *Eidetic* essence? Has "this operation" been subjected to eidetic variation? Has sufficient effort gone into the task of breaking up the monolithic demonstrative pronoun *this*?

" . . . that *I hear/understand myself* at the same time that I speak . . . ." Yet if the voice of The Phenomenologist preserves silence, in what sense does it ever really speak at all? Does the ear of The Phenomenologist ever hear anything like a melody or a tone, does it ever hear its own voice? Or does it not rather exercise a mathematically trained yet woefully impoverished *imagination* and then *write*.

To be sure, it is not The Phenomenologist's voice as such that Derrida has in mind.

> Such is the essence or normative quality of speech [*parole*]. It is implied in the very structure of speech that the speaker *hears himself*: both that he perceives the sensible form of the phonemes and that he understands his own expressive intention (VP,87/78).

Yet this subtle shift from *voix* to *parole*, the very structure of speech, should give us pause: if the phenomenological voice guards silence, then it certainly *never* breaks into speech. Even if Derrida is granted full liberty to invoke the "essence" and "very structure" of speech (but invoked *how*? eidetically? apodictically? adequately?), it is uncertain whether and in what way Husserlian lucubration might engage speech. Derrida is, therefore, right to continue, "Now, to account for the phenomenonological power of the voice, we shall have to specify the concept of pure auto-affection precisely and to describe what, in it, makes it open to universality."[10] Auto-affection is the dissimulative reduction of "even the inward surface of one's own body," writes Derrida, going down the throat of the phenomenology of the *corps propre* which, as we shall see he will claim to have eschewed. This "inward surface" is of course the gorge, the throat which tradition has torn inside out. Auto-affection *appears* to dispense with the body image and space in general, achieving an illusory self-proximity. More than proximity, we might add: perfect superposition, *volle Deckung*, of voice and phenomenon. Such self-proximity, more a proprietary holding than mere propinquity, has various names in philosophy: subjectivity, the *für sich*, consciousness and self-consciousness, the sphere of immanence. Not even spoken dialogue can shatter the crystalline purity of this monologue: to speak to another is to make him "*repeat immediately* in himself the *s'entendre parler* in the very form in which I produced it," and such tacit reproduction "*gives itself out* as the phenomenon of a mastery or a limitless power over the signifier." After describing the sovereign mastery of speech, which bestows on me my interiority and allows me to box the ears of all the others I address, box them and take them home with me, Derrida brings these paragraphs to dramatic peripety and denouement in one brief sentence: "This proximity is broken when, instead of hearing myself speak, I see myself write or gesture" (VP,90/80): *Incipit scriptio. Incipit tragoedia.*

It is unfair of me to truncate Derrida's presentation at this point. For the crucial demonstration – the generation of space and the effraction and engorgement of any pure "inside" with the protowriting of traces, the traces themselves proliferating by the fission of the living present in the process Derrida calls *differânce* – occurs only now, in the next few pages of chapter six. It is a devastating demonstration indeed, bringing to bear both the Hegelian dialectical and the Heideggerian ecstatic analyses of *time* on the Husserlian philosophy of *meaning*. Yet I will stop now, to recapitulate Derrida's descriptions and to suggest how the resonance of another phenomenological voice, that of Maurice Merleau-Ponty, might alter the course of Derrida's demonstration while conducting it to the same end. For "the irreducible openness in the inside," and "the eye and world within speech" (VP,96/86) emerge in the colloquy of both thinkers. In which neither gets his ears boxed.

It is a curious colloquy, to be sure, inasmuch as Derrida so seldom mentions Merleau-Ponty.[11] Yet it is difficult to imagine him being indifferent to the most important thing that happened to phenomenology in France. In a sense, we have Derrida's reply to "The Philosopher and His Shadow"; but where is the response to "Eye and Mind" or *The Visible and the Invisible*? Indeed, where is the response to *The Phenomenology of Perception*?

Derrida explicitly denies that "the phenomenology of one's own body" will enable us to comprehend fully the movement of idealization (VP,84/75), and at the very end of *Voice and Phenomenon* he repudiates phenomenology as such, which, he writes, "is always phenomenology of perception" (VP,117/104). The first phrase clearly refers to Merleau-Ponty; the second, too, appears to do so. Yet appearances, even at the end of metaphysics, can be deceptive. For the "perception" Derrida means is Husserlian proximity to the *Urquelle* of *Evidenz* in the "living present," the latter conceived ultimately as the *Quellpunkt* for internal time-consciousness and for all the contents of consciousness. Yet the thrust of Merleau-Ponty's phenomenology – stressing description rather than reflexive analysis, the always-already-there character of the world, the impossibility of complete reduction, the merely apparent independence of eidetic essences, and the "infinite meditation" or interrogation that can never be certain where it is headed – is to unsettle all the mechanisms and presuppositions of Husserlian phenomenology. As for the first phrase, on the lived body, in *Voice and Phenomenon* there is an *I* which, whether within reduction or outside of it, offers a compelling decription – a *scription*, no doubt, but one that is *about* something, a *de-scription* – of what happens when the *I* raises its voice. When that *I* speaks, it invokes an experience – *one* experience, a sharply profiled if terribly elusive experience – of mortal speech. If the *I* were not to speak, if there were no experience, no phenomenological voice giving-itself-out-as, if there were *no giving*, Derrida would have nothing to write home about. Concerning that experience, Merleau-Ponty might compell questions like the following (in reply to the eight points elaborated on pp. 55–56 above).

1. Must the voice function in unfailing complicity with idealization? Or might the voice itself, especially if it is engorged by Jacques Derrida or Maurice Merleau-Ponty, hear the dull reverberations of all its supposedly "pure ideas?"

2. Can the *speaking* voice – leaving the *phenomenological* voice to enjoy its chronic laryngitis – ever refrain from plunging into the space of the world? Is not the space of motility, the motility of glottis, tongue, teeth, lips and lungs, inevitably a space in the world, a space of situation rather than location? Are not the presumed infinity and universality of thought mere sedimentations of speech?

3. Is it phonality as such that is decisive for the tradition of intellectualism, or is it not rather the perceptual faith of anonymous visibility, along with the *disponibilité* of acquired speech and the hypocritical sentiment of eternity, that conjure the putative transparency of thought?

4. Need phonality and phonetic writing always and everywhere express themselves as technical mastery? What about the writer of fiction, who never knows what he will write until it is written? What of the proverbial orator or lover who can't wait to hear what he will have had to say? And how did Mallarmé become possible?

5. Does not Husserl's initial, pristine notion of intentionality subvert the genetic intent of both the reduction and constitution, so that phenomenological consciousness, far from being the pure self-presence of the *ich kann*, is cast forth again and again into the medium of an already constituted *Lebenswelt*?

6. Is it not precisely the voice-in-communication that introduces alterity into the speaking subject, allowing the speaker to deform acquired speech in order to say something new, although never allowing him to know for certain whether he is speaking or listening to language?

7. Are not my words – if I am speaking here and now – so alive that they leap into the space of the world, drawing me in their wake out of myself and making me an "allocutor," someone who speaks and is spoken *to* and who is never perfectly coincident in time?

8. Is it not the nonacoustic signifier, preeminently the written sign, that grants access to a monumentalized, scripturalized, immortalized infinite? Is not the most intriguing aspect of Derrida's analysis

of the voice the fact that *it never speaks* but only writes phenomenological or deconstructive tracts? Is there not a sense in which Derrida is so entirely right because he is so completely wrong? So that the result would be not a contradiction or a confusion but an *ambiguity*?

With regard to Derrida's remarks on "the phenomenological value of the voice" (see p. 58 above) Merleau-Ponty would perhaps intervene only at step three, where the phonetic signifier "seems to fade away at the very moment it is produced," thus allowing a kind of frictionless ascent into the realm of the signified. Here Merleau-Ponty would surely agree that such ascent is possible, although he would dispute its inevitability. But let me now give him the opportunity to comment for himself in detail.

Merleau-Ponty Writes

Both in the *Phenomenology of Perception* and the later writings, Merleau-Ponty emphasizes the rootedness of speech *and* writing in the spatiality of the gesturing body, one's *own* body, alive. Talking and writing alike can be described in terms of motility, kinesthetic stuctures, and the duly "deconstructed" body schema or body image. Is there not in Derrida's descriptions – in spite of his demur in *Voice and Phenomenon* and his rejection in *Grammatology* of what he calls "transcendental kinesthetics" – a residual genetic claim, a claim that spatialization as such is a matter of *écriture* or, at least, of an *archi-écriture*? Yet precisely that *archae*ological claim should give us pause, in the way that Foucault's archaeology of reason, madness, and power gave Derrida pause. If a genetic phenomenological residuum is found here, can we not at least try to dissolve it in a structural (if not structuralist) account of body space? Would writing, defined as the compromise transaction of hand and eye (G,409), derive its irreversibility from the temporalizing linearity of phonation? Or would writing be that gesture which is defined in the first place as a *prise* on the world of paper, parchment, or stone, a gesture that contains all its movements globally and that is prefigured in the two-handed, oriented, bilateral body-in-the-world?[12]

But let me hasten on to the second-order sense of body, according to which the signifier itself is flesh. In "On the Phenomenology of Language." Merleau-Ponty discusses the "quasi-corporeity of the signifier."[13] Here, as everywhere, he acknowledges the diacritical and differential nature of signification; precisely this "action at a distance" in language makes signification "an eminent case of corporeal intentionality." Just as the spatiality of my body is neither a location in geometric space nor a mental representation, so too speech and writing are neither physical causalities nor pure ideas. They have a *gestural* sense. Such sense Merleau-Ponty defines as a *trace*; that is, a meaning that is never wholly transparent or fully present. Yet, for Merleau-Ponty, the traces of speech and writing diverge in directions quite opposed to those sighted by Derrida.

In the *Phenomenology* (especially the chapters on "The Body as Expression, and Speech" and "The Cogito") Merleau-Ponty accounts for the intellectualist tradition of atemporalizing idealization in terms of *acquired* or *sedimented* expression. The *disponibilité* of achieved expression – *disponibilité* being the very word Derrida employs to express such mastery – creates the illusion of free-floating ideality. Although Merleau-Ponty does refer to examples of spoken words,[14] his analyses of sedimentation usually involve the *written* word, words on paper, which the eye in reading seems to follow yet actually *sees through* to the things signified. As we read the second *Meditation*, we glide across the printed lines of this particular musty artifact up to the ozone layer of the *cogito*. Derrida's eye follows the traces of these very lines, but it begins to hear Descartes whispering off the page. As a kind of proto-parole. Precisely in his insatiable reading, Derrida quits the eye and ultimately even the ear. He goes for the throat.

Both Merleau-Ponty and Derrida focus on the temporal character of expression, written and oral, although Derrida has much more to say than the former about how the time of the voice unfolds in and as the space of writing. And both thinkers celebrate the mysterious power of language to deform itself in order to say something new, Derrida in the dissemination of possible meanings or "blancs" in a text, Merleau-Ponty in the voices of silence – especially in the "musical ideas" of the novelist and poet.

In the manuscript on which Merleau-Ponty was working when he collapsed, *The Visible and the Invisible*, a remarkable anticipation – with a difference – of Derrida's treatment of the voice is found. That book was originally one part of a two-pronged project. Under the title *The Origin of Truth*, it was to have shown how a phenomenology of perception would proceed to the cultural and intellectual world, the realm of ideas. Simultaneously, a work entitled *Introduction to the Prose of the World* was to show how all ideas, whether musical, poetic, phiosophical, or mathematical, were forms of embodied expression: language would not be the clothing but the very flesh of thought. The latter work was abandoned, though its thesis never was; and the "origin of truth" became the fragment we possess today as *The Visible and the Invisible.* (Incidentally, there is some value in thinking of Derrida's *Of Grammatology* as situated at the point of convergence of these two fragments of Merleau-Ponty's project, even though *Of Grammatology* is doubtless more a reading of prose than a singing of the visible world.)

The central chapter of *The Visible and the Invisible* is entitled "The Intertwining – the Chiasm."[15] If the chiasm is Merleau-Ponty's answer to the question of "the origin of truth," then Derrida's reply to it can be readily imagined. Yet one should not be too quick to assume that for Merleau-Ponty origin means replete presence. If he closes his chapter with a reference to "ultimate truth," it is not in order to bathe that chapter in pure light but to allow it to return to an inexpungible obscurity and essential ambiguity. Merleau-Ponty's "ultimate truth" is given the title *reversibility.* It is not dialectical reversal or synthesis of any kind, but a "mystery as familiar as it is inexplicable"(VI,172). The reversibility by which my look seems both to strip and to envelop the things seen, "clothing the world with its own flesh" (VI,173); by which vision seems sovereign yet formed at the heart of the things we see; by which tactility is touched in turn by things it went out to manipulate, the hand itself proving to be as tangible as the eye is visible; such reversibility is no intellectualist sleight of hand. The word *reversibility* designates not transparency but the thickness of the body and the depths of the world. For Merleau-Ponty – who throughout the 1950s is reading Heidegger, as is Derrida – reversibility is a paradox of Being, not of Man: " . . . the body pertains to the order of things, as the world is universal flesh" (VI,181).

After discussing the reversibility of vision (the seeing/seen, the sensing/sensible), Merleau-Ponty proceeds to the question of expression, but not before developing his notion of intercorporeity, not before offering his astonishing description of the patient and silent labor of desire, lovemaking as the paradox of expression. Only then does the phenomenological voice come to speak in his text. Likewise, in *Signs,* which continues on the path opened up by the chapter "Others and the Human World" in the *Phenomenology,* Merleau-Ponty interprets Husserl's insistence that transcendental subjectivity is an intersubjectivity in such a way that inter*corporeity* invades and permeates the once sacrosanct sphere of immanence. As Merleau-Ponty extends his analysis of reversibility beyond the circle of visibility and intercorporeity, he invokes the movements of the human countenance, expressive gestures, "and, above all, these strange movements of the throat and mouth" which are called the voice.

Merleau-Ponty begins by echoing Hegel,[16] for whom sound [*Klang*] constitutes the first reverberation of subjectivity in nature, and then refers to specifically human sounds:

> Like crystal, metal, and many other substances, I am a sonorous being. Yet the vibration of me [*à moi*] I hear from within; as Malraux says, I hear with my throat [*je m'entends avec ma gorge*]. It is a matter in which, as he also says, I am incomparable; my voice adheres to the mass of my life as no one else's voice does. Yet if I am close enough to someone talking to hear his or her breath, to hear the effervescence or the fatigue, I attend in them, almost as I do in myself, the terrifying [*effrayante*] birth of vociferation. Just as there is a reflexivity of touch, of the view and of the system tactility/vision, so is there also a reflexivity of the movements of phonation and hearing: they have their sonorous inscription, the vociferations have in me their motor echo. This new reversibility and the emergence of the flesh as expression are the point of insertion of speaking and thinking in the world of silence. (VI,190)

A marginal note asks whether this reversibility of expression is new at all, or whether the perceived world is not always bubbling with speech and thought: the very notion of passage from a silent to a talking world will have to be overcome. And there are even more severe problems with the description than this one. I shall proceed to them directly – after repeating one phrase from the description in order that it may exercise its full impact on the project we associate with the name Jacques Derrida. Merleau-Ponty writes that a reversibility or reflexivity "of the movements of phonation and hearing" exists and he accounts for that reversibility in this way: such movements "have their *sonorous inscription*, the vociferations have in me their motor echo." If something like a Merleau-Ponty/Derrida colloquy (never a debate!) develops, might it not hinge on the question of the relation of *sonorous inscription* to *archaic writing*? And would not such a colloquy link phenomenology and deconstruction to engorged philosophy?

Gorgo Listens

Merleau-Ponty is not satisfied to have expanded my hearing of my own speech *avec ma gorge* to hearing another speaker who is close to me; he introduces into his account a kind of divergence (*écart*) that enables me to hear myself from the outside, as it were, in the world. Along with my "heard voice" there is, he says, "my articulated voice"

(VI, 194–95). By that he appears to mean something different from what Derrida and Rousseau call the consonantal, algebraic voice (G, 443–44). From the very outset of speech, according to Merleau-Ponty, I am for myself not only a *locutor* but also an *allocutor*, someone speaking to and spoken to, even if I am only talking to myself. "To the extent that what I say has meaning, I am for myself, when I speak, another 'other'; and to the extent that I understand [*comprends*], I no longer know who is talking and who is listening" (S,121). Only through such intentionality or directionality can there be a *delocutor*; that is, the speech (of) which one is speaking. If we think of the figures on the Cozumalhuapa stele in the Dahlem Museum in Berlin, figures whose discourse with one another is portrayed by coiling ribbons of speech flowing from the mouth of each to the mouth (not the ears) of the other, then we must understand that both figures of the discourse embody and enact together what we call *language*. The articulated-reticulated bands go from gorge to gorge *through the medium of the world*.

Such reversibility, which is really a kind of *doubling*, is in danger of working to well – the intellectualist danger, par excellence. My speech, says Merleau-Ponty, "offers itself and all speech to a universal Speech" (VI,202). What would this articulated voice be which, while not dead, is outside of me as a second-order hearing? What makes this description so problematic – crying out, as it were, for deconstruction – is the fact that Merleau-Ponty seems to suppress the *effrayante* character of the birth of voice, the *frayage* or *breaching* of the gap, the gap I call Gorgo, in order to ascend to a "sublimated" and more highly rarified, "subtle," and "transparent" form of flesh. To incarnate this second-order reversibility of expression, he even conjures a quasi-Coleridgean glorified body, so that at the very moment when he wants to emphasize the fact that invisibility is *of* the visible, and speech and thought *of* the world, his writing slips into an all-too-familiar metaphysical register. Similarly, in *Signs* (S,100–01; 120), Merleau-Ponty persists in the notion of truth as "the presence of all presents," affirming the Husserlian fabulation of "living presence" as the *fons et origo* of all meaning, even though his own analysis of human temporality ought to have occluded such presence utterly. Yet Merleau-Ponty himself always and everywhere resists the inclination to ascend. At the end of his chapter on the chiasm, he plays on the word *entendre*, so central to Derrida's descriptions. To understand *is to hear*. Speech and ideality adhere to the world of perception, so that the putative progression *voir, parler, penser* is itself reversible and returns us to the flesh of the visible.

In Merleau-Ponty's progression, *voir, parler, penser,* Derrida would deconstruct the first term, which is also the last term, fearing that if all phenomenology is phenomenology of perception it will take visibility as its *Urquelle* of evidence. For Derrida, the second term, *parler,* occasions a dreamy ascent to the third, *penser,* which is unmentionable. Fearing that for Merleau-Ponty the intertwining works too well, Derrida seems determined not to allow it to work at all: he will not let us look at the world, it seems, but only at the World Book.

And yet! The scene of writing is *of the world;* the play of writing is the play *of history.* If the philosopher cannot quit the Hegelian gallery of spirit's heroes, a gallery that is in fact a labyrinth, he can surely learn that his own maze and the world are not coterminous. He must learn amazement. Foucault accuses Derrida of *la petite pédagogie,* with all the little scholars rapt to His Master's Voice. If we want to say that Foucault's accusation is unfair, as I am convinced it is, then we must insist on the worldly engagement – and engorgement – of deconstruction. We must insist on the phenomenological and even ontological weight (forgive these words; I know: they stick), we must insist on what I have called the frontal-ontological character of contemporary thought.

What of this voice, then, and what of the invaginated site of the metaphysics of *Sein und Schein*? (*Invagination,* incidentally, is Merleau-Ponty's word, along with the words *écart, dêhiscence, différence,* and *inscription.*) Is the voice *the* secret of idealization? Or is Merleau-Ponty right to ask (VI,211), "The proposal to demand of experience itself its secret – is this not already an idealist outlook on things?"

If it is not *the* secret of experience, and if deconstruction has made the intimacy of all "experience" suspect, the voice nonetheless remains one of the obsessions of an engorged philosophy. The flesh of the voice heard and understood remains *effrayante.* More Gorgo than Gorgeous. Why, after all, is the threat of mutism a knife at the throat, a total threat, a shadow of what Freud calls *Kastrationsangst*? Laryngitis, the burlesque of mutism, is comic in the way that jokes about circumcision are comic. Even the alienation of my voice from me in a tape recording evokes embarrassment, rage, and something like shame at the public exposure of my sphere of immanence ("Oh, but you *do* sound that way!" the others assure me, these idiots who have no call to be between my ears), a rage and shame that would be appropriate to the full frontal exposure of me naked to ridicule. And the gorge itself, this "isthmus" with its "sensitive valve?" How explain the burning resentment, the fury I feel at the onset of a simple sore throat? In many languages, a sore throat has the name *angina,* related to the word *Angst*. And when the word *angina* is pronounced in any Western tongue it reminds the speaker of yet another matrix, and the topic of "language and desire" becomes more intricate than I had hoped. This sleeved site, so susceptible, so vulnerable: the site of metaphysics from Plato through Hegel, the site of phenomenology and deconstruction alike.

After defining the enigmatic Zarathustra-type as the very paradigm of Dionysian philosophy, a philosophy that thinks the most abyssal thought – symbolized by the black snake bit fast in the shepherd's throat – Nietzsche asks, "What language would such a spirit speak when talking to itself alone?" He replies, "The language of *dithyramb*."[17] His example is the *Nightsong*, a song of "the desire to desire." Its opening lines:

> It is night: now all leaping fountains talk aloud.
> And my soul too is a leaping fountain.
> It is night: only now do all lovers' songs stir.
> And my soul too is a lover's song.
> An unsated, insatiable thirst is in me;
> it wants to be voiced. A craving for love
> is in me; it speaks the very language of love.
> I am light: O that I were night! But this
> is my solitude – that I am girded in light.
> *Ach, dass ich dunkel wäre und nächtig*!
> O that I were dark and of the night!
> How I would suck at breasts of light!

Notes

*On the title: see my brief essay, "Engorged Philosophy: A Note on Freud, Derrida and Differance," in *Derrida and Differance*, eds. David Wood and Robert Bernasconi (Warwick: Parousia Press, 1985), pp. 9-16.

1. Jean-Paul Sartre, *La Nausée* (Paris: Gallimard, 1938), p. 141.

2. See Jacques Derrida, *L'écriture et la différence* (Paris: du Seuil, 1967), pp. 335-37.

3. Jacques Derrida, *La voix et le phénomène* (Paris: Presses Universitaires de France, 1967), trans. David Allison, *Speech and Phenomenona* (Evanston: Northwestern University Press, 1973). (Henceforth cited as *VP*; French ed. page/American ed. page.)

4. Samuel Taylor Coleridge, "Dejection: An Ode," in *Selected Poetry and Prose of Coleridge*, ed. Schneider (New York: Holt, Rinehart and Winston, 1965), p. 128, 11. 53-58.

5. I am indebted to David Wood for directing me to James's remarkable pages. See William James, *The Principles of Psychology*, two vols. (New York: Henry Holt, 1890), vol. I, pp. 299–302.

6. *Ibid.*, p. 301.

7. *Ibid.*, pp. 301–02.

8. *Ibid.*, p. 305.

9. See David Wood, "Time and the Sign," *Journal of the British Society of Phenomenology, 13*, 2 (May 1982):149.

10. See *VP*, p. 88/79; see also Jacques Derrida, *De la grammatologie* (Paris: Minuit, 1967), pp. 405ff. (Henceforth cited as *G*.)

11. Derrida cites Merleau-Ponty in *L'Origine de la géométrie* (Paris: Presses Universitaires de France, 1962), on pp. 71, 116–118, 122, and in *De la grammatologie* on pp. 155 n.4 and 219 n.6. In both places the bone of contention in Husserl's relation to ethnological science and the problem of historical-cultural relativism. Derrida rejects Merleau-Ponty's reading of the later Husserl, one which would see a "striking difference" between the early and the late writings. Derrida is tempted to uphold a view that is "diametrically opposed" to Merleau-Ponty's: he argues that Husserl excludes the historical realm more and more as his work proceeds – whatever the usual understanding of Husserl's *Krisis* may lead us to believe. Perhaps the most intriguing of these references is Derrida's rejection of "existential" psychoanalysis of the style promoted by Merleau-Ponty. See *G*, p. 219 n.6. Finally, see Derrida's forceful rejection of Sartre and Merleau-Ponty in *Philosophy in France Today*, ed. Alan Montefiore (Cambridge: Cambridge University Press, 1983), p. 38. (My thanks to Robert Bernasconi for these references!)

12. It would be worthwhile to describe in great detail the Derridean and Leroi-Gourhanian "transaction" in terms of the spatiality of the lived body. The project would involve both of Husserl's assistants, Oscar Becker and Martin Heidegger, and would require an expansion of Derrida's remarks on indication [*Zeigen, Anzeichen*] and an introduction of *Greifen*, our grasp of the writing stylus, as a form of what Merleau-Ponty, after Gelb and Goldstein, called "abstract movement."

13. See Maurice Merleau-Ponty, *Signes* (Paris: Gallimard, 1960), pp. 110–11, for this and the following. (Henceforth cited as *S*.)

14. See Maurice Merleau-Ponty, *Phénoménologie de la Perception* (Paris: Gallimard, 1945), pp. 461–62, on the word *sleet*.

15. Maurice Merleau-Ponty, *Le Visible et l'invisible*, ed. Claude Lefort (Paris: Gallimard, 1964), pp. 172–204. (Henceforth cited as *VI*.)

16. See Sections 299–302 of G. W. F. Hegel, *Enzyklopädie der philosophischen Wissenschaften im Grundrisse* (1830), eds. Friedrich Nicolin and Otto Pöggeler (Hamburg: F. Meiner, 1969), pp. 247–50. See also Jacques Der-

rida, "Le Puits et la pyramide," in *Marges de la philosophie* (Paris: Minuit, 1972), pp. 79–127, esp. pp. 101–11.

17. Friedrich Nietzsche, *Ecce Homo*, in the *Kritische Studienausgabe*, eds. G. Colli and M. Montinari (Berlin: de Gruyter; Munich: DTV, 1980). vol. 6, p. 345.

Part III.
The Limits of Representation

5. Representation and Its Limits in Descartes

Dalia Judovitz

In his essay "The Age of the World Picture," Martin Heidegger describes the essence of modernity as established by Descartes in terms of the reduction of the world to a picture: "The world picture does not change from an earlier medieval one into a modern one, but rather the fact that the world becomes a picture at all is what distinguishes the character of the modern age."[1] In this essay, I will explore Heidegger's contention that the modern age is defined by the reduction of the world to a picture by examining the status and function of representation in Descartes. The concept of representation will be in question as the paradigm of a new set of relations between the Cartesian subject and the world. Representation will be understood not merely as a picture of the world, but rather as signifying the possibility of apprehending and grasping the world as a pictorial schema. Although the Renaissance and the Baroque philosophical and literary traditions recognize the allegorical and conventional function of representation, as exemplified in the Shakespearean dictum "The world is but a stage . . . ," in Descartes's work, representation takes on a new meaning. It ceases to function as a convention, and it acquires the objective character of truth as certitude based on the extension of epistemological principles to philosophy. In addition to its objective character, representation also implies a new agency, the construction of the subject (*cogito*), which governs its order axiomatically.

Representation is in question not in its traditional sense as rendering or presenting as an image, but rather as the index of the reduction of the world to a set of standards or norms, to a prototype. The limits of representation do not concern the character of the world-become-picture, but the conditions of possibility for reducing it to a pictorial schema. My analysis will show that representation (which as a prototype posits the conditions of possibility for all other pictures) involves the exclusion of the visual character of the image in favor of its figural interpretation. The notion of representation in Descartes is thus delimited in two different senses. By positing the conditions of possibility, or schema, through which the world can be grasped, representation has a transcendental function. As a prototype, it both subtends and determines the order of things. However, the power of representation, as a will to objectify the world, can be posited only through the production of another limit. The visual content of representation is excluded in order to promote its figural and symbolic interpretation. The concept of representation is thus symptomatic of a crisis: the reduction and dephenomenologization of the visual image, in favor of its interpretation as a rational symbolic form.

The formal and normative character of representation is based in Descartes's mathematization of knowledge, on his upholding mathematical certitude as the model for all other knowledge. I show that Descartes's interpretation of representation relies not only on the concept of *universal mathematics* (science of measure and order) but also on the philosophical and rhetorical traditions of the arts of memory and the Baroque. In doing so, I hope to modify the mathematical character of the epistemological requisite that Heidegger claims Descartes applies to the world.[2] Unlike Michel Foucault, who, in *The Order of Things*, echoing Heidegger, suggests that Descartes inaugurates the age of representation, I suggest that Descartes's particular foundational interpretation of representation involves the culmination and also exhaustion of the Neoplatonic and Baroque philosophical and literary traditions.[3] It is important to remember that the Neoplatonic philosophical and rhetorical traditions of the arts of memory already present a highly sophisticated understanding of representation and its pictorial and figural status. The Neoplatonists use allegorical representations as the figures of knowledge: emblematic images and rhetorical devices function as the loci or commonplaces for mnemonic devices. Frances Yates,in *The Art of Memory*, has shown that the Neoplatonist thinkers Campanella, Ficino, Bruno, and many others rely on allegorical figures or prototypes. Giulio Camillo uses a theatre (the very metaphor of representation) in order to define it allegorically as the general paradigm of knowledge.[4] Descartes's own search for a universal science as developed in his early writings (the *Preambles* and his correspondence of 1619) indicates his knowledge of the Neoplatonic tradition and the influence of the arts of memory as a rhetorical and allegorical tradition on the formulation of his project.

Descartes also found echoes of this Neoplatonic concern for representation in his own context, that of the French Baroque, which in both literature and philosophy (the movement of *libertinage érudit*) is concerned with the materialist character of representation. For the materialist philosophers (Gassendi, the brothers Patin, and others) and writers (Théophile de Viau, Charles Sorel, and Scarron) of the 1620s. representation is not as yet established as a formal schema.[5] Rather, baroque representation is defined by its lack of closure, formal unity, and metaphorical character – in other words, by the impossibility to enclose the world within a picture defined as a frame. For the Baroque tradition, described as an "eros of vision." *representation* takes on a new meaning: it no longer reflects being in a Platonic sense; rather, the essence of all representation is appearance. The most perfect representation or copy (*trompe l'oeil*) is nothing more than just that, representation. For the Baroque, representation is always allegorical: it is excessive, a site of endless doubling, proliferation, and illusion.[6] No representation has privilege over another, since the most perfect representation is nothing more than representation, *i.e.*, a material illusion based on convention or allegory. Baroque representation is described by its lack of a formal and foundational character, which is the expression of the crisis of knowledge of the period. The problem for the Baroque is that it cannot delimit knowledge and determine it as a stable theory, as an epistemology. This can be seen most clearly in Montaigne's *Essays*, where the essay as a formal expression of knowledge about the world is always tentative and open in its structure. Instead of providing a theory of knowledge for the world, the essay problematizes what it means to know, *i.e.*, interpretation.

Descartes's search for certitude in the *Rules for the Direction of the Mind* and *Discourse on the Method* can be seen as the reaction against the Baroque interpretation of representation as material illusion (*trompe l'oeil*). Certitude is a concept so clear, distinct, and transparent that it appears to escape and deny its own representational and material status. Descartes's relation to representation is critical of the Baroque interpretation of representation in visual and hermeneutic terms. For Descartes, representation is not only derivative in the Platonic sense, but also misleading as a guiding principle for knowledge. In Rule 1 of *Rules for the Direction of the Mind*, Descartes denounces resemblance because it produces an illusory sense of knowledge, one that denies the differences between things. He observes that when human beings notice a resemblance between things, they ascribe to each, even in those respects in which they differ, what they found true of the other.[7]

His attack on resemblance creates the effect of a break with the previous traditions, especially those of the Baroque that use resemblance as one of their models of knowledge. In Montaigne's *Essays*, resemblance is used as a convention with the recognition, however, that all resemblance implies a representation with a difference: "Resemblance does not make things as much alike as difference makes them dissimilar."[8] Resemblance for the Baroque is not a guiding convention, the basis of a theory of knowledge; it is merely one convention among others. For Montaigne, all representation is but interpretation. The sense of a break that is announced by Descartes's attack on resemblance must consequently be viewed with circumspection. Descartes's sense of crisis with regard to resemblance entails the critique of the Baroque concept of resemblance as a paradigm for representation. Decartes thus presents mathematical certitude as the answer to a crisis in the order of representation, whose conventional and problematic status was already amply understood and explored by the Baroque tradition. But this crisis is a fiction. Descartes's doubts regarding representation are merely the expression of his interpretation of representation according to mathematical constraints as a certitude.

Descartes's critique of resemblance in the *Rules* is accompanied by the elaboration of a new definition of knowledge based on what he calls *universal mathematics*, a conceptual interpretation of mathematics as a science of measure and order that functions both as a generalized logic and a symbolic language. It is based on several traditions, bringing together the mathematics of antiquity and the Renaissance with rhetorical and logical principles that include the arts of memory and Baroque paradigms. Although Descartes contends that his new science is purely a science of measure and order, a closer inspection of the *Rules* reveals that his concept of logical method and the order of arguments and reasons is also informed by rhetorical and logical commonplaces from the arts of memory and Baroque traditions. Whereas Heidegger and Foucault stress the mathematical character of Descartes's new science, I suggest that the Cartesian interpretation and application of *universal mathematics* is not purely mathematical as a science of measure and order.[9] Rather, by contextualizing Descartes's elaboration of his new science through other traditions, mnemonic, rhetorical, and logical, the mathematical character of his philosophy can be seen in its broader and schematic sense as the emergence of a theory of figuration.

This influence is most visible in Descartes's description of the formal principles of his new science: deduction and intuition. Deduction involves the breakdown of any argument into a "series of facts" that have a causal relation to each other insofar as "certain truths can be known from others" (Rule 6). By enumerating facts into a series of interconnected arguments or concatenations, Descartes arrives at the possibility of reducing these interconnected chains or links to a new kind of unifying vision, that of intuition. In Rule 3, Descartes defines intuition as follows:

> It is in a similar way (by clear and distinct vision) that we know that the last link in a long chain is connected with the first, even though we do not take in by means of one and the same act of vision all the intermediate links on which that connection depends, but only remember that we have taken them successively under review and that each single one is united to its neighbor, from the first to the last (HR 1, 8).

The metonymic movement of deduction is supposed to be so rapid as to reduce these interconnected chains to a final intuitive figure, whose character is both causal (it acts as a common unifying figure) and perceptual (described as clear and distinct idea). Descartes explains in Rule 7, that he learned to pass from the first link of the chain to the last so rapidly that "no stage in the process was left to the care of memory, but seemed to have the whole in intuition before me at the same time" (HR 1, 19). Thus, intuition is presented as a substitution and displacement of memory, and yet its schematic character (Rule 12) as the reduction of metonymic chains to a causal and common figure relies onthe same principles as the arts of memory. The Neoplatonic tradition uses commonplace figures in a schematic sense: as emblems, compendious abbreviations, and mnemonic devices. But the problem is that Descartes ceases to consider intuition as a device or a convention. Rather, he recognizes it as an end in itself, thus confusing its conceptual status with its perceptual status. Intuition as clear and distinct idea has the character of visual sensation, and yet, this perceptual dimension of the image in Descartes is elided by its conceptual function as a figure of thought.

Descartes's elaboration of intuition borrows the allegorical conventions of the arts of memory, those of metonymy and figurality in order to produce a new symbolic order in the *Rules*. This new order reduces the concatenation of philosophical arguments (discursive principles) to the intuition of a common image (figural principle). The concept of intuition elaborated by Descartes is the expression of both the traditions of mathematics and of the arts of memory. Its formal structure relies not merely upon concepts of mathematical figure, but also upon notions of rhetorical and logical figure. What is particularly striking, is the extent to which Descartes's reliance on the Neoplatonic and Baroque traditions (demonstrated by his correspondence, the *Preambles* and the *Rules*) exhausts and displaces it through the elaboration of his new paradigm based on epistemology. This is because Descartes presents the judgments by intuition, those of clear and distinct ideas, as the solution to what he perceives as the crisis of representation, of doubt and deceptive appearances that describe Baroque tradition. Although intuition and deduction are posited as the solution to the previous paradigm based on resemblance, this so-called solution preserves within its own structure the traditions and the contradictions it was intended to resolve.

Descartes's denunciation of visual resemblance (tied to illusion and appearance) is accompanied by his positing a new concept of representation based on figurality. He rejects knowledge based on ocular vision in favor of a formal system that schematizes the visible according to logical and rhetorical paradigms. The order of reasons is now based on a rhetorical rather than visual commonplace, discourse is reduced to figure and the structure of the arguments to intuition or metaphor.

Intuition stands simultaneously for the denunciation of one kind of vision, which can lead to error, and the affirmation of a new kind of vision that schematizes the visible.[10] This ambivalent relation to the visual, its exclusion and subsequent recovery as a schematic figure in the order of discourse, marks Descartes's special interpretation of representation. The concept of representation in the *Rules* thus emerges in its foundational sense as the axiomatic schema of the world. This interpretation of representation involves a change in its meaning and status as pictorial image. Representation in Descartes can no longer be understood purely as an image, since its visual pictorical status has been put into question by Descartes's critique of resemblance. Rather, the exclusion of the visual content of representation is recovered in terms of its formal figural character, the reduction of the chains of reason to intuition. Consequently, representation functions as a symbolic schema or commonplace that frames and establishes the conditions of possibility of all images intended to reflect or display an understanding of the world.

Descartes's *Rules* thus presents a concept of science whose order exceeds the purely mathematical definition of the science as measure and order. Consequently, Cartesian mathematics is not purely "mathematical." Rather, the Cartesian epistemology developed in the *Rules* must be considered in the broader sense as a theory of representation that inherits certain formal features of traditional mathematics. Foremost among them is the notion of certitude and axiomatic truth. But Descartes's interpretation of mathematics also involves a conceptual move. He posits a new symbolic order that is also informed by the rhetorical and logical traditions preceding him.

Descartes's new mathematical order in the *Rules* and elaborated in *The Discourse on the Method* challenges the privilege heretofore accorded to the divine order, and changes its character as well. Nature is now brought before man as the objective, and placed in the realm and within the schema of a conventional order of knowledge. Cartesian method is erected as a rational set of relations and a nomative evaluation of the world. Rather than merely describing things, it actually prescribes them by setting them up in advance hypothetically as a prototype. Since mathematics axiomatically constructs the objects it proposes to recognize, it discovers only that which it produces. It pursues only those questions to which it has possible answers. Descartes's elaboration of method thus expands the meaning of theory of representation outlined in *Rules*. By extending his mathematical/rhetorical approach to philosophy, he posits a new demand upon philosophical thought – that its truth be defined as adequacy and verification of its axiomatic propositions. Philosophical truth thus comes to express the objective character of representation, and not as it pretends, an objective description of the world. The new philosophical language encompasses both man and nature in its hypothetical outreach. Neither can be conceived outside the structure of representation – measure, order, and figure. Rather, they must be understood as products of its axiomatic character, its schematic outline. Representation thus imposes a hierarchical relation to the world, one where presentation of the character of objects under consideration is subsumed within its own conventional order.

Descartes's new mathematical rhetorical order thus emerges as more than just an epistemology. It is a theory of representation, the affirmation of the subject's precedence over what there is, now become a picture. As a theory of representation, it confuses the order of signs with that of the world, thereby confusing the conventional order for the natural order. Not surprisingly, Descartes's mathematical language has claims of absolute objectivity or truth. But the objectivity of this mathematical language is nothing more than the result of adequation between the thing reduced conventionally to a sign and the order into which it appears to belong "naturally."

Descartes's elaboration of epistemology, as a theory of knowledge based on mathematics and rhetoric, has not merely philosophical but also scientific and technological consequences. By technology, I do not mean merely the threat posed by machines. Rather, I claim with Heidegger that this technological threat is inherent in the essence of the Cartesian philosophical position.[11] For Descartes, science does not proceed from the particular, the experiment, but rather from the universal order that anticipates it. The unknown in Descartes must always be already figured or represented in the order of the known. Descartes's claims to objectivity are based on this absolute determinism, in which truth is merely the statement of adequation to a priorly posited proposition. Descartes's epistemology is not purely a discourse of knowledge, but also a discourse of power affirming the subject's ability to propose, create, and manipulate the conditions of possibility of the truth of things. The potentially lethal machines and apparatus produced by this technological viewpoint emerge as a subsidiary effect, set into motion by the redefinition of man in rational terms that affirms through representation his mastery of nature and the world.

The second characteristic of representation as a new theory of the world is thus revealed. By forcing and framing the world into a particular order, this mathematical rhetorical demand reduces the world to an object that has the character of a picture. But this picture is not just a regular picture, a representation in the mimetic sense of the word. Rather, it is a model, a set of norms for what the world should look like. Representation now comes to mean that which is determined in such a limited way as to function purely as repetition, adequation, and confirmation; that is, literally as *re-presentation*. The essence of representation is technological insofar as this schema that it applies to the world frames it in such a way that the world can only appear or be figured within its limits and as its verification. Thus, the age of representation or world picture has less to do with representation as a visual picture than with representation as a frame and model for the world. By setting up the truth of representation in terms of certitude, Descartes breaks with the previous interpretations of representation, in order to restrict and foreclose its meaning in an objective sense. The question of technology, as the threat posed by machines to man, must be understood above all in terms of the technologization of thought, as made possible through the rational structure of representation.

Where does the subject fit into the picture? In the *Rules*, the Cartesian subject is defined as a purely formal position within representation.[12] Its role is that of a neutral and empty substrate (not unlike the axiomatic subject of geometric proofs) that circumscribes the sphere of all that can be represented. The concept of representation implied in Descartes's mathematization of nature cannot be conceived as a staging independent of the elements staged. Representation also involves the organizer of the spectacle, even if this position is purely hypothetical. The objective character of Descartes's philosophical position thus emerges as an illusion fostered by a system of representation governed by axiomatic limits, by an absence. Unlike Montaigne, Descartes is unable to represent the act of representation: the difference operated by language and rhetoric upon the figures of both domains, philosophy, and literature. Instead, the refusal to recognize the mediational character of representation is compensated by the dissimulated presence of the subject of representation, the organizer of the spectacle. The rhetorical space of this masked subject will foster the hermeneutical illusion of personality, intention, and individuality, *i.e.*, subjectivity interpreted in the various guises of subjectivism. The very "emptiness" of the subject, its impersonality and abstraction, thus constitute the substrate for the illusion of personality, of the human as subjective being. However, the extended list of the Cartesian *dramatis personae*, the anonymous subject of the *Rules*, the autobiographical subject of the *Discourse*, and the personal subject of the *Meditations*, are nothing more than figures standing in for the anonymous subject of truth, that governs the very principle of figurality.

In *The World*, the horizon of subjectivity is expanded. There Descartes posits a hypothetical imaginary world in order to explain the workings of the present one. The only problem with this fictional world is that Descartes identifies it later in the text in an unmediated way with the real one. His interpretation of the axiomatic in fictional or imaginary terms in the *World* extends human creative ability to bring together the potential and the actual, the axiomatic and the real. These qualities, heretofore applied traditionally to God, are subsumed into the formal structure of subjectivity. Although the subject is presented in negative terms, the "I" is "emptied out" of all worldly content; it gains both in the *Discourse* and in *Meditations* in its formal position to manipulate not only the world, but also itself. The subject's formal essence is constituted by its transcendental position as the logical function that acts upon the conditions of possibility for the existence of all other empirical entities. The subject in Descartes creates itself, its own conditions of being, but in doing so it must negate itself and "empty" itself of all social, historical, and empirical reality. This can be seen in the *Discourse* (Part 4) and in the *Meditations* (Part 3), where the subject (*cogito*) is described in purely negative terms, as an entity that can exclude itself from and deny its social, historical, and physical context. Thus the truth of its existence as subject, the proposition "I think, therefore I am," verifies not its specific empirical content but rather its general possibility to exist, as a trancendent, anonymous, and impersonal entity.

The Cartesian interpretation of subjectivity in the *Discourse* entails an interpretation of consciousness that is exhausted by its purely formal or logical function as warrant of representation. The very foundation of the subject requires the destruction and exhaustion of its content, its de-essentialization, in order to promote its formal, transcendental function. This de-essentialization of subjectivity is even more clearaly visible in the *Meditations*, where the subject is no longer defined in inferential terms, but rather as a virtual entity: "I am, I exist." Here, even, the inference from thought to the existence of the subject is broken, so that the subject emerges as an entity whose essence is defined by its ability to speak, to perform, in other words to establish and define autonomously the conditions for its own existence as representation. Although Descartes later in the *Meditations* qualifies the subject as a thinking thing, this qualification does not modify its predetermined truth as a representation that cannot gain access to or be conscious of its own truth. The subject of the *Discourse* and the *Meditations* is a virtual subject, the subject of truth, which though governing and included axiomatically in all representation, cannot really experience itself, having been reduced to a schema.

The Cartesian definition of man in the *Meditations* in terms of a thinking substance thus further modifies its subjective content by foreclosing the possibility of its definition in a modern sense as a psychological and intentional entity, and also the reflection regarding its existential status as "self" and "self-consciousness."[13] However, the negation and exhaustion of the subject's material, historical, and social substance – its essential content – is compensated by the gain of the subject's formal position through its theological redefinition in terms of will. The negative definition of the *cogito* in the *Discourse* is expanded through hyperbolic doubt in the Meditations. The hyperbolic doubt argument seeks to produce through the metaphorical figure of the evil genius an all-powerful doubt, a doubt that extends beyond the confines and encompasses the limits of subjectivity. Descartes recognizes that the problem of doubt and deception lurks within not only the paradigm of resemblance *The Rules*), but also any traditional interpretation of subjectivity. Through the fiction of the evil genius, he constitutes an exteriority that superceeds the totality of subjectivity. Consequently, he is able to shift the problem of the subject's inability to define its own truth, to the problem of having that truth defined through the intervention, the deception of an exterior agency. This exteriorization of doubt beyond the limits of subjectivity allows for a far more total, absolute (hyperbolic) doubt. This total doubt implies the contradictory redefinition of subjectivity: its expansion through its capacity to produce an absolute, that of hyperbolic doubt, as well as its delimitation and foreclosure through the fiction of an outside generated by the subject. The fiction of an excess beyond the subject is played off against that of its exhaustion as representation and as a self-generating entity.

The hyperbolic doubt argument leads to a rationalization and economization of subjectivity, which is constituted as the interplay of an excess beyond representation (the figurative function of the hyperbole) with the constitution of the subject as a result of this liminal play. The subject is defined in the *Meditations* both as site of excess, and of consumption and completion, since its meaning is circumscribed and delineated through hyperbolic doubt. The notion of subjectivity thus emerges in liminal terms as the interplay between a totality made possible by the excess of the hyperbole, and also as the exhaustion fostered by the containment of the subject within the limits of a rational economy. The subject becomes through representation the constitutive unit of a rational order that preordains its expenditure.

The elaboration of subjectivity from the *Rules* to the *Meditations* emerges as a position both liminal and excessive. Its liminal character is defined by its own character as object, as a fixed axiomatic entity, as a set position that governs representation. Its hyperbolic character expands the meaning of subjectivity to a point that challenges the capacities to represent heretofore reserved to God alone, and also, paradoxically, forecloses its meaning. For the subject now becomes that entity that controls both its relations to the world and itself, and through the economy of this interplay, further raltionalizes or determines its own structure and meaning. The hyperbolic doubt argument highlights another major aspect of representation, that of its economic character. Representation thus comes to mean, in terms of subjectivity, the possibility of its reduction to an economy that delimits both its meaning and circulation. The picture of subjectivity in both the *Discourse* and the *Meditations* has no relation to an empirical individual; it is not a picture in the ordinary sense of the word. Rather, this picture is nothing more than a frame, constituted by the liminal interplay of an economy of determination and undetermination.[14]

The subsequent elaboration of the epistemic subject in theological terms in the *Discourse* and the *Meditations* leads to a redefinition of subjectivity in terms of will. By will, however, I do not mean a particular attribute of the subject or a faculty, but rather the ability of the subject to further "perfect" its already perfect – mathematically certain or objective – essence. This notion of will is not supplementary to subjectivity; it is its true expression insofar as it belongs inherently to its essence.[15] The will emerges as the index of a new set of relations established between man and God, which also shapes the character of man's relation to the world, *i.e.*, representation. Descartes's use of theology in order to better ground subjectivity and his mathematical order leads to the actual disenfranchisement of the transcendental-divine order by the humanly created mathematical and axiomatic order. Rather than delimiting the meaning of subjectivity – marked as it must be by imperfection and by its finite understanding – Descartes actually expands the horizon of subjectivity, since it is through will that the human being can aspire to a perfection heretofore ascribed to God alone.

Although in the *Meditations* Descartes recognizes the fact that man's understanding is finite, this acknowledgement is coupled with the realization that man shares God's infinity in the faculty of the will. Man's will is infinite; it has the capacity to go on perfecting and improving itself endlessly. The function of the will is to compensate for the limits of understanding. Thus, a new dimension of subjectivity comes to the fore. Instead of acknowledging its obligation to Christian revelation and doctrine, the subject now emerges as that entity who, through representation, legislates and perfects its own relation to itself. The "willful" character of representation is not to be understood as a desire or a striving for something, but as a command, as the interiorization of a demand by the subject upon itself. Consequently, what is paradoxical is that the traditional arguments that previously established God's priority over man as infinity and perfection now become means for affirming man's priority to himself, as the will and capacity to propose and secure the subject's self-definition – in other words, as representation. It is ironic, however, that the character of subjectivity as will is described by its infinite perfectibility and expansibility; and yet, the truth of the subject, about itself and the world, is contained by certainty. The subject, as an interpretation of consciousness, can no longer have access to its truth about itself, since it has been predetermined by certitude and foreclosed by representation. Subjectivity thus refers less to man than to the subject's always-already-conscious truth about itself, *i.e.*, the truth of its perfectibility as completion and self-determination, that is, certitude.

This new metaphysical position occupied by the subject is not to be confused with either God or man. Rather, the subject is a conflation of the two positions, through the displacement of the transcendental by the axiomatic, and yet, identical to neither human nor divine viewpoint. This new position is essentially technological; it is negative insofar as it elevates the axiomatic to the status of the transcendental. This subject is inhuman insofar as it is cut off from its essence, and circumscribed by its relation to the world (the willful character of representation as dominance, measuring, executing, and disposition over things).

The paradox, then, is that the subject cannot be identified with man or the limits that circumscribe the human, as in, for instance, Montaigne's elaboration of the self. Descartes reaches the position anticipated by Montaigne's injunction:

> People try to get out of themselves and to escape from the man. This is folly; instead of transforming themselves into angels, they turn themselves into beasts; instead of lifting they degrade themselves. These transcendental humors frighten me, like lofty and inaccessible heights.[16]

Montaigne's reluctance before "transcendental" and "supercelestial" behavior, which, as Heidegger also claims, goes hand in hand with "subterrestrial conduct," expresses his own interpretation of humanism, one that scales down the idea of man through the exigencies of conduct and the limits imposed by death. In Montaigne, this interpretation of man as self-consciousness leads neither to a depletion of the essence of man nor to the extravagant position of the subject as sovereign guarantor of representation. Rather, Montaigne's humanism inseparably unites theory and practice, defining the human being as a process, a movement, a passage. The essence of the self can be defined by itself outside its textual frame and the project for writing or "essaying" on diverse subjects. Rather, it emerges as a fragment within the text, a citation among citations – never purely text, but always already an "intertext." The self in Montaigne thus exists otherwise than as the subject, *i.e.*, a proposition, a mode of self-assent that as representation presents the illusion of autonomy.

In comparing the two authors, Montaigne and Descartes, one begins to realize the fundamental difference that characterizes their respective interpretations of man as "self" and as "subject." Unlike Merleau-Ponty, who in "Everywhere and Nowhere" saw the self as a precursor of the subject, I think that it is a question of two very different kinds of entities.[17] The construction of the "self" requires neither mathematical constraints nor the unbridled expansion of the subject in its assumption of an autonomous and sovereign position in the order of things. The "self" finds it impossible to conceive itself outside the constraints of representation, which, as Montaigne points out, conditions our perceptions of the world since all our quarrels are about words. Descartes's interpretation of man as "subject" not only makes speaking about "'man' proper" impossible, but makes speaking about his humanism ironic.

The establishment of the Cartesian subject enabled the systematic study of man in the human sciences. And yet, these so-called human sciences are already based on an interpretation of man as subject, thereby making it impossible to ask the question of who "man" is or might be. The fundamental paradox is that the human sciences are the extension of a de-essentialized and inhuman subject, an axiomatic position that can hardly be subsumed under the aegis of humanism proper, such as Montaigne's. The inhumanity of the Cartesian subject is described by its negative self-definition, which leads to the objectification of both itself and the world. The willful character of representation and the power inherent in the subject's relation to its own definition and that of the world announce the nihilism intrinsic to the very foundation of modern metaphysics.

Heidegger claims that Neitzsche's elaboration of nihilism as the essence of the modern age is but the completion of the subjective position outlined by Descartes.

> Western history has now begun to enter into the completion of that period we call the *modern*, and which is defined by the fact that man becomes the measure and the center of all beings. Man is what lies at the bottom of all beings; that is, in modern terms, at the bottom of all objectification and representabiity. No matter how sharply Nietzsche pits himself time and time again against Descartes, whose philosophy grounds modern metaphysics, he turns against Descartes only because the latter *still* does not posit man as *subjective* in a way that is complete and decisive.[18]

He considers Nietzsche's elaboration of the will to power as the fulfillment of the Cartesian definition of the subject as will and representation. Nietzsche's nihilism or the devaluation of values is the expression of the metaphysical position outlined by Descartes: the de-essentialization of the subject, the redefinition of the subject as will to representation and the displacement of the divine order. From a metaphysical viewpoint, modern nihilism is not merely an ethical issue, but rather the expression of a crisis that haunts the character of modernity as established through representation and subjectivity. By positing both the subjective and the objective positions, Cartesian representation cannot be regarded as a neutral position. It has implicit values. The Cartesian position is nihilistic insofar as it interprets representation as neutral and objective without recognizing its conventional schematic nature. The question of values for modernity must be seen in relation to and as the expression of Descartes's negative ontology, one where the essence of the subject is defined through negation, through its denial as a social, historical, and empirical entity in order to attain its transcendental status. Likewise, representation is also defined as a picture, but its character is that of a schema or prototype that is itself merely a frame with no content.

The consequences of the concept of representation (the world become picture) now emerge clearly. If representation is always in crisis or an "end," this is because of the exhaustion of its essential possibilities as represented image. Descartes doubly delimits representation, first through the exclusion of the phenomenological character of the image as a visual artifact and second by interpreting it in purely formal terms, as a prototype. Representation as the index of the self-legislated access and relation to the world by the subject has the character of "closure." This "closure" or "end" of metaphysics does not mean the actual cessation of history. Rather, as Derrida claims, the closure of representation is the expresion of the historicity of modernity.[19] This is why modern metaphysics cannot be simply overcome and surpassed. The possibility of postmodernity would mean the overcoming of what is today considered as the modern: our definition of representation, subjectivity, and the task of thinking. If modernity appears to be always in crisis, it is because this crisis is part and parcel of its definition, its ontology. Representation is postmodern only when it reinflects and reinscribes within thought, art, and ethics those categories excluded and reified by its foundation. A critique of representation from a postmodern perspective would entail redefining its formal schematic character, so that the oppositions embedded in it would be set free to new determinations. This would mean, echoing Heidegger's words, "the surrender of previous thinking to the determination of the matter for thinking."[20]

Notes

1. "The Age of the World Picture," in *The Question Concerning Technology and Other Essays*, trans. W. Lovitt (New York: Harper & Row, 1977), p. 130.

2. Cf. Martin Heidegger's analysis of Descartes's concept of *mathesis* in *What Is a Thing?*, trans. W. B. Barton and V. Deutsch (Chicago: Henry Regnery, 1967), pp. 64–111.

3. Cf. Michel Foucault, *The Order of Things* (New York: Vintage Books, 1972), chapter "Representation." My reading differs with Foucault's insofar as I show that Descartes's concept of representation relies on the paradigms of the age of resemblance, which also has a concept of representation, although not in a foundational sense. The Foucauldian notion of epistemic rupture thus emerges as the expression of a crisis inherent in the Cartesian definition of representation.

4. See Francis A. Yates, *The Art of Memory* (Chicago: University of Chicago Press, 1974).

5. For an analysis of the philosophical movement of *libertinage érudit*, see René Pintard, *Le libertinage érudit dans la première partie du XVIIe siècle* (Paris: Boivin, 1943), and for the problems of the literary Baroque see M. Raymond, *Baroque et Renaissance poétique* (Paris: Corti, 1955) and J. Rousset, *La littérature de l'Age Baroque en France* (Paris: *PUF*, 1974).

6. For an epistemological analysis of the Baroque concept of allegory, see Walter Benjamin, *The Origin of German Tragic Drama*, trans. S. Osborne (London: *NLB*, 1977).

7. *The Philosophical Works of Descartes*, trans. E. S. Haldane and G. R. T. Ross, 2 vols. (Cambridge: Cambridge University Press, 1969), vol. 1, p. 1. (Henceforth *HR*.)

8. *The Complete Essays of Montaigne*, trans. Donald M. Frame (Stanford, *CA*: Stanford University Press, 1965), Vol. III, chap. 13.

9. Cf. Martin Heidegger's discussion in *What Is a Thing?*, pp. 98–112 and M. Foucault's comments in *The Order of Things*, "Representation."

10. Cf. Jean-François Lyotard, *Discours, Figure* (Paris: Kliensieck, 1972), pp. 13–14. His general discussion of the opposition of the discursive and the figural is essential to my critique of representation.

11. See Martin Heidegger, "The Question Concerning Technology," in *The Question Concerning Technology and Other Essays*, pp. 3–35.

12. The analysis of subjectivity that follows is a summary of my analysis *Subjectivity and Representation: The Origins of Modern Thought in Descartes* (Cambridge: Cambridge University Press, 1987).

13. Cf. Jean-Luc Nancy's *Ego sum* (Paris: Flammarion, 1980), for a seminal discussion of the formal character and literary function of the Cartesian subject.

14. The concept of economy and its function in Descartes is alluded to in Jacques Derrida's "Cogito and the History of Madness," in *Writing and the*

Difference, trans. Alan Bass (Chicago: University of Chicago Press, 1978), pp. 51–54.

15. For an analysis of the concept of the will in Descartes and Nietzsche, see Martin Heidegger, *Nietzsche: Nihilism*, vol. IV, trans. Frank A. Capuzzi and David F. Krell (San Francisco: Harper & Row, 1982), pp. 85–158.

16. *Essais*, III, 13, 1096.

17. Maurice Merleau-Ponty, "Everywhere and Nowhere," in *Signs*, trans. Richard C. Cleary (Evanston: Northwestern University Press, 1984), pp. 153–54.

18. Martin Heidegger, *Nietzsche: Nihilism*, vol. IV, p. 28.

19. See Jacques Derrida, "Cogito and the History of Madness," pp. 31–63; also see Robert Bernasconi's analysis of closure in "Derrida on Levinas: The Question of the Closure of Metaphysics" (unpublished manuscript).

20. Martin Heidegger, "The End of Philosophy and the Task of Thinking," in *Basic Writings*, ed. David F. Krell (New York: Harper & Row, 1977), p. 392.

6. Hegelian Dialectic and the Limits of Representation

Deborah Chaffin

Why discuss the Hegelian view of representation? With the possible exception of the dialectic, no other aspect of Hegelian thought has been subject to as much criticism. Indeed, not only have Hegel's own views on representation become quite familiar, but so too have the so-called limits of this view. It is almost taken for granted today that Hegel's interpretation of representative activity – the site of language, speech, and writing – presents us with the clearest instance of Hegelian idealism. Thus, something suggests that yet another discussion of Hegel and the limits of representation will simply involve retilling old fields – a classic example of laboring and suffering in the vapors of a "pessimistic gloom."[1] Yet such a view would surely be mistaken. As I will show in what follows, there is good reason for returning once again to the Hegelian text.

This attempt to rethink and situate representation within the Hegelian project has been prompted by the challenging interrogations of Heidegger and Derrida. On the face of it, these two thinkers appear to offer very different critiques of Hegel's theory of representation. By emphasizing the appropriation of objects and return to self which is present in the movement of representation, Heidegger treats representative activity as *the* essential feature of the Hegelian absolute. On the other hand, Derrida's analysis points out the *lack, contingency,* and even *ignorance* present in representation for Hegel. For Derrida, such a lack leads to the necessity of viewing representation as *merely preparatory,* as a subject matter itself subject to another Hegelian *Aufhebung*. Far from being the embryonic form of the absolute, as in Heidegger, Derrida views Hegelian representation as simply a way station in the march of the absolute.

Although I believe that these analyses may be crucial for an understanding of the projects of Heidegger and Derrida, I have less interest in expounding their positions than I have in exploring the ways in which Hegel's interpretation of representation, and language in particular, is subsumed by these thinkers in the interest of identifying Hegel as a decisive stage in the history of metaphysics.

Accordingly, in what follows, I will first outline the place assigned to representation in the interrogations of Hegel by Heidegger and Derrida. For it just may be the case that they have isolated only one aspect of Hegel's reflection on representation and treated it as if it were the whole. I then offer a reconstruction of Hegel's reflections on representation situating this theory within the context of his account of intelligence, or what he calls "subjective spirit." Within this context, we can see why Hegel's account actually forces him to break with representationalism as an adequate theory of intelligence. For, at the highest level of thinking, the concept is not an inert entity we bring to presence, it is rather the activity we *are*.

Heidegger and Derrida: Their Interrogations of Hegel

In his reflections on *Hegel's Concept of Experience (1942–1943)* and in the transcribed notes from a 1968 seminar on Hegel's *Differenzschrift*, Heidegger argues that representation is *the key* to the meaning of the Hegelian absolute. As Heidegger puts it, "All . . . moments of absoluteness have the character of representation."[2] Situated within the general project of determining the meaning of the absolute, Heidegger offers an interpretation of representation elevating it to the position of being the *ground* of Hegel's metaphysics. It is important to note that the question of representation is, in this way, made into a pivotal stage in Heidegger's "destruction of the history of ontology."

In his lifelong dialogue with Hegel, Heidegger continued to view representation as *the* fundamental characteristic of Hegelian idealism in its relation to Being.[3] Indeed, Hegel's advance beyond the Cartesian view of self-consciousness lies in the fact that he no longer viewed knowledge as an instrument, as a *means* for grasping "what truly is." With Hegel, according to Heidegger, "what truly is" is determined as "Spirit: that which is present and by itself in the certainty of unconditional self-knowledge" (HBE,118). Thus, Hegel will not allow a distinction between knowing and that which is known: for truth has become ". . . knowing the self-certainty of self-consciousness in its unconditional essence and thoroughly to be in this knowledge as knowledge."

(HBE,121). In other words, for Hegel truth has become the absolute self-certainty of knowing.

Because truth has become a matter of knowing itself, Heidegger can speak of the Hegelian absolute as absolving itself from any relation to its objects, from anything other to it (HBE,118–22). Indeed, the absolute appears as *parousia*: In Heidegger's words,

> The presentation of the absolute is an essential mode of presence [*parousia*]. As such, *i.e.*, as being present [*Anwesen*], it is the Being of beings that are as *subjects* . . . . The subjectness [*Subjektität*] of the subject is the Being of the subject [*Subjektsein des Subjekts*], that is, of the subject-object relation (HBE,122).

In other words, this subject through which the absolute comes to presence has ". . . its being in the *representing* relation to the object" (HBE,121). Thus, representation becomes the *ground*, or the *foundation* for the coming to presence of the absolute.

In the representing act, the subject both returns to itself (it renders the object as present to *it*) and it becomes aware that as subject *it* is essential to the presentation of any object at all.[4] Thus, on the basis of re-presentation, the subject makes a *self*-discovery: the discovery that the essential relation between subject and object is one of *subjectness (Subjektität)*. And as Heidegger will argue, subjectness is the domain of the presence of the absolute, that is, subjectness is Heidegger's interpretation of what one commentator has called "the structural meaning of Spirit.[5]

According to Heidegger's reading, then, the subject itself comes to be (*west*) in its *representing* relation to the object. Such representative activity presents the object only insofar as it is an object given for a subject. It is in representaiton that the subject first knows itself as subject. Here, self-certainty has become the mode of being of subjects; and self-certainty, or subjectness, is *to be in* a subject-object relation. Hence, through his examination of the single moment of "representation" in Hegel's system, Heidegger seeks to establish the basic ground of Hegelian thought: namely, that subjectness, or the *self*-discovery revealed in representaiton, is the *parousia* of the absolute.

According to Heidegger's "metaphysical" reading, Hegelian representation is actually *the* essential way in which the absolute, or spirit, manifests itself as the site of elevation above the world of objects and as the return to self. Hegel is viewed as "classically" metaphysical insofar as representation is precisely that kind of thought which aims to discover the unique and ultimate word that allots to each present being the character of presence – an approach which consists, finally, in "identifying" beings in their totality.[6]

Derrida takes a somewhat different approach to the problematic of representation in "The Pit and the Pyramid: An Introduction to Hegel's Semiology," – and also in the essay "From Restricted to General Economy: A Hegelianism Without Reserve." In both of these works – and especially in the "Introduction," – we see the *seriousness* which Derrida accords Hegel, as well as absolute knowing. What Derrida claimed of Bataille's dialogues with Hegel, we could as well claim of him: He does not allow himself to merely *abstract* concepts from the Hegelian system or to *manipulate* isolated propositions, ". . . drawing effects from them by transportation into a discourse foreign to them . . . ."[7] But, as will be seen, this carefulness does not prevent Derrida from bringing into question the *meaning* or *guiding concept* of the whole of Hegelian reason. Indeed, Derrida can put the Hegelian project in question precisely because he has thought the whole as such, in its totality, without ignoring its systematic necessity.

As in Heidegger, Derrida's interrogation of the Hegelian theory of representation takes place within the context of a presentation of the history of metaphysics. Yet, as he argued in the first part of *Of Grammatology* and in *Speech and Phenomena*, such a history can be most fruitfully pursued in terms of a history of the concept of the sign. For Derrida, ". . . the history of truth, of the truth of truth, has always been . . . the debasement of writing, and its repression outside 'full' speech."[8] Hence, the analysis of Hegel's interpretation of speech and writing – of his theory of representation – is the strategy Derrida uses in order to show, finally, that Hegelian thought is indissolubly linked to the "modern" metaphysics of presence *as* self-consciousness, the metaphysics of the idea as representation.[9]

Derrida begins with an architectonic reading: he points out that the theory of the sign has a very determinate place within the Hegelian system. Occuring in the third part of the *Encyclopedia of Philosophical Sciences*, the theory of the sign is that moment in the science of the Idea when the Idea has come back to itself out of the otherness of nature. As Derrida puts it: "The theory of the sign . . . belongs to the *science* of the moment when the idea comes back to itself after having . . . lost awareness, lost the consciousness and meaning of itself in nature, in its Being-other."[10] Representation, then, becomes an essential structure of the Idea's return to self-presence. Accordingly, we have the "first, most general" determination of the sign: it ". . . is a form or movement of the Idea's relation to itself in the element of spirit, a mode of the absolute's Being-near-to-itself" (PP,74).

But here the sign – or representation – has been identified as merely one mode of the absolute, one moment or movement in the development of spirit. In its first phase, as subjective, spirit "moves" only in relation to itself and "psychology" is the science of spirit determining itself in itself, as a subject for itself. As subjective, however, spirit is only an ideal totality of the idea – it possesses only internal freedom. And the arbitrariness of signs rests on the inscription of representation and semiology within the science of psychology. Thus, according to Derrida's analysis, the sign can only appear ". . . as a mode or determination of subjective and finite spirit as a mediation of transgression of itself, a transition within the transition, a transition of the transition" (PP,74).

In Hegel, the sign is treated as a moment of transition: as the transition between the productive imagination and memory. Generally, the representing act is a transition between intuitive intelligence (which does not alter the intuited content) and pure thought (which is a living and dynamic activity): it is an active comprehension that what was merely contingent in intuition is, in fact, a necessary condition of what intelligence has itself become. Thus, Derrida's focus on the provisional character of the sign and representation, allows him to present Hegel as having made a traditionally metaphysical move. As the site of transition, the sign is merely ". . . the bridge between two moments of full presence" (PP,71).

The sign is a self-production of intelligence; for with the sign intelligence has produced *itself* in the world as a *thing*. As Derrida remarks, "This singular thing is the *sign*; it is engendered by a fantastic production, by an imagination that shows signs of itself, making the sign as always, emerge from itself in itself" (PP,78). But, for Derrida, this sign-producing activity is only another indication of the "idealizing mastery" operative throughout all the activities of intelligence. It is an indication of yet another attempt on the part of the subject to appropriate and constitute nature in its own terms.

Finally, Hegel's semiology, his theory of speech and writing, is another means by which " . . . spirit, elevating itself above the nature in which it was submerged, at once suppresses and retains nature, sublimating nature into itself, accomplishing itself as internal freedom, and thereby presenting itself to itself for itself" (PP,76). Thus, Derrida's critique of Hegel's theory of the sign centers around the fact that, in Hegel, the sign is itself a moment in the development of rationality in the sight of truth. Because the concept of the sign has been determined by Hegel as a lack of full truth, it can be subsumed into a *progression* – the development of rationality, the development of absolute knowledge.

Therefore, although Derrida and Heidegger have quite different emphases in their respective critiques, a relation between the two has emerged. Both focus on the moment of representation in Hegel's text in order to show that Hegel himself is a "representative" thinker: the entire movement of spirit is seen to be included *within* the circle of absolute knowledge, which means that spirit itself only comes to be within discourse, within the system or the work of signification. This "history of meaning" is reassembled and represented by Heidegger and Derrida through the figure of the representing subject. In this figure, the heart of Hegelian metaphysics is laid bare; a metaphysics that links the sign to the concept, to truth and presence.

But what does this privileged example signify *for Hegel*? Does he elevate the *structure* of representing activity into the model of thinking itself? Does he treat the sign, and representation generally, as ignorant of spirit's proper depth? Is the sign, in other words, always already in the service of presence, at work for the history of meaning?

The Hegelian Theory of Representation

In a fragment he wrote between 1822 and 1825, Hegel characterized spirit in the following way:

> Where does it come from – nature; where does it tend – to its freedom. Its being is this motion of freeing itself from nature. This is its very substance to such an extent that it is not permissable to speak of it as a fixed subject [*feststehenden Subjecte*] which does and brings about this or that, as if such activity were a matter of chance, a kind of condition, by means of which the subject is constituted ". . ."[11]

It is this "motion of freeing itself" which is the explicit subject matter of the third part of the *Encyclopedia of Philosophical Sciences*, the "Philosophy of Subjective Spirit."

Specifically, it is in the division of psychology that Hegel develops the moments *through* which spirit becomes *conscious* activity. That is, the goal of Hegel's psychological investigation is to show the *reality* of reason, to exhibit reason as the *täitige Macht selbst* or active power. The development of the two previous moments of subjective spirit had different goals: the anthropological and the phenomenological moments of subjective spirit have shown reason to be the "goal" and "standpoint" of nature and consciousness respectively, but they have not shown the reality of reason.

The activity of intelligence is concerned, then, with "finding reason." And since it is theoretical spirit which is investigated here, the activity of intelligence can be assumed to be concerned, at first, with the empty form of finding reason. Accordingly, the single activities of intelligence are immediately described and understood *in themselves* as moments of reason itself (EPS,463A,209).

As demonstrated in the discussion of Derrida, intelligence, or theoretical spirit, is represented (*dargestellt*) by Hegel as having three moments: intuition, representation (*Vorstellung*), and thought. These "moments" should not be pictured as actually distinct however, for they are described by Hegel as being coactive, as being three *functions* or *processes* of intelligence. Thus, as categories of thought, they do not signify ontological reality as that which comprehends all that is, but rather the *transitions of* thought itself. When he describes the transition from intuition to representation, for example, Hegel does not appeal to an independent reality which can be sensed or intuited; he refers instead to the operations of intuiting and thinking. The transition occurring between intuiting and representation is a transition that has occurred within these operations themselves. Thus, at the level of intellectual activity, an implicit assumption exists that it is possible to know rationally. This is the *merely formal* certainty of intelligence. And it is the task of the psychology to show *how* this formal knowledge of certainty becomes determinate knowledge (EPS,445,103–17).

Initially, intelligence finds itself determined: first, as intuition, intelligence ". . . still has the form of *immediacy*, and consequently the appearance [*Schein*] of being self-external [*sich ausserlich*], of being like consciousnes in that it relates itself to the rational as to something *outside it* which it does not mediate but merely *finds*" (EPS,445,111–12). Second, the activity of intuiting itself seems contingent. Yet, this indistinct immediacy of the object and of the intuiting subject's activity leads the subject to direct its attention to what has occurred. Furthermore, the immediacy of this initial act of attention hides the fact that a transition in thinking itself has occurred. Thought only becomes aware *after the fact* that in attending to the object intuited, a transition has occurred within thought itself.

The transition becomes explicit in representation. Because representation has the form of universality, it is able to distinguish the activity of immediate intuition from the content intuited, thus transforming the sensible appearances which intuition has always already mediated.

This transformation takes place throughout the moments of representation. In recollection, the first moment of representation, intelligence has become introspective and is able to form images, based on its retention of content from past intuitions. The sensible appearances of intuition are universalized in the representative act by means of a discriminating attention. For Hegel, this discriminating attention *is* the imagination (EDS,445–59,157–99). In this movement, the possible relations between images expands, and attention may even be directed toward the activity of relating itself. Hence, intelligence can move, through representation, to the explicit positing of its own activity.

Intelligence explicitly posits its own imaginative activities in the formation and usage of signs, or language in general, for signs, or language, are objective and existent things external to intelligence. Because they are external, signs escape the provisional character of the consciousness which produces them. According to Hegel,

> . . . intelligence . . . *appears* in taking up sensuous content and forming representations for itself out of this material . . . it then gives its independent representations a definite determinate being [*ein bestimmtes Dasein*], . . . a meaning [*Bedeutung*] (EPS,458A,177).

For Hegel, the sign indicates the very movement of intelligence itself. Since language is the result of the intelligence's *own* activity, signs re-present the dynamic of intelligence itself.[12] This aspect of representation is seen perhaps most clearly in memory, and specifically, in mechanical memory. In mechanical memory, intelligence has no need to refer beyond the name to the intellectual activity of meaning. Mechanical memory is concerned with names and nothing else. Again, for Hegel,

> It is well-known that one only knows something entirely by rote when one finds the sense of the words to be of no account; . . . . The ability to retain by rote series of words the connectedness of which is devoid of understanding . . . is therefore so truly remarkable because it is the essence of spirit to be with itself, *whereas here* it is as it were inwardly externalized . . . . Spirit is with itself only as the unity of subjectivity and objectivity ". . . it makes itself inwardly into an externality as memory ". . . (EPS,463A,209).

By means of memory, spirit is therefore being, a mere space of names as such, senseless words. But, as subjectivity, spirit is also the power of words or the bond between them.

By focusing on memory, the final moment in the development of representative intelligence, the moment which becomes thought proper, we can see *why*, for Hegel, representationalism could *not* be the final nature of thought.[13]

As a theory of perception and the intellectual activities involving sensory moments, representationalism allows one to understand how an individual mental object (an image) can come to represent a universal (a meaning). Yet representationalism can never give one certainty that knowledge is of things as they are apart from such activity. For Hegel, we must have a nonrepresentational foundation for our intellectual activities, otherwise one would be caught in subjective idealism; that is, we could never know if our knowledge was of the object or only of our particular understanding of the object. In short, one must be able to know the universal since we are so prone to use the universal even in merely representing an object to ourselves, even in representing ourselves. And in self-understanding – including the most subjective moments, of imagination, of fantasy – one begins with the knowledge that individuals are not merely sums of things; individuals are self-particularizing or self-specifying – what Hegel calls "concretely universal."

Thus, for Hegel, representation is limited: as an activity of intelligence, representationalism remains on the level of opposition and finitude.[14] The merely representing subject can never be the basis of philosophical truth. Furthermore, the problematic of representation is a very limited perspective from which to view the Hegelian text. Hegel is concerned throughout his work to describe another meaning of subjectivity: as the power of negativity, the subject is able to construct a world. When the absolute is conceived as *self-development* and creative interpretation, it is unnecessary to conceive of absolute knowledge as knowledge in its totality, complete and unchanging.

Although Hegel believed that thinking is, in part, the rule-governed use of symbols and signs ("only through words can we think"), he also believed that only the intelligent manipulation of signs or symbols can be identified with thought. For, as Nietzsche points out in *On Truth and Lie in an Extra-Moral Sense*, ". . . between two absolutely different spheres, as between subject and object, there is no causality, no exact correlation, and no expression, but, at best, an *aesthetic* relation; . . . an allusive transposition, a halting translation into an entirely foreign language; but, in any case, there must be an intermediary sphere and a mediating force, freely composing and freely inventing.[15]

Such a usage of language is active in the sense that it is *self-developing*, it is both cause and effect; moreover, it is also inseparable from its objective instances. Thus, one can understand the Hegelian absolute as this universal self-constituting activity – an activity which becomes self-conscious only when one has *knowledge* of it. As Hegel says,

> The philosophical cognition of spirit is difficult since it involves our being concerned with the most concrete and developed form attained in the *self*-actualization of the Idea . . . (EPS,I,3).

Thus, at the highest level, the concrete universal, or the Idea, must be *realized* – it is not something one merely represents, but is the activity one is. And, again, as Nietzsche knew so well, "Ultimately, the individual derives the values of his acts from himself; because he has to interpret in a quite individual way even the words he has inherited. His *interpretation* of a formula at least is personal, even if he does not create a formula: as an interpreter he is still creative."[16]

Hegel's complete theory of subjective spirit thus bespeaks his peculiar "Copernican" assumption that there is a unity to reason such that theoretical activities are meaningless apart from an active orientation of thinking itself. Such an orientation is not captured by the figure of the merely representing subject. Spirit, as the concrete universal, aims to interpret the world successfully. Such "interpretations" or "determinations" simply define the content of the world according to particular orientations. Hence, the determinations of thought are responsible for the actuality experience involves, not for the "objectivity" or "structure" of experience itself.

Perhaps, then, in the final instance, Hegel's claims about the nature of absolute knowledge are actually much more modest than either Heidegger or Derrida suggest. Viewed from the perspective of the problematic of language and representation, language, for Hegel, does not give way to an all-encompassing conceptuality, for conceptuality, or the absolute, is, in its origin and in its movement, fully bound up with the finitude of thought, and it has been the task of the analysis of "subjective spirit" to show that this is so.

Notes

1. Friedrich Nietzsche, *The Gay Science*, trans. Walter Kaufmann (New York: Vintage, 1974), sect. 347, p. 288.

2. Martin Heidegger, *Hegel's Concept of Experience* (New York: Harper and Row, 1970), p. 39; *Hegels Begriff der Erfahrung*, in *Holzwege* (Frankfurt am

Main: Vittorio Klostermann, 1972), p. 125. I have frequently altered the "standard" (anonymous) English translation. (Henceforth cited (German edition) as *HBE.*)

3. Martin Heidegger, "A Heidegger Seminar on Hegel's *Differnzschrift,*" trans. W. Lovitt, *Southwestern Journal of Philosophy,* Fall 1980, vol. XI, No. 3:33–35.

4. This particular way of expressing this movement was suggested to me by the insightful and exciting "Between Hegel and Heidegger," Dennis Schmidt, *Man and World,* 15, 1982:17–31.

5. *Ibid.*, p. 21.

6. Michel Haar, "Nietzsche and Metaphysical Language," in *The New Nietzsche,* ed. David B. Allison (Cambridge: Massachusetts Institute of Technology Press, 1985), pp. 7–8.

7. Jacques Derrida, "From Restricted to General Economy: A Hegelianism Without Reserve," in *Writing and Difference,* trans. Alan Bass (Chicago: University of Chicago Press, 1978), p. 253.

8. Jacques Derrida, *Of Grammatology,* trans. G. C. Spivak (Baltimore: Johns Hopkins University Press, 1976), p. 3.

9. Jacques Derrida, *Speech and Phenomena,* trans. David B. Allison (Evanston: Northwestern University Press, 1976), p. 3.

10. Jacques Derrida, "The Pit and the Pyramid: Introduction to Hegel's Semiology," in *Margins of Philosophy,* trans. Alan Bass (Chicago: University of Chicago Press, 1982), p. 74. (Henceforth cited as *PP.*)

11. G. W. F. Hegel, *The Encyclopedia of the Philosophical Sciences,* trans. Michael John Petry (Dordrecht and Boston: D. Reidel Publishing, 1977), vol. I, p. 91. (Henceforth cited as *EPS.*)

12. John Burbidge, *On Hegel's Logic: Fragments of a Commentary* (Atlantic Highlands: Humanities Press, 1981). Since he is the single interpreter of Hegel's *Logic* who takes the development of the "Philosophy of Subjective Spirit" to have a direct bearing on the purely logical investigations of the *Science of Logic,* I have found Burbidge's reflections most helpful.

13. This point was suggested to me by Willem de Vries, "Hegel on Representation and Thought," a paper presented at the 1982 meetings of the Eastern Division of the American Philosophical Association.

14. Dennis Schmidt, "Between Hegel and Heidegger," p. 25.

15. Friedrich Nietzsche, *On Truth and Lie in an Extra-Moral Sense,* in *The Complete Works of Nietzsche,* vol. 2, ed. Levy (London: Foulis, 1911), p. 184.

16. Friedrich Nietzsche, *The Will to Power,* trans. W. Kaufmann and R. J. Hollingdale, ed. Walter Kaufmann (New York: Vintage, 1968), sect. 767, p. 403.

7. Heidegger and the Limits of Representation

Dorothea Olkowski

The question of the limitations of representation is one that Heidegger seldom confronts in the sense of standing directly opposed to it. Only in the essay, "The Age of the World Picture," does he address himself to the role of representation in thought in an oppositional manner. What distinguishes the modern age is that the world becomes picture because "man" looks upon it and represents it; thus, it has the character of a subjective perception.[1]

In the Modern Age, to represent is to bring what is present-at-hand before oneself, to force it into this relationship as the norm. "Man" puts himself into the scene in precedence over what is in order to unify the otherwise fragmented signifying system (AWP,131).

When "man" begins to represent, to set out before and in relation to himself, the world becomes a picture while "man" becomes *Subiectum* and takes precedence over all other possible centers of relationship. The act of bringing what is present-at-hand before oneself, the determination of this relationship as the norm, and the precedence of "man" over every other possible center, creates a unified system, a significational norm within which only what can be referred to man as an element of his "lived experience" is taken seriously (AWP,134).

Modern representing [*Vor-stellen*] is not, however, unprecedented. Heidegger points to Plato's refusal of the Parmenidean pronouncement that thought and being are the same, as the presupposition of Modern representing (AWP,130). If thought and being are one, the world is not a picture because the apprehension of "what is" is demanded and determined by Being. The Greeks, says Heidegger, were looked upon by that which is, beheld by it, included and maintained within its openness, even if driven about by its oppositions, exposed to its confusions, and marked forever by its discords. Prometheus is tied to the rock, Pentheus dismembered by the Bacchae, Actaeon changed into a stag and torn to bits by his own pack of hounds. The world is not a picture.

But in Plato, the beingness of what is gets redefined. Plato determines that the beingness of what is is *eidos*, that is, aspect or view (AWP,131), and this, says Heidegger, is the presupposition for the world's having to become picture. "Man" establishes himself as that setting in which whatever is must present itself, so man becomes the representative of that which is (AWP,132).

When the world becomes picture and man brings his life as *subiectum* into precedence over other centers of relationship, man conceives of his position as a world view (AWP,134). Thus, the relationship between individuals, when each is conceived as *subiectum*, produces a confrontation of world views (AWP,134). No longer driven by the oppositions and confusions of Being, we are now marked by the discordance of world views, the difference of representations, the desire of appropriation.

But how is it that "man" becomes *subiectum* and the "world" becomes his representation? Into what orbit has the system of significance entered such that is becomes fragmented, and what is the sense [*sens*] of its drive to unification?

In *The End of Philosophy*, Heidegger writes that in the "beginning of its history," Being opens itself as emerging and unconcealment.[2] A house, for example, rests, preserving the completion of what is moved, what has been in motion, a gathering of all the movements of a production (EP,5). For Aristotle, *ousia*, substance, the "individual man or horse," is not capable of motion.[3] This *energeia*, this *Entelecheia*, having itself in the end, "presencing without production," is *to eschaton*: complete, entire, perfect (EP,5).

However, this is not simply a question of tying Prometheus to a rock because this notion of Being arises only in opposition to the Platonic *eidos*, an "aspect" that has been transformed to *aitia*, cause. *That* a thing is stands firmly over against *what* a thing is. Not only does Prometheus "rest" tied to the rock but also, a vulture is sent to continuously nibble at him, the reminder of his transgression of the authority of the Father of the Heavens; the symbol of the cause of his punishment.

In Heidegger's reading of the history of Western thought, cause dominates every coming-to-be (EP,13). God, as highest being, is pure actuality. Always fulfilling whatness, God is the causality of all real things (EP,21), and existence, like Prometheus's fate, becomes dependent upon causality. Reality lies in the effector.

In this shift, "God effects the world within which man is the true effector" (EP,19). As pure actuality, God is the source and place of salvation and blessedness, as well as the cause of the real. Man, in turn, must "make sure of his salvation," find his assurance, by determining "the essence of certainty in himself in accordance with the essence of certainty in general,"[16] that is, in accordance with that of God.

Assured in its salvation, bowing down to that real being who directs all human activity, freeing itself for the *lumen naturale*, the human being is appropriated by an authoritative, native certainty guaranteeing what is brought before it.[17]

No longer does "what is," the Greek *hypokeimenon*, emerge in the resting preservation of what is completed. Rather, certainty has become the condition of the possibility of what is brought before us and re-presented. What effects and is effected in its constancy, the *subiectum*, is the ground upon which other things are placed": the ground for bringing about what is real.[18] Thus, although Heidegger does not say so in this text, it must also be the ground for all representational construction, a ground presupposed by *eidos*.

What is constant is the system of human predicating behavior: the *ratio*. The *subiectum* is not yet the subject; it is the significational system. Therefore, the proposition characterizes "what is" in terms of discursive categories.[19] We have not yet entered the age of the world picture insofar as the *ratio* of certainty is representational thinking as a constant significational system and not the *cogito*.

However, the *subiectum* and the ratio certainly presuppose the world's becoming picture. By bringing something before itself, every effecting (every representational thinking) represents precisely what is effected, and so it *is* representation. Reality and representation are thought as one, and the beingness of beings is the same as representation.[20]

Heidegger shows how the belonging-together of reality and representation, as it is thought by Leibniz, anticipates the emergence of subjectivity and the age of the world picture. The significational system is here characterized as *la force*, the transitional essence of striving representation, in accordance with which every being *is*. Every representation is from a single point of view, that of the monad. Yet each is in transit from one perception to another in accordance with the underlying, supporting, unifying unity.[21]

The many perceptions are unfolded in this unity which determines each in its being. *La force* retains the character of highest being, the causality of all real things, *suprema substantia*. This supreme "effecting" emanates to the real, individual beings which then can mirror the universe from their point of view; thus they also each originate, imitating the divinity.[22]

Appropriating a world as a perspective, each monad mirrors originally from its point of view. Representing from its point of view, it represents itself, is a representing something. This representative presence is, says Heidegger, accomplished by a kind of ego, as its own essential activity.[23]

Nascent ego is transformed into subjectivity when the character of representation is thought along with will. As the representedness of self-representing, the beingness of beings as will portrays itself, attains itself, transcends itself (in the unifying unity), thus has itself, *is* being (EP,56). The Kantian "I think" means "I represent something as something," "I let something stand together before me," and it is this which determines its unity (EP,57).

It is this history that Heidegger thinks when he writes about modern representing as *Vor-stellen*. The story of Metaphysics from Plato to Nietzsche has lost sight of Being that opens itself out as emerging and unconcealment. *Vor-stellen* now dominates; "man" takes precedence over all other possible centers of relationship.

That the world becomes a picture is not, however, strictly a function of projection. "Man" is also looked upon by what is, defined by its institutions, reduced by its mechanistic rationale, fabricated as one of its events. With regard to Being, there is a remainder, an *Enframing*, "the manner in which something holds sway" (AWP,136), the mode in which Being chooses to come into presence in a certain age, so that not only the mode of representation gives Modern thought its character, but also the way human beings in general articulate themselves upon the "essence of an age" (AWP,137).

The *Ge-stell* (framing) is then the trace, the remainder of the Greek emerging and unconcealing of Being; it is the gathering of the bringing forth, the letting-come-forth.[4] Because the *Ge-stell* is the "essence of an age," its nature today is that of modern technology. This trace appropriates everything into an "assured availability," a distorted derivation of the *poiesis* that lets what is present come forth into unconcealedness.[5]

Art critic Craig Owens notes that art history has always defined representation in terms of *Vorstellung*, a kind of symbolic activity, and *Darstellung*, in the sense of a theatrical presentation.[6] As the latter, representation is the tangible, physical presence of a thing that is visually replicated, while in its symbolic function, the image substitutes for an absence, a part substitutes for a whole.[7]

Owens quotes from Heidegger's *Origins of the Work of Art* to articulate this structure. In this text, Heidegger states, in terms meant to be ironic and critical of the tradition, that:

> The work makes public something other than itself; it is an allegory. In the work of art something other is brought together with the thing that is made. To bring together is, in Greek, *sumballein. The work is a symbol* (OWA,22). (Emphasis added.)

In this text, allegory is consigned to the symbolic, and the symbolic is understood as the representational mode which Heidegger wished to supplant. Thus, the significance of Heidegger's narrative of Metaphysics. Heidegger seeks to allow presencing to show itself, to let the work speak, not as *eidos, energeia, actualitas, perceptio*, monad, or will, but as the gift in whose giving Being vanishes in Appropriation.[8]

As *Vorstellung*, substitute, the thing presences in terms of the present, the "now." In the essay "*Ousia* and *Grammé*," Jacques Derrida shows how this sense of Being manifests itself within the horizon of meaning provided by time. Lacing together the texts of Heidegger and Aristotle, Derrida points to the precomprehension of time in discourse in which a being is grasped in its being as presence, and meaning is understood only in terms of its reference to a determinate mode of time: the present, the "now."

Yet, the now is not itself temporal; it becomes temporal only in ceasing to be, in being negated by another now, in proceeding to the no-thingness of being which is just-past or not-yet.[9] To be a being, a thing must remain free of time; beingness is being-present, the presence of the present.

In Aristotle, time cannot be a determination of beings because it neither exists for itself nor belongs to things as an objective determination. Nor is it, as Derrida implies, a pure form of sensibility, the form of what occurs in the soul, the form of all phenomena in general (OG,70). But insofar as the now acts as a unit of measure, that allows one to distinguish before and after, the now, being *in act*, is opposed to movement. Before and after are the nonbeingness of time, diminishing affectations of the present (OG,76).

Since each now, each present, is in act, each now is the impossibility of coexisting with another now. Yet several nows are maintained together in a synthesis, and this is the creation of time (OG,80). It is also the creation of representation. A moment of time, the not-yet or the just-past substitutes for an absence; a part substitutes for a whole. Starting from the notion of the "now" as in act, the essence of presence can only be captured in each successive now, that is, in the creation of representation, the repetition of each now in the succeeding now. Representation as the deferred presence of the now is the only way we can grasp the essence of the present.

Thus, in *On Time and Being*, Heidegger recognizes the necessity of rethinking the notion of time in its relation to Being, for "we represent time – the unity of present, past, and future – in terms of the now" (TB,11). This, writes Heidegger, is measuring and calculating time; it is not the presencing of the gift. *To presence* means to last in present being, a lasting that comes toward us human beings, (TB,12), so that even what is no longer present in the sense of the "now" presences immediately in its absence (TB,13).

What Heidegger means is that presencing is not equivalent to the "now" of this moment. What has been, also presences, and in this presencing is extended. What is *coming* toward us and is not-yet present presences, and in this, presencing is offered (TB,13). When there is presencing, it is then, the presencing of what is absent. It is the reciprocal relation of what is not-yet and what is no-longer that "at the same time" gives and brings about the present (TB,13).

Presencing opens up a "time-space" that must be distinguished from the time represented as a line thought in the sequence of "nows." Rather, to "true-time" belongs dimensionality. Dimensionality consists in "a reaching out that opens up, in which futural approaching brings about what has been, and the reciprocal relation of both brings about the opening up of openness" (TB,14–15). Dimensionality is what enables us to represent and delimit an area of measurement.

Heidegger names this dimensionality that brings future, past, and present into their interplay, "the first, original, literally incipient extending in which the unity of true-time consists": nearhood, the nearing of nearness (TB,15). It is the "matter" of philosophy (TB,19). It "keeps open the approach coming from the future by withholding the present in the approach" (TB,20).

It can be said of this fourth dimension that it *absents* the present in order to make space for the past and future. Is not the fourth dimension another name for the absent present, the reciprocal relation that takes place *at once*, the deferred presence of the now, the creation of representation, the gap between beings and presencing? Is it not space that always gives time, insofar as time has been thought by analogy with the line? If this is so, then one must not wonder what Heidegger means when he asks, at the end of his discussion of "opening and presence," "In what circle are we moving here, inevitable?" (TB,72).

The temptation to represent time as a line is clear, but a multiplicity of now-points represented as a line are a multiplicity of immobilities, a series of successive arrests that do not give time. Heidegger, however, maintains the conception of nontrue-time by analogy with a line as the succession of nows. As part of time, each now exists potentially only, a line is what would exist were the now *in act*. But a line *in act* is a circle. To be *in act* is to be full and complete. A full and complete line is a circle, otherwise, it would only be an unrelated series of arrested limits. The circle removes this limit by regenerating the same point, the end reproducing itself in the beginning and the beginning in the end. Temporality, as conceived in the history of Metaphysics, is not a line, but a circle.

The circle encompasses origin and end within itself: to begin, to be the "first, original, literally incipient extending" is also to end; to move toward the future is to move toward the past; to be absent is also to be present. It is within the framework, the *Gestell* of the circle, that Western representational thinking has defined itself, repeated itself and represented itself, eventually producing consciousness, the subject that takes precedence over all other centers of relationship in the pure presentation of each "now" point on the circle.

Given the ambiguity of a thing, a jug, Heidegger begins to think from the "nothing of the jug,"[10] which is the absence of presence. Heidegger projects thingness in the form of the emptiness and void that it shapes as a vessel. The jug character is the poured gift of pouring out. In presencing as a thing, it brings the fourfold in their remoteness near to one another, and this "appropriating mirror play" is what we call the world (T,177,179). As the absence of presence, the jug represents the world.

Given the task of thinking, Heidegger writes that thinking must prepare for its future, its transformation, by learning what remains reserved, what remains concealed in the history of philosophy from its beginning to its end (TB,59–60). What is necessary, says Heidegger, is to become aware of "opening," the open for everything that is present and absent (TB,65). But following the circle, from what remains to what is not-yet, only what is already traced in the representation of the beginning in the end is found.

Given the detachment of a work of art, Heidegger claims that the work does not represent, but that whenever art happens there is a beginning, a thrust out of nothing, something is brought out of the source of its nature in a founding leap (TB,65). As the presence of an absence, a thrust our of nothing, a founding leap, the work of art is a pictorial representation "useful" in the discovery of the world of the peasant woman. Heidegger projects a forestructure whose path follows the concepts of earth, world, the fourfold, and is coded by the poetics of the soil (OWA,63–64). In this representative function, the work of art gets instrumentalized so that one forgets the work as art and sees only the world of the peasant woman.

In each case, the circle belongs to the structure of meaning Heidegger deploys, and the circle is the limit of representation. It remains necessary, Heidegger asserts, to think by determining the matter at hand (TB,61). If one just stares at something, or stands in front of it silently, one fails to understand it. One must recognize that the thing has an involvement disclosed in one's undertanding of the world.[11] Interpretation remains operative in the realm of what one wishes to know.

Because in understanding the world, existence is always understood along with it, understanding takes on a certain projective character (BT,146,186). It sketches out its own possibilities and in so doing develops itself. This development of understanding is the meaning of interpretation; it is the working out of possibilities projected in understanding (BT,148,188).

Therefore, interpretation is always grounded in something we have in advance, a totality of involvements which is already understood; something seen in advance, what is held so as to be conceptualizable; something grasped in advance, a definite way of conceiving an entity (BT,150,191) Without this structure, understanding is struck dumb and the entity remains unintelligible.

Following Heidegger, one is compelled to follow the circle: Not only is the main step from work to art a circle like the step from art to work, but every separate step that we attempt circles in this circle (OWA,18). Or again in the lecture on the end of philosophy:

> We still need an education in thinking .... In this respect, Aristotle gives us a hint in Book IV of his *Metaphysics* .... 'For it is uneducated not to have an eye for when it is necessary.' The sentence demands careful reflection. For it is not yet decided in what way that which needs no proof in order to become accessible to thinking is to be experienced .... Only the peculiar quality of that which demands of us above all else to be admitted can decide about that. But how is this to make the decision possible for us before we have not admitted it? In what circle are we moving here, inevitably? (TB,19).

But is it after all impossible to think within the circle as long as one is careful not to make man into the dominating subjectivity? Michel Foucault, for example, argues that because representation is not consciousness, we may not be able to escape its law, insofar as what can be known in the human sciences is always given to representation.[12]

In this light, Heidegger attempts to rethink the unity of time and Being apart from consciousness, in terms of Appropriation. "What determines both time and Being, in their own, that is, in their belonging together we shall call: *Ereignis*, the event of Appropriation" (TB,19). Appropriation brings the two "matters" together and maintains and holds them together. Heidegger points out that neither Appropriation nor Being is either a subject or a predicate (TB,21), so that Appropriation can never be placed in front of us, or set out before it and in relation to us as what is present-at-hand.

By thinking Being and following what is "its own," what is proper to it, Being proves to be the gift of presence granted in the giving of "true-time," and Being vanishes, is absent, in Appropriation. Thus, the denial and withholding of the present play within the giving of the unity of time and Being in Appropriation (TB,22).

Because he believes that he has removed time from the structure of the "now," when, in fact, he has only withdrawn it from the straight line, Heidegger says that Appropriation *is* not, in the sense of being "now" present, that Appropriation simply appropriates. However, since Heidegger is compelled to follow the circle, Appropriation remains the trace, the presence of what is absent, be it Being or time.

Additionally, Appropriation must be questioned with regard to the "its own" of Being, the property of Appropriation, the sense in which Appropriation preserves what is its own. In an essay titled, "Representation, Appropriation and Power," Craig Owens explores how representation is constituted as an apparatus of power (RAP,17) within the Classical system of representation, what Heidegger has called the unifying *ratio*, the significational system whose constitution lies in the will understood as lying in essential unity with appearance, ideal representation (EP,57).

In this regard, Owens quotes Marx from "A Contribution to the Critique of Hegel's Philosophy of Right." "'By calling the people his private property, the king is merely declaring that the owner of private property is king.'" Owens clarifies this quote as follows:

> In the Classical system of representation, then,the subject of representation is posited as absolutely sovereign. In other words, the person who represents the world is transformed through the act of representation from a subjective being enmeshed in space and time – which he is, in a sense, possessed – into a transcendent, objective Mind that appropriates reality for itself and, by appropriating it, dominates it (RAP,17).

In other words, the representation of any individual who substitutes for things his individual representation of them, thus for whom the representation is a transparency through which reality is contemplated, this representation is only the mirror of what belongs to the Sovereign, the significational system, the unifying *ratio*, which appropriates reality for itself, or in Heideggerian terms, preserves its own (RAP,16–17).

The subject is transformed into an abstract, transcendent Being unable to appear in its own representation, though it nonetheless recognizes itself therein. Although absent, it remains present (RAP,19). Michael Foucault offers the example of Velasquez's "Las Meninas," in which the painting, along with all the figures and properties in it, is focused on a single central point which is, however, external to the painting, absent from the scene. This singular focus is the Appropriation and the property of the Sovereign who acts as model, who although absent from the picture plane, is mirrored on the surface of the canvas, and so is present.

If one gazes upon the spectacle represented there, what one sees is the vision of the Sovereign, the unifying *ratio* that sustains individuals and their world (RAP,17). Whoever or whatever determines the *ratio* maintains itself as the absent source of power. Whatever vision does not conform to the *ratio* is *Expropriated*, stripped bare, silenced, left without hope of recognition. As Heidegger claims, Expropriation is Appropriation.

With this in view, is not Heidegger's rethinking of time and Being as the event of Appropriation simply not the last gasp of power, a last attempt to master what is? Human being stands within true-time, perceives Being, belongs to Appropriation. We are mastered by what is and we project it onto things as Heidegger projects the fourfold, that is, the absence of technology, back onto things, the beginning in the end and the end in the beginning.

Recognizing this vicious circle, the postmodern sensibility has refused the mastery of the circle of representational systems. This requires that one neither brackets nor suspends the representational circle, nor directly opposes its mastery and so becomes part of its system. Rather, the alternative is to subvert, disperse, and counter the system of mastery.

Artist Martha Rosler, for example, alternates photographs of New York Bowery storefronts with typewritten words signifying inebriety. The photographs and the written words are technically bland, a refusal of mastery. But an even stronger refusal lies in that the words do not supply appropriate captions for the photographs, completing what is absent in them, nor does the artist photograph the inhabitants of Skid Row, thus victimizing them and constituting herself as moral master.[13]

Gilles Deleuze dodges the logic of essences that establishes the present in memory in representations; diverts the logic of concepts that establishes the present as knowledge of the future, and disdains judgment that measures events by searching for origins. He suggests that events repeat themselves as singular universals, indefinite and phantasmic repetitions, and that the individual encounter with such repetitions is only thought as mime, a repetition without a model.[14]

In this analysis, Heidegger's valuable insight that it is technology which Enframes us in the Modern era, and that the destruction of much that is valuable to individuals is tied to technological-calculative "man" positing himself as the master must not be disregarded at the risk of losing the human trait of thinking. However his method of immersion, working from within the *ratio*, the very structure he seeks to supplant has continually, constantly, endlessly encircled him within the limits of representation.

Notes

1. Martin Heidegger, "The Age of the World Picture," in *The Question Concerning Technology and Other Essays*, trans. W. Lovitt (New York: Harper and Row, 1977), p. 131. (Henceforth cited as *AWP*.)

2. Martin Heidegger, *The End of Philosophy*, trans. Joan Stambaugh (New York: Harper and Row, 1973), p. 4. (Henceforth cited as *EP*.)

3. Aristotle, *Physics*, trans. Hardie and Gaye, in *The Basic Works of Aristotle*, ed. Richard McKeon (New York: Random House, 1970), ch. IV, bk. 2.

4. Martin Heidegger, "The Origin of the Work of Art," in *Poetry, Language, Thought*, trans. Albert Hofstadter (New York: Harper and Row, 1975), p. 84. (Henceforth cited as *OWA*.)

5. *Ibid.*, p. 85, translator's remark.

6. Craig Owens, "Representation, Appropriation and Power," *Art in America* (May, 1982):13. (Henceforth cited as *RAP*.)

7. Craig Owens, "The Allegorical Impulse: Toward a Theory of Postmodernism, Part I," *October* (12, 1980):81.

8. Martin Heidegger, *On Time and Being*, trans. Joan Stambaugh (New York: Harper and Row, 1972), p. 22. (Henceforth cited as *TB*.)

9. Jacques Derrida, "*Ousia* and *Grammé*: A Note to a Footnote in *Being and Time*," trans. Edward S. Casey, in *Phenomenology in Perspective*, ed. F. Joseph Smith (The Hague: Nijhoff, 1970), p. 62. (Henceforth cited as *OG*.)

10. Martin Heidegger, "The Thing," in *Poetry, Language, Thought*, trans. Albert Hofstadter (New York: Harper and Row, 1975), p. 169. (Henceforth cited as *T*.)

11. Martin Heidegger, *Being and Time*, trans. John Macquarrie and Edward Robinson (New York: Harper and Row, 1962), pp. 150, 191. (Henceforth cited as *BT*.)

12. Michel Foucault, *The Order of Things*, trans. anonymous (New York: Vintage Books, 1973), p. 361.

13. Craig Owens, "The Discourse of Others: Feminists and Modernism," in *The Anti-Aesthetic*, ed. Hal Foster (Port Townsend, WA: Bay Press, 1983), p. 68.

14. Michel Foucault, "Theatrum Philosophicum," in *Language, Counter-Memory and Practice*, ed. Donald F. Bouchard, trans. D. F. Bouchard and Sherry Simon (Ithaca, NY: Cornell University Press, 1977), p. 179.

Part IV.
Overcoming Metaphysics and the Revaluation of Values

8. Heidegger on Nietzsche: The Question of Value

Dick White

Nietzsche proclaimed himself both Antichrist and antinihilist, and he sought to overcome metaphysics. Nevertheless, according to Heidegger, his determination of Will To Power as *letztes Faktum*, and his project of revaluation in accordance with Will To Power, identify his thought as essentially nihilist and as the proper fulfillment of the metaphysical tradition. For Heidegger, Nietzsche is the last metaphysician, and the Will To Power represents the final possibility of metaphysics because it is the explicit recognition and endorsement of the violence of this re-presentational thinking. Indeed, the Will To Power grasps the Being of beings solely in terms of its possible value for the preservation and enhancement of human power.

In this respect, Nietzsche's thought is held to express the total domination of technology and the triumph of a global planning, which secures and arranges everything with a view to its own aggrandizement. Heidegger claims that the Will To Power provides the metaphysical basis for technology, and that technology itself is nothing other than completed metaphysics. Hence, after Nietzsche, philosophy as such becomes irrelevant. Finally, then, the Will To Power is to be understood as the consummation of nihilism, for in its relation to technology it is revealed as the most adequate expression of the disclosure of Being, in its complete withdrawal from man into oblivion and nothingness.

Heidegger's interpretation is both exciting and compelling. It leads to a better understanding of the history of philosophy, as well as to the way in which Nietzsche is essentially the philosopher of our times. Nevertheless, Heidegger's interpretation is perhaps only truly coherent once the traditional priority of metaphysics is accepted over all the other domains of philosophy, including that of ethics. For this is what Heidegger claims when he states that "ethics and psychology are grounded in metaphysics,"[1] or that value is simply the weakest and most confused of all the offspring of ἀγαθόν[2].

Certainly, on the strength of this traditional ordering, Nietzsche's stress on revaluation can be construed as metaphysical, even in spite of itself. Given the priority of metaphysics over ethics, it is apparent that every ethics and value-positing necessarily involves a particular metaphysical perspective. As in Descartes, ethics is understood as the fruit of a tree whose roots are metaphysical.

Nevertheless it can also be argued that the acceptance of metaphysical priority predisposes Heidegger to ignore the workings of Nietzsche's ethical and practical project, as something actually secondary to the metaphysics it represents. It follows that Heidegger's metaphysical reading of Nietzsche can be challenged on the grounds that it obscures as much as it illuminates.

In fact, Nietzsche is the philosopher who asserts the absolute "primacy of the practical" and who effects through laughter a complete *reductio ad absurdum* of all metaphysical questions. Heidegger's metaphysical reading of Nietzsche dictates a univocal determination for each of Nietzsche's key concepts – the Will To Power, Eternal Recurrence, and Overman could *not* be admitted as fundamental metaphysical principles if they did not each possess one basic serious meaning from which every other determination followed. By emphasizing the ethical intention of Nietzsche's thought, then, I will suggest that Heidegger's reading of Nietzsche is inadequate since it fails to grasp the multiplicity in use, meaning, and origin, which such concepts *do* reveal in their practical aspect.

I begin with a discussion of value and its relation to Will To Power. After considering the irreducible difference between Nietzsche's Master and Slave, I show that the metaphysical treatment of Will To Power is flawed because it is undiscriminating. Finally, I argue that Heidegger's position on will and value has some very dangerous implications, and that in the encounter with nihilism it is Nietzsche who really has the most to teach us.

I.

According to note 715 of Nietzsche's *Nachlass*, which Heidegger quotes at length "The standpoint of 'value' is the standpoint of conditions of preservation and enhancement for complex forms of relative life-duration within the flux of becoming."[3] Thus, a *value* is an ideal or a goal that can inspire life to reach beyond itself and so augment its Will To Power. Nietzsche's complaint, of course, is that the bourgeois Christian values of modern Europe no longer act in such a way: indeed, they actually diminish and dilute life by emphasizing those "passive" virtues that allow weakness to continue in "wretched contentment" under the mask of goodness.

What is significant, though, is that with Nietzsche's discussion in *The Genealogy of Morals* and *Beyond Good and Evil,*[4] the concept of *value* is given a *double* origin, in the affirmation of the Noble Master and the vengeance of the Slave. As I will show, such a double origin implies a double meaning, which effectively undermines any attempt to determine the nature of value and, hence, Will To Power, outside of all particular perspectives.

For Nietzsche, the Master type is autonomous in that his creation of value is an act of strength and self-affirmation, rather than a response to something outside of himself. For the Master, "good" is the name and celebration of life as it shines forth in his own existence: his value-creation is a consecration and endorsement of this existence, as something utterly singular and differentiated from the rest of creation.

By contrast, the Slave feels his own impotence in comparison with the Master. Out of the spirit of revenge, he denigrates the Master and the Master's values as "evil." The Slave would like to be a Master, but the only way he can forget his own wretchedness is by reducing everything else to his own wretched level. The value-creation of the Slave is inspired by vengeance, weakness, and fear; his values are primarily the values of utility – moral and social conformity, science, and "progress" – which serve to normalize society by suppressing individual difference. Nietzsche understood that such values have secured the Slave's control of the earth:

> For . . . we can see nothing today that wants to grow greater, we suspect that things wil continue to go down, down, to become thinner, more good-natured, more prudent, more comfortable, more mediocre, more indifferent, more Chinese, more Christian – there is no doubt that man is getting better all the time.[5]

In short, the Slave's mode of valuation is fundamentally different from the Master's. Certainly, for both Master and Slave values *are* "the conditions of preservation and enhancement of Will To Power." But what constitutes preservation and enhancement from the Slave's perspective is entirely different from what constitutes preservation and enhancement in the eyes of the Master.

For the Slave, these are understood in purely appropriate terms, as the gradual assimilation of all that is strange and different. With such a conception of value, the Will To Power can only be grasped as a totalizing force which aims at complete spiritual and political domination. *This* Will To Power is a will to possess power, a will to assimilate and control all that is outside of itself.

The Master experiences preservation and enhancement in quite different ways. Certainly not as power over others, but as power over oneself, as a continual movement of self-overcoming and self-refinement, in the manner of a work of art. This leads us to a version of Will To Power that cannot really be thematized, since it would then become prescriptive in the slavish sense: as a set of rules and regulations or "procedures" for increasing power. Instead, the Master's Will To Power can only be suggested or evoked, through the image of the Greek hero or the philosopher of the future; or else in poetry, with the evocation of a gift-giving virtue as the supreme generosity of soul.[6]

The Will To Power is Nietzsche's ruling principle of interpretation. But this does not give it an incontrovertible status. As Nietzsche says elsewhere, "'Essence,' the 'essential nature' is something perspectival and already presupposes a multiplicity."[7] By showing the irreconcilable difference between Masters' and Slaves' conceptions of value, one can argue that even Nietzsche's ruling principle presupposes a multiplicity. Indeed, the Will To Power is a principle of interpretaion that must itself be interpreted.

II.

And so, the question to ask now is "How does Heidegger interpret the Will To Power?", which is to say, "*Whose* version of the concept does he grasp?" In itself this is an illuminating question, because it shows the difference between Heidegger's early treatment of Nietzsche in the lecture courses of 1936 and 1937 and in his later essays of the 1940s.[8]

In "The Will To Power As Art," Heidegger is basically sympathetic to Nietzsche's position, grasping Will To Power in terms of his own categories of resolve and openness to oneself; arguing very forcefully that the Will To Power is not a blind compulsion, or the striving that arises from a lack that has power as its goal. Here the basic determination of Will To Power is that of "commanding" – certainly not as mere "ordering about," but as self-commanding which implies power over oneself.[9]

In the first lectures, the Will To Power is seen to emerge from the "raging discord" of art and truth, in which relationship "truth" is understood as the preserving aspect which freezes and secures one particular perspective on existence, while "art" is the enhancing aspect which celebrates existence by discovering new perspectives and visions of the real.

Yet, what is so curious about Heidegger's discussion is that here he yokes together what he regards as Nietzsche's paradigm cases – the Slavish project of truth and the Noble project of art – as constitutive moments of a *singular* Will To Power. Such a reading of Nietzsche's statement, "value is the condition of preservation and enhancement of Will To Power," is thus an attempt to overcome irreducible differences in perspective within the enclosure of an all-encompassing metaphysical principle. Instead of arguing that different types have different conceptions of value, and hence Will To Power, Heidegger would understand the Will To Power as a unitary phenomenon which contains the struggle of these different motives within itself. As he writes, "Both values determine in their value relation the unitive essence of the intrinsically value-positing Will To Power."[10]

This implies, contrary to what Nietzsche asserts,that the Slavish and Noble perspectives are equally dependent upon each other: For Heidegger, the Will To Power as art presupposes and requires the existence of a preestablished perspective of truth, even though it is always in violent conflict with that truth. In this way, "Art and truth are equally necessary for reality. As equally necessary they stand in service to one another and go counter to each other."[11]

In his later work, Heidegger's rejection of the original separation of Master and Slave becomes even more pronounced as the "raging discordance" between art and truth seems to give way to a mutual complicity of these two values in the technological domination of the earth. As he writes in *Overcoming Metaphysics*,

> The two constitutive 'values' (truth and art) in the concept of the Will to Power are only circumscriptions for 'technology,' in the essential sense of a planning and calculating stabilization as accomplishment, and for the creating of the 'creators' who bring a new stimulus to life over and above life as it is, and guarantee the business of culture.[12]

Thus, in the later essays on Nietzsche, the Will To Power is grasped in purely slavish terms, as a blind appropriation that aims to reduce everything to a uniform level so as to control it more efficiently. In this respect, "values" are now cynically understood in terms of pure calculation and utility: a value, whether it is art or truth, is whatever promotes assimilation and control. In this way, the *actual* form of Will To Power – technology – is treated as if it were the *necessary* result of value-positing as such (including any "revaluation" from the perspective of "life").

In fact, it can be argued that Heidegger's later work on Nietzsche is primarily the occasion for a confrontation with technology, as the modern epoch of nihilism, and only secondarily a coming-to-grips with Nietzsche's own thought. Heidegger grasps technology as completed metaphysics, and he holds the Will To Power to represent the fulfillment of the metaphysical project, insofar as it brings metaphysics to the manifestation of its essence: in this way, Heidegger's preoccupation with the problem of technology leads him to attack the Will To Power as the essence of this global movement, which assaults and organizes everything and everyone within the uniformity of its domain. As he writes in "The Word of Nietzsche,"

> . . . in deliberately willing the Will To Power as the being of whatever is; and . . . in rebelliously withstanding and subjugating to itself every necessary phase of the objectifying of the world [willing as Will To Power makes] secure the stably constant reserve of what is for a willing of the greatest possible uniformity and equality.[13]

Clearly, what Heidegger is describing in his meditations on technology is the complete triumph of the Slave, which Nietzsche had already alluded to in his diagnoses of contemporary values and "modern man." But in reading the Will To Power as a univocal principle, Heidegger remains insensitive to the prospect of "Nobility," which Nietzsche elaborates as an alternative value-positing to that of the Slave. Except perhaps for the early descriptions of the Will To Power as "releasing all things to their own essence,"[14] Heidegger refuses to allow for the possibility of a mode of willing that is not ultimately domineering, in the sense of forcing whatever is into the confines of its own projection. But this is crucial; for it means that Heidegger is led to reject the entire ethical/practical dimension of Nietzsche's philosophy as something which is tainted by the nihilism he discovers in Will To Power. More than this, the rejection of Will To Power *en bloc* effectively closes the door to *every* practical response to nihilism, as already engaged in the original sin of value-positing. For Heidegger, no distinction exists among different types of values or among values of different types. Given his reading of Nietzsche, every *kind* of willing and every version of the practical is rejected indiscriminately, since it necessarily partakes of the nihilism it seeks to overcome.

III.

Following this interpretation of Will To Power, Heidegger's rejection of willing and value-positing of every kind has tremendous implications, both for his own philosophy and for the encounter with nihilism itself. Thus, in his later work, Heidegger regards the two basic activities of "willing" and "thinking" as in complete opposition to each other. Certainly this is a traditional view – that "thinking" is careful and responsive but can achieve nothing in the world, whereas "willing" can effect the most dramatic changes though it is ultimately arbitrary and blind. However by making willing and thinking mutually exclusive, Heidegger is brought to his provisional and frankly unsatisfactory stance of "willing not to will."[15]

For the later Heidegger, philosophy is no longer capable of having any effect upon the future of the world. Consequently, the thinker is not called upon to act as wise man or to give practical advice: the rigidity of the thinking/willing opposition determines every form of philosophical self-assertion as overreaching and ultimately "impious." Instead, the thinker must now prepare himself with anticipatory resolve for the possible grace of Appropriation (*das Ereignis*). As Heidegger remarks in the *Spiegel* interview,

> . . . philosophy will be unable to effect any immediate change in the current state of the world . . . . The only possibility available to us is that by thinking and poetizing we prepare a readiness for the appearance of a god in [our] decline, insofar as in view of the absent god we are in a state of decline.[16]

In terms of its direct effect upon the world, philosophy is now useless. But in accepting this, Heidegger does not admit any reduction in the status of philosophy. Rather, he claims philosophy represents the most perspicuous and decisive form of Being's involvement with man. For Heidegger, the modern technological age is grounded and fulfilled in the metaphysics of Will To Power; similarly, in other discussions of Plato's truth or Descartes's method, Heidegger assumes that the trace of Being's epochal determination is always most manifest in philosophy: "Metaphysics grounds an age."[17]

One of the consequences of allowing philosophy such a privileged realm of disclosure, however, is to render the problem of nihilism as first and foremost a problem of philosophy. Clearly, this does not mean that nihilism is a philosophical pseudoproblem or that philosophers are the direct cause of nihilism through their refusal to consider the meaning of Being. Rather, it means for Heidegger that all of the usual phenomena associated with nihilism – decadence, spiritual decline, world-weariness, lack of meaning, etc. – are merely symptoms that derive from the fundamental event of the oblivion of Being; and *this* achieves its most manifest and paradigm form in philosophy. It follows that the confrontation with nihilism is most *authentically* a purely philosophical confrontation. Hence, any attempt to overcome nihilism through moral revaluation actually contributes to it, by failing once more to recall what has been forgotten:

> The default of Being is expressly, if unknowingly, misplaced in its default by the nature of metaphysical thinking, as thinking in values, whereby the very misplacing does not know itself as such. The nothing of Being is sealed in the interpretation of Being as value. It belongs to this sealing that it understand itself as the new 'yes' to beings as such in the sense of Will To Power, that it understand itself as the overcoming of nihilism.[18]

Nietzsche would probably reject this supreme elevation of philosophy as yet another example of the arrogance of German scholarship. Obviously it is a painful circumlocution that grasps a concrete phenomenon like nihilism, and secures it within the jurisdiction of "thinking" by asserting the preeminence of its philosophical manifestation. Indeed, the effect of Heidegger's circumlocution is perhaps most perilously to reduce the pain and nausea of nihilism, by first removing it from everyday experience and then recovering it as an obstacle to "thinking." Perhaps in this way one suffers what Heidegger describes elsewhere as the "pain" of the last men: for with such a conception of nihilism, is not the greatest danger of all that we will "feel no pain?"[19]

By contrast, precisely at this point, Nietzsche's confrontation with nihilism is most inspired. Certainly, Nietzsche has an overall account of nihilism, in terms of the "devaluation of values." But quite apart from simply "describing the situation," Nietzsche's writing is also *performative* in that he uses parable, parody, and thoughts that are a torment and an affliction, to *force* one to become aware of one's impoverished situation and to wrench one out of wretched contentment.

Consider Nietzsche's doctrine of Eternal Recurrence, for example. Nietzsche realized that for the modern Slave, the thought of eternal recurrence was potentially the most devastating thought of all: The life that can only endure earthly existence by fixing onto other worldly hopes or the ultimate peace of nothingness is utterly crushed by the revelation of present nausea continuing throughout eternity. As he says, "This is the most extreme form of nihilism: the nothing (the 'meaningless') eternally."[20] Thus, the doctrine will either drive the Slave to complete despair or else it will at last provoke him to a self-affirmation in which he finally wills himself by willing the eternal return of his own willing. In this way, the Slave becomes a Master.

Nietzsche intends the thought of eternal recurrence as a constant torment and nightmare from which it is impossible to escape. To press a confrontation with this thought, to make it *more* than just a thought-experiment, he sought to sketch it as a scientific proof, or else he thought of it as a new religion, his own "noble lie," and a doctrine that is going to "sift men."[21] In this respect, the thought of eternal recurrence is intended to mold the future of humanity.

Thus, instead of reconvening the problem of nihilism at another level, Nietzsche deliberately seeks to afflict individuals with the full horror of their everyday existence, so that eventually they are compelled to take charge of themselves and come to a decision concerning their own existence. In this respect, the Noble Master and the Slave, with the various forms they assume in Nietzsche's work, represent the two most basic possibilities of being. In response to Heidegger's reading and in the confrontation with nihilism, what we must now do is recall to ourselves the suppressed figure of Nietzsche's Master, as the possibility of an affirmative willing which would *not* seek the endless appropriation of everything that is. For with such a figure, nihilism is overcome.

IV.

In conclusion, Nietzsche is a 'philosopher of will," but not because he continues the will-based metaphysics of Leibniz, Hegel, or Schelling; or because he follows Schopenhauer by proclaiming will as the "ground" of all that is: In Nietzsche, such metaphysical ultimacy is rejected as expressing nothing more than a need for security. Far from being the "last metaphysician," Nietzsche is most aptly described as the *first* philosopher of will, because he violently rejects the traditional theoretical issues of metaphysics and epistemology, in order to force individuals beyond mere contemplation to a standpoint of active willing. Nietzsche understood that nihilism was the product of Slavish values; therefore, he proposed an alternative value-positing from out of the Noble perspective of life.

In fact, Heidegger's own encounter with nihilism suffers in comparison: for as I have suggested, the latter is an oblique approach that mutes the horror of this Waste Land by taking it up into the question of Being. While Nietzsche can evaluate contemporary existence by making constant distinctions, genealogies, and diagnoses of the Will To Power and its various types, Heidegger's indiscriminate rejection of will and value bring him to an undiscriminating encounter with the modern world. What is clearest of all is that in the battle between Heidegger and Nietzsche, the efficacy of the "practical" is most at stake. And while Heidegger objects that Being has been "made into a value," his response of rejecting valuation in its entirety cannot be accepted.

Notes

1. Martin Heidegger, *What is Called Thinking?*, trans. J. Glenn Gray (New York: Harper and Row, 1968), p. 89.

2. Cf. Martin Heidegger, "Plato's Doctrine of Truth," trans. John Barlow, in *Philosophy in the Twentieth Century, Vol. 3*, ed. William Barrett and Henry Aiken (New York: Random House, 1962); 263; also Martin Heidegger, *Introduction to Metaphysics*, trans. Ralph Mannheim (New Haven, CT: Yale University Press, 1973), p. 196ff.

3. Friedrich Nietzsche, *The Will to Power*, trans. W. Kaufmann (New York: Vintage, 1966), sect. 715. For Heidegger's discussion see Martin Heidegger, "The Word of Nietzsche," in *The Question Concerning Technology*, trans. W. Lovitt (New York: Harper, 1977), pp. 53–112; also Martin Heidegger's later essays on Nietzsche, published in volume two of *Nietzsche* (Pfüllingen: Neske, 1961), trans. F. A. Capuzzi in *Nietzsche, Volume 4: Nihilism* (San Francisco, CA: Harper, 1982), sect. 10.

4. Friedrich Nietzsche, *On the Genealogy of Morals*, trans. W. Kaufmann (New York: Vintage, 1969), first essay; "Beyond Good and Evil." Cf. especially sects. 241, 260, 261.

5. Friedrich Nietzsche, *On the Genealogy of Morals*, I sect. 12.

6. Cf. Friedrich Nietzsche, "Thus Spoke Zarathustra," in *The Portable Nietzsche* trans. W. Kaufmann (New York: Vintage, 1968), pp. 186–87.

7. Friedrich Nietzsche, *The Will to Power,* sect. 556.

8. See the "plan of the English edition" at beginning of Martin Heidegger, *Nietzsche, Volume 1: The Will to Power as Art,* trans. D. F. Krell (San Francisco, CA: Harper, 1982), where a useful chronology is provided.

9. Martin Heidegger, *Nietzsche, Volume 1,* p. 41.

10. Martin Heidegger, *The Question Concerning Technology,* p. 86.

11. Martin Heidegger, *Nietzsche, Volume 1,* p. 217.

12. Martin Heidegger, *The End of Philosophy,* trans. Joan Stambaugh (New York: Harper, 1973), p. 94.

13. Martin Heidegger, *The Question Concerning Technology,* p. 102.

14. Martin Heidegger, *Nietzsche, Volume 1,* p. 137; also p. 131: "For Nietzsche, art is the essential way in which beings are made to be beings."

15. See, for example, Part 2 of Heidegger, *What is Called Thinking?*; Martin Heidegger, *Discourse on Thinking,* trans. John Anderson and E. Hans Freund (New York: Harper, 1966); Martin Heidegger, *On Time and Being,* trans. Joan Stambaugh (New York: Harper, 1977). For a discussion of thinking and willing, cf. most obviously, Hannah Arendt, *The Life of the Mind* (New York: Harcourt, Brace and Jovanovitch, 1978).

16. Martin Heidegger, "Only a God can Save Us," trans. William Richardson, in *Heidegger: The Man and the Thinker,* ed. Thomas Sheehan (Chicago: Precedent, 1981), p. 57.

17. Martin Heidegger, *The Question Concerning Technology,* p. 115; for the discussion of Plato and Descartes, cf. Heidegger, "Plato's Doctrine of Truth," and Heidegger, *Nietzsche, Volume 4,* sect. 15–21.

18. Martin Heidegger, *Nietzsche, Volume 4,* p. 219.

19. Martin Heidegger, *What is Called Thinking?,* especially first three lectures.

20. Friedrich Nietzsche, *The Will to Power,* sect. 55.

21. *Ibid.,* sect. 56; cf. also sections 1053–67.

9. Devaluation and Destruction: On the End of Metaphysics and the Revaluation of All Values

Richard Taft

In the question of "Nietzsche/Heidegger," I want to situate my remarks precisely at the "/". That is to say, I do not attempt to explicate, correct, or defend Heidegger's interpretation of Nietzsche as it occurs in the *Nietzsche* volumes and in many shorter pieces, nor do I attempt to compare and contrast the thought of the two men with respect to various common philosophical issues or problems, as if the topic were "Heidegger on Nietzsche," or "Nietzsche and Heidegger." Instead, I attempt to disclose a hinge or point of contact between the two which can serve as a basis for an *Auseinandersetzung*, thereby yielding fruitful insight into the work of both. That point of contact is, in simplest terms, their respective ways of taking up the metaphysical tradition.

Certainly since the last part of the nineteenth century, and arguably even before that, the notion of a radical interpretive involvement with the metaphysical tradition has an increasing significance for European philosophy. In this essay, I concentrate on two of the most significant contributors to this philosophical tendency, Nietzsche and Heidegger, for both of whom a radical critical stance with respect to the tradition was more than simply a by-product of their thought, but in fact in many ways it came to embody the richest fruit of their philosophical activity. This can be seen concretely by comparing Nietzsche's project of a devaluation and subsequent revaluation of all values with Heidegger's project of a destruction of the metaphysical tradition and a retrieval of that which made such a tradition possible in the first place. This comparison is possible and fruitful to the extent that both Nietzsche's and Heidegger's projects are ultimately enacted at the level of a radical critique of language.

I.

On its most general level, Nietzsche's self-appointed task can be characterized as the passionate and violent overturning of the systematic, whether "system" be conceived of in terms of religion, morality, philosophy, or language. Modern man's "will to a system," in whatever form it might take, is the source of a pervasive blindness and sense of suffocation Nietzsche sees as endemic to his world. Thus, he writes, "I mistrust all systematizers and I avoid them. The will to a system is a lack of integrity."[1]

For this essay, I must limit my remarks on Nietzsche's devaluation and revaluation of all values to his critique of Philosophy as it occurs in *Twilight of the Idols*.

In *Ecce Homo*, Nietzsche says of *Twilight of the Idols* that it is

> . . . an exception among books: there is none richer in substance, more independent, more subversive [*Umwerfenderes*] – more evil. If you want a quick idea of how before me everything stood on its head, begin with this essay. What is called *idol* on the title page is simply what has been called truth so far. *Götzen-Dämmerung* – that is: the old truth is approaching its end.[2]

Insofar as *Götzen-Dämmerung* has a "subject," it is a consideration of "old (read: conventional) truths," or idols. But what is most radically significant about this book is not a discussion of conventional metaphysical truths or systems, however illuminating (or the reverse) these discussions might be. Rather, the radical dimension of *Götzen-Dämmerung* is indicated by its subtitle: "How One Philosophizes with a Hammer."

Nietzsche's style, at least in this work, is characterized in terms of "convalescence" – a familiar word to the reader of *Zarathustra*. Recall that in the earlier book, the chapter in Part III headed "The Convalescent" ("*Der Genesende*") describes the creation in seven days of Zarathustra, teacher of the most abysmal thought, namely, Eternal Recurrence.[3] In *Götzen-Dämmerung*, convalescence is associated with another thought, a "question mark so black, so tremendous that it casts shadows upon the man who puts it down,"[4] namely, the Revaluation of all Values. *Convalescence* is described here in terms of two apparently quite different images: on the one hand, it is described in terms of healing wounds; on the other hand, it is a "sounding-out of idols."[5] These two modes of convalescence indicate two prongs (what, after Derrida, we might call two spurs[6]) of Nietzsche's style, which I call a style of dance (in which one "runs into the sun every moment" – note the "wound" being healed here: "a heavy, all-too-heavy seriousness") and a style of the hammer (the idols are "touched as with a tuning fork" to "hear as a reply that famous hollow sound which speaks of bloated entrails"). This book, with its style(s) of Dance and the Hammer, is Nietzsche's "great declaration of war" against the Eternal Idols or the old truths,[7] a war which is fought as an enactment of the Devaluation and Revaluation of all Values. The idols or old values which he confronts include such metaphysical fossils as the systems of orthodox Christianity, Philosophy, and the conventional Morality which goes with them. Curiously, in so doing, Nietzsche has declared war on truth, the "highest" value of them all. In this book, Nietzsche sounds out the philosopher with his hammer and the wound lies exposed. In the face of this exposure, with all of its serious overtones, he responds not by arguing for a "better" set of concepts with which to understand things, but adopts instead a more subtle strategy: "The last thing *I* should promise would be to 'improve' mankind. No new idols are erected by me; let the old ones learn what feet of clay mean."[8] A new doctrine would not heal the wound, but only cause it to fester, even if invisibly. However, what is most radical in this remarkable work is not its "content" but its strategy – its style(s).

But, of course, it is quite fair to ask what is meant by Nietzsche's "style." One could attempt a more or less conventional analysis of Nietzsche's style of writing, taking pains to categorize his various images carefully, his uses of verse and unusual sentence structure, and the frequency with which he repeats key terms. One example of this sort of thing is Silk and Stern's *Nietzsche on Tragedy*, which among other things carries out an extremely detailed analysis of what they call Nietzsche's "style" in *The Birth of Tragedy*.[9] With respect to the present work, for example, Nietzsche tends to employ metaphors of death when speaking about philosophy (*e.g.*, graves, grave diggers, mummies) as well as terms suggesting stagnation (the most notable of these being "Egyptification," which suggests both the process of embalming once-living bodies and the activity of entombing them in huge and lifeless momuments of stone), to which he opposes life, activity, sensuousness. Furthermore, he continuously sets up oppositions which he refuses to resolve, claiming instead that there is the need for an enemy.[10]

I argue that however useful some of the results of such analyses might be for "Nietzsche Scholarship" (an expression which never ceases to sound funny – one must always wonder what this edifice would sound like if struck by Nietzsche's hammer), they effectively conceal what is most radical about Nietzsche's style(s). If an appeal to authority is more forceful in making this point, consider Nietzsche's own assessment of style: "Good style *in itself* – a pure folly, mere 'idealism,' on a level with the 'beautiful in itself,' the 'good in itself,' the 'thing in itself.'"[11] Clearly the question of style is not approached on its most fundamental level in terms of a structural ideal to be held up, examined, and commented upon.

The problem of Nietzsche's style(s) is one of language, not of structure. The radicality of his style(s) is due to entrapment within the metaphysics of language to the extent that his style(s) is his way of sounding out yet another idol, namely the metaphysical conception of language. This was alluded to in the section of *Götzen-Dämmerung* on "Reason in Philosophy," to which I referred earlier. At the end of the fifth part of that section, having already exposed God as the emptiest of concepts, Nietzsche writes, "I am afraid we are not rid of God because we still have faith in grammar."[12]

In light of the limitations which govern our normal use of language at all times, how are we to understand the radicality of Nietzsche's style(s) which, if successful, seeks to strike the metaphysical system of language with a hammer, but somehow has to do so from within language itself? For Nietzsche (and for us) the key to radical style(s) is learning to think and learning to write, both of which *can* be akin to dancing.[13] Nietzsche's style(s) must be seen on the most radical level as a "dancing" with concepts and words – with writing. It is only in and through such "dancing," which will always serve to cultivate tensions within conventional forms of expression, that Nietzsche can "write with a hammer." Thus, it is important to see that on their most radical levels, his style(s) enact a fundamental challenge to textuality, by which I mean not only a challenge to the conventions of a written text, but also – and perhaps more significantly – to textuality in the broad, contemporary sense which it comes to have for writers like Derrida.

To see the best sense in which Nietzsche's style(s) enacts such a radical challenge, it must be understood how this style(s) has its origin in his understanding of language. His earlier essay, "On Truth and Lie in an Extramoral Sense," has one obvious point in common with *Götzen-Dämmerung*: both are devoted to the task of exposing the nature of truth the way it is normally understood. Here, as he will again show in his later book, truth is the product of conventions, or more specifically, it is established through the "legislation of language" [*die Gesetzgebung der Sprache*] in which certain words come to be the agreed-upon designations for certain things ("Truth and Lie" 371/81). The issue then arises as to the adequacy of these designations which are produced, after all, only on the basis of convention. Nietzsche argues that these conventions are fundamentally arbitrary, and that in fact the use of language is based on metaphor rather than logic.

It is extremely important to see in all of this that, while the "truths" expressed according to linguistic conventions are illusory and while they cannot have the degree of certitude to which they lay claim, at no time does Nietzsche suggest something like a program to "perfect" this "weakness" in our language. At no time does he try to deny the problems caused by the conflict between language's metaphorical roots and our logical presuppositions about it, nor does he try to replace the conflict; he tries only (only?) to recognize and exploit it. Language, with its inherent conflict, presents Nietzsche with a *stylistic* problem. He sees the "hardening and congealing of metaphors" ("Truth and Lie" 378/87) that occurs in everyday language, and it is to counteract this tendency which he sets as his most important task. He provides a typically masterful description of how his subversive stylistic skirmishes can and do succeed:

> . . . That immense framework and planking of concepts to which the needy man clings his whole life long . . . is nothing but a scaffolding and toy for the most audacious feats of the liberated intellect. And when it smashes this framework to pieces, throws it into confusion, and puts it back together in an ironic fashion, pairing the most alien things and separating the closest, it is demonstrating that it has no need of these makeshifts of indigence and that it will now be guided by intuition rather than concepts . . . . There exists no word for these intuitions; when man sees them he grows dumb, or else he speaks only in forbidden metaphors and in unheard-of combinations of concepts. He does this so that by shattering and mocking the old conceptual barriers he may at least correspond creatively to the impression of the powerful present intuition ("Truth and Lie" 382–83/90).

This is the finest *description* of Nietzsche's style(s), of dancing with words and concepts, that could be hoped for, just as *Thus Spoke Zarathustra* is probably his finest enactment of the same. It is important to see from this description how and why the problem of style, the nature of language and truth, and the significance of art are all radically intertwined. It is only because of this radical intertwinement that art can serve as "the great stimulus of life" in the way he envisioned. The artist who embodies Nietzsche's "free intellect" attacks the "congealed metaphors" which pass as conventional truths (or idols), and in so doing exposes the metaphorical, illogical, uncertain essence of language – although of course it is no longer "essence" as an abstraction. The essence of language is revealed quite correctly and vividly in and through the living, dancing style(s) of Nietzsche's mature works. In this sense, which is simultaneously radical and concrete, style is act and act is style.

II

I now move abruptly to the other side of the "/". In the first part of this essay, I illustrated that a fundamental consequence of Nietzsche's thought is the development of a particuar sort of critical relationship to the metaphysical tradition, a relationship which I described in terms of Nietzsche'a style(s) and his project of a devaluation/revaluation of all values. In turn, I illustrated the way this fundamental relationship came to necessitate an attempt on Nietzsche's part to enact a radical critique of language.

At this point, however, in spite of all of his insights, Nietzsche's project of devaluation/revaluation continues to be constrained and limited in effectiveness because he remains bound by traditional concepts and traditional conceptual oppositions even while he seeks to subvert them. Furthermore, for Nietzsche, language remains something essentially under human control, something like a tool which an artist, for example, can use to his own ends, and this state of affairs persists in spite of his devaluation of the logical and revaluation of the metaphorical as seen in "On Truth and Lie." I now consider Heidegger's relationship to the metahysical tradition and show how, at least in one respect, Heidegger takes Nietzsche's thought a step further by radicalizing his understanding of language.

Heidegger informs us repeatedly that metaphysics has "ended," that we are living and thinking in a "post-metaphysical" or "post-philosophical" epoch.[14] This notion of an "end" of metaphysics is of central importance throughout Heidegger's work, indeed to the extent that one cannot fully appreciate the depth and radicality of the *Seinsfrage* apart from it. In light of this situation, which has somehow brought metaphysics to a closure, one might ask with Heidegger the question "What now?" Philosophy as metaphysica has ended, but what of thinking? Taking the title of one of Heidegger'a later essays as our guide, one might ask: "What now is the task of thinking if it is no longer to be metaphysical thinking?"

Even in his early lecture courses, those now appearing in the *Gesamtausgabe* which imediately predate and in effect constitute his early working-out of the problematic of *Sein und Zeit*, Heidegger was concerned with this issue, even if not explicitly. The genesis of this question and Heidegger's attempts to grapple with it is seen in the notion of "retrieval" [*Wiederholung*], an idea which he retained throughout his thinking. From his earliest lectures and writings, *Wiederholung* is an integral part of Heidegger's attempts to radicalize philosophy, to direct his thinking to the roots or source of Western philosophy. From the outset, *Wiederholung* is described as a nontraditional (which is to say radical) way to take up traditional philosophical thinking. In his 1925 lecture course, *Prolegomena to the History of the Concept of Time*, in a section entitled "The Taking-Up of the Tradition as Genuine *Wiederholung*," Heidegger writes, "The taking-up of the tradition is *not* of necessity traditionalism and the taking-over of prejudice. The *true retrieval* [*Wiederholung*] of a traditional question lets its external, traditional character just disappear and goes back before the prejudice."[15] In this lecture course, as in *Sein und Zeit*, the question Heidegger attempts to radically determine is the *Seinsfrage*. He wants to take up this question in a way that will enable him to retrieve and think again the originary granting of Being from out of which metaphysical tradition and all of its inherent prejuices developed.

Clearly, Heidegger's attempts at a retrieval of this originary granting already at work in *Being and Time* can be seen, as well as in the early lecture courses. It becomes particularly noticeable when he tries to think-*through* a traditional metaphysical concept in a way which simultaneously thinks-*by* that concept by revealing that from out of which the concept arose. While on the surface this appears to be merely a systematic disclosure of the presuppositions of traditional metaphysics, much more than this is, in fact, at work. As merely one example from among many, recall Heidegger's discussion of ἀληϑειά in §44 of *Being and Time*. In this section, he undertakes a discussion of the everyday understanding of truth, which has its source in the Greek word ἀληϑειά, to show that there is a primordial ontological sense of truth as unconcealment which underlies and makes possible everyday understanding. Heidegger's discussion of truth serves to disclose an apsect of the traditional, everyday undertanding of truth which has remained concealed, unthought, unsaid since the beginning of Western philosophy, namely unconcealedness as the source of truth.

Even though he later repudiates certain of the particulars of this analysis of truth,[16] there appears to be a basic procedure Heidegger's thinking follows as he attempts to retrieve the originary source of Western metaphysics. His thought always begins with the traditional, everyday understanding of a concept (*e.g.*, "truth" or "language" or "art"), then begins to develop various implicit but unthought aspects of these concepts, and moves finally to a consideration of what it is which grants thought about these notions in the first place. This is made explicit in a later essay when Heidegger characterizes retrieval in terms of a "step back": "The step back goes from what is unthought . . . to what gives us thought.[17]

The closure or concealment of the Ontological Difference, characteristic of the end of metaphysics for Heidegger, is most obviously manifest in the way we conceive of language today. Contemporary philosophical debate about the essence of language has been dominated by the notion of language as essentially a tool which man can use or not, as he sees fit, and whose primary function is the conveying of information or data. This instrumental view of language is further attested to by the prominence of the science of linguistics, in which language is treated as an object, the properties of which man can scientifically investigate in much the same way that he would investigate the chemical properties of a mineral.

While Heidegger's concern with retrieving the source of language's essence through a destruction of traditional metaphysical concepts of it occurring throughout these writings, we recall two such discussions in particular at this point as representative of what I call Heidegger's style of *Wiederholung*. In the second part of a lecture series bearing the title "What is Called Thinking?", Heidegger undertakes a careful reading of a particular fragment of Parmenides. Here, it is not necessary to pursue the fine points of that discussion beyond noting how Heidegger first sets up the problem (Figure 1). As is usually the case when he discusses the writings of the Greeks, Heidegger takes exception with the conventional translation of the fragment. In particular, he claims that the translation is a nicely syntactic proposition ("One should both say and think that being is"), while in fact what Parmenides wrote is paratactic, or is independently ordered *without* the use of connectives. Thus before discussing what the fragment says, Heidegger retranslates it in a way which clearly reveals the paratactic character of the original Greek ("Needful: the saying also thinking too: being: to be").[18]

Summary of Heidegger's treatment of Parmenides' Fragment:
(*What is Called Thinking?*, Part II, Lectures VI–XI, pp. 172–244)
(*Was heißt Denken?*, pp. 106–149, 163–175)

I. Χρή τό λέγειν τε νοεῖν τ' ἐόν ἔμμεναι.

II. One should both say and think that Being is.

III. Χρή : τό λέγειν τε νοεῖν τ' : ἐόν : ἔμμεναι

IV. Needful : the saying also thinking too : being : to be

V. It is useful : the laying before also taking to heart too : Being : beings

IV. To let something be what it is: : the Ontological Difference

FIGURE 1

This distinction between syntactic and paratactic saying, and Heidegger's insistence that paratactic saying is the language of thinking, is vitally important for his retrieval of the source of language's essence. What makes paratactic saying the language of thinking is the fact that it speaks even where there are no words, whereas syntactic saying by its very nature strives to establish a fixed relation between the parts which are said by means of particular connectives. This fixed relation, of course, is defined by the relationship between the subject and predicate in propositional language, the language of modern metaphysics and technology. Paratactic saying, on the other hand, by speaking even when there are no words, serves to disclose the play of presence and absence which is characteristic of ἀληθεία and which is granted as *Ereignis* occurs. Paratactic saying is the language of thinking because it allows the unsaid to disclose itself as such.

The significance of Heidegger's insistence on the importance of paratactic saying is clearly seen if the outcome of his discussion of Parmenides's fragment is noted, namely the disclosure that what called forth thinking at the beginning of the Western tradition, and what was concealed even in Parmenides's fragment, is the difference between Being and beings – the Ontological Difference. While this thought-provoking difference was concealed in Parmenides's fragment, it was retrieved through Heidegger's insistence on and careful questioning of the paratactic nature of the fragment.

By way of a second example, notice that in attempting to consider Heidegger's retrieval of the fourfold and the granting of *Ereignis*, in his later essays a curious impasse is found. It is at this point in his thinking that Heidegger's own language becomes increasingly "poetic" or "metaphorical" or even "mystical" as some have charged. It is often the case that commentators on this aspect of Heidegger's thinking simply fall into a stylized repetition of Heideggerian "jargon," and in so doing completely miss what is thought-provoking in these unusual essays. The impasse is clear: why is writing about Heidegger's lectures on poetry so difficult, and how can the danger of merely turning Heidegger's thinking into a collection of platitudes be avoided? Given what has been discussed, that part of the problem is probably a problem of language. Heidegger himself had alluded to this in "The Origin of the Work of Art" when, in the context of stressing the privilege of poetry, he said, "To see this, only the right concept of language is needed."[19] It is certainly the case that Heidegger's later thought about poetry resists any attempt at mere "exposition" in the form of a traditional commentary. Indeed, his essays, which at first glance give every appearance of being commentaries on specific poems themselves, in fact enact a destruction of the very enterprise of such a commentary. Thus, a writer trying to write an exposition of Heidegger's later lectures and essays on poetry finds himself in the curious and frustrating position of trying to accomplish something which the very text he is working on seeks to undermine. Not surprising, the results of such efforts are disappointing.

What then are we to say about these writings? What is most obvious and most curious in Heidegger's writings about poetry and the fourfold when thought of in contrast to "The Origin of the Work of Art," for example, is a change of style. Heidegger moves from a style emphasizing strife and battle, holding-open and setting-in-place, to one which emphasizes dwelling-within and letting-be, in short, *Gelassenheit*.

This change of style goes along with several points already addressed. First, and perhaps most significantly, with his writings on the fourfold, Heidegger effectively dispersed whatever dialectical residues might have remained, however unintentionally, in his later writings. In addition, with his discussions of the fourfold and the granting of *Ereignis*, Heidegger surmounted a simple dependence on propositional language. Instead, he has taken up a style which questions presuppositions about the very nature and function of language. This style, which develops out of what Heidegger calls the "unsaid," indeed constitutes the greatest obstacle to reading his later writings since it forces one to reassess relationships to languages. To summarize, in his later writings, Heidegger has developed a style of retrieval [*Wiederholung*].

But what *is* the fourfold? This question is in fact an absurdity on a par with the question "What *is* Being?" or "What *is Ereignis*?" for "fourfold" certainly does not name a being but names that which grants beings their Being. In less convoluted terms, it is only because man dwells within the fourfold that beings can emerge as such.

Now, consider the essay " . . . Poetically Man Dwells . . . " as an attempt to disclose the sense in which art, now considered exclusively in terms of poesy to which Heidegger ascribes a privileged place within the arts, is capable of enacting such a dwelling within the fourfold. This essay is a perfect example of what I referred to as a "style of retrieval." By taking as his starting point three words from one of Hölderlin's poems, lifted completely out of their original context, Heidegger proceeds by gradually reconstructing the original poetic context of the poem, by reintroducing one or two at a time the lines which Hölderlin had written on either side of the three words which Heidegger takes as both his title and his point of departure. The "result" is a fairly large chunk of the original context of the words "poetically man dwells," but in the process of restoring their context, Heidegger develops a quite unorthodox reading. Rather than proceeding as an exegetical commentary on Hölderlin's poem, which deals with a text that is always present before the reader as something to be "grasped," Heidegger proceeds by questioning a fragment in such a way as to explore dimensions of it that go far beyond the explicit intentions of its author. He only restores the original context on the basis of his own reading, which in turn provokes one to read the original text in a "new" way, in terms of what remained unsaid in Hölderlin's text even as it granted Hölderlin's saying of that text.

What is most at issue in this essay is the idea of "dwelling," which has a great deal of importance for Heidegger's later thought. Heidegger develops the notion of dwelling, and ultimately of poetic dwelling, on the basis of Hölderlin's poem: "When Hölderlin speaks of dwelling, he has before his eyes the basic character of human existence."

One can now see clearly why Heidegger places such importance on poetry as the most important level of artistic activity. Poetry, as an originary happening of language which is at the same time within language, is significant for "postmetaphysical" thinking because it is able to provide an avenue of access to the unsaid. Poetic language, like the paratactic language of Parmenides, lets language speak even when there are no words. Thus, poetry serves to situate a thought-provoking play between what Heidegger calls the "said" and the "unsaid." The happening of this play in turn allows *Ereignis* to disclose itself as the happening of difference as such.

By virtue of its ability to provoke the disclosure of *Ereignis*, poetry has brought thinking to the edge of metaphysics to the extent that it has the potential to disclose the limits of the metaphysical-technological worldview through a disclosure of the limits of everyday language. At the same time, in part through its encounters with poetry, thinking is granted the possibility of transgressing those limits. Thinking as the transgression of the limits of metaphysics is what Heidegger means by "overcoming" metaphysics.

By way of a conclusion, I want to return briefly to the notion of style. For Nietzsche, the notion of style has both a surface meaning (how he actually constructs text) and a more radical significance (which discloses a strategic level operative in his writings).

Using this notion of style as a springboard, I then developed the notion of a style of *Wiederholung* as a way of referring to a strategic dimension of Heidegger's texts which occurs on the level of a radical critique of language, and which is also reflected in some peculiarities found in some of his later essays. For me, the notion of a style of *Wiederholung* in Heidegger is significant because it in effect designates the strategy Heidegger employs to bring thinking to the edge of metaphysics. It is, in turn, helpful to keep this notion of style as strategy in mind as one reads Heidegger's treatment of other philosophers – of Nietzsche, for example – because in so doing we can see how these writings transgress the limitations of traditional commentaries and actually bring thinking to the edge of metaphysics.

Notes

1. Friedrich Nietzsche, *Götzen-Dämmerung* (Stuttgart: A Kröner, 1954), Aphorism 26; *Twilight of the Idols*, in *The Portable Nietzsche*, ed. Walter Kaufmann (New York: Penguin, 1977), p. 470.

2. Friedrich Nietzsche, *Ecce Homo*, "Warum ich so gute Bücher schreibe," in *Werke. Kritische Gesamtausgabe*, ed. G. Colli and M. Montinari (Berlin: de

Gruyter, 1968), vol. VI, p. 352; *Ecce Homo*, "Why I Write Such Good Books," in *The Basic Writings of Nietzsche*, ed. W. Kaufmann (New York: Modern Library, 1968), p. 770.

3. Friedrich Nietzsche, *Also Sprach Zarathustra*, in *Werke. Kritische Gesamtausgabe*, vol. VI, p. 271; *Thus Spoke Zarathustra* in *The Portable Nietzsche*, p. 332.

4. Friedrich Nietzsche, *Götzen-Dämmerung*, p. 51.

5. *Ibid.*

6. Jacques Derrida, "The Question of Style," in *The New Nietzsche*, ed. David Allison (New York: Delta, 1979), p. 176ff.

7. Friedrich Nietzsche, *Götzen-Dämmerung*, pp. 51–52.

8. Friedrich Nietzsche, *Ecce Homo*, trans. W. Kaufmann, pp. 217–18.

9. Cf. Friedrich Nietzsche, *Ecce Homo*, ch. 10, "Style and Philosophy."

10. Friedrich Nietzsche, *Götzen-Dämmerung*, pp. 78–79.

11. Friedrich Nietzsche, *Ecce Homo*, in *Werke*, vol. VI, p. 302.

12. Friedrich Nietzsche, *Götzen-Dämmerung*, p. 72.

13. *Ibid.*, pp. 103–04.

14. Cf. Martin Heidegger, "The End of Philosophy and the Task of Thinking," in *On Time and Being*, trans. John Stambaugh (New York: Harper, 1977) and Martin Heidegger, "The Question Concerning Technology," in *The Question Concerning Technology and Other Essays*, trans. W. Lovitt (New York: Harper, 1977).

15. Martin Heidegger, *Prolegomena zur Geschichte des Zeitbegriffs*, ed. P. Jaeger (Frankfurt: Klostermann, 1979), p. 187. (Translation mine.)

16. Martin Heidegger, "The End of Philosophy and the Task of Thinking," p. 70 and especially note 5.

17. Martin Heidegger, *Identity and Difference*, trans. John Stambaugh (New York: Harper, 1969), p. 50.

18. Martin Heidegger, *Was Heisst Denken?* (Tübingen: Niemeyer, 1971), pp. 108–14, 166–68; *What is Called Thinking?*, trans. J. G. Gray (New York: Harper, 1972), pp. 175–86.

19. Martin Heidegger, "Der Ursprung des Kunstwerkes," in *Holzwege* (Frankfurt: Klostermann, 1972), 5th ed., p. 60; "The Origin of the Work of Art," trans. Albert Hofstadter, in *Poetry, Language, Thought* (New York: Harper, 1971), p. 73.

10. Foucault and Nietzsche: Affectivity and the Will to Power

Garth Gillan

One of the marks of any particular belief, Nietzsche thinks, is that, in the agon, the "For and Against" of the instincts, it strives for domination.[1] Each belief, each perspective or interpretation of reality, is an expression of the will to power in life. This is true of the belief in the "soul" and of the belief in "truth" and the "good." "Truth" is the kind of error that makes possible human survival according to certain dominant values (WP,493,272). Knowledge expresses the instrumentality of power: the range of the calculable and necessary for a species to survive. The desire for knowledge grows in exact measure as the will to power, the desire for the mastery of its environment, grow in a species (WP,480,266). Truth is the correlate of the enhanced power that it provides, in terms of the advantages that it brings; in other words, the criteria for truth express what truth ought to be if it could be recognized (WP,455,249).

For Nietzsche, therefore, the will to power does not express the metaphysical reality of the concepts of soul, truth, knowledge, truth, and the good. For metaphysics, Nietzsche substitutes the idea of eternal recurrence. In order to explain the emergence of the soul and the ideas of truth, beauty and the good, the concept of the will to power operates within a different substitution: the transformation of sociology into a "theory" of the forms of domination. Such forms of domination can be known by means of another substitution that exchanges epistemology for "a perspective theory of the affects" that orders the affects in terms of their superiority and spirituality (WP,462,255). The will to power is then not a unity, but a rubric for a multiplicity of affectual configurations and regimes each tied to the drive to survive in a series of conflictual and agonal situations.

Nietzsche's thought is enigmatic, because it tries to capture the enigmatic within itself: it is a disclosure that in its aphoristic style refuses to close the breach that the terror of ever recurring reality has created between concepts. The gaps between words and things cannot be closed: "Are not words and sounds rainbows and illusive bridges between things which are eternally apart?", asks Zarathustra.[2] Language is not anchored in things, names are illusive, because words dance over and around objects. The very pattern of that dance is enigmatic. It unfolds perceptions that fail to bring into focus unitary things as the pledge of their eternal veracity, but issue simply from multiplicity. Aphoristic language is a discourse recoiling in aversion from the idea of "one total view of the world" (WP,470,262). It is enigmatic because it is fascinated by contestation, opposition, and illusion. Nothing anchors the multiplicity of perspectives; no substantial unitary subject can espouse one total viewpoint, a privileged viewpoint, a pragmatic perspective from which all the others can be judged true or false. There is only the will to power striving in each dominant value. "My hypothesis;" Nietzsche states, "the subject as multiplicity" (WP,490,270).

"Belief in the body," Nietzsche writes in *The Will to Power* "is more fundamental than belief in the soul: the latter arose from unscientific reflections on the agonies of the body (something that leaves it. Belief in the truth of dreams)" (WP,491,271). The proper register of Nietzsche's discourse of the will to power is the physiological level where the domination of instincts and values appears as conflict and striving for mastery. The belief in the body delimits the terrain where conflict can install itself, where the "For and Against" of values can assume concrete figures in the opposition of classes, races, values and moralities.

There is no immediate transition from Nietzsche's conception of the will to power to Foucault's formulations of the power/knowledge couple, nor from Nietzsche's theory of affects to Foucault's analysis of the affective dimensions of discursive practices, from the *libido sciendi* of eighteenth century medicine in *The Birth of the Clinic* and the appearance of madness in the fear inspired by bourgeois paternalism in *Madness and Civilization* to the affective mechanism of sexuality in the first volume of *The History of Sexuality.* There is, in fact, no transition, as if it were a question of intellectual history; there is only a textual transposition that expresses a movement of displacement. Foucault transposes the question of the will to power into the register of discursive practices, and he displaces Nietzsche's concern for the psychological, from the primacy of belief in the body over the belief in the soul into an historical space. The body is not a natural, founding subject as it was for Merleau-Ponty, it is a movement upon which history inscribes its dark past.

For Nietzsche, language plays over things and inhabits the distance that eternally separates them; for Foucault, language is the discourse spread out among events and emerging from struggle and reversals of values, concepts, institutions, and emotions. The displacement of the will to power into the objectifying power of discursive practices in turn makes possible a transposition of the body. The belief in the soul transposed into the body is the epistemological site for the analysis of the interplay of knowledge and power. The body provides, in its institutionalization in the asylum, clinic, and prison, the concrete details for the coupling of power and knowledge in specific discursive systems, orders, and disciplines that delimit the true from the false. But is it more than a site? The body for Foucault is the space of affects in whose oppositions and reversals, degradations and spiritualizations, the body itself is individualized and torn apart. The interplay of affects in the history of modern subjectivity polarizes the space of the body, brings it into communication with itself, constitutes it as an object for the gaze of others and conforms it to the social space it must inhabit if it is to move, remain stationary, reproduce, live, or die. It is equally through the positioning of affects that the body gains its interior space, is doubled and turned inward, to become a subjectivity recoiling from its objectification.

But the body is not the object of Foucauldian discourse. Foucault's successive analyses of affectivity, knowledge, and institutionalization, and the concrete coupling of power and knowledge that arise from them focuses upon history. Foucault writes apropos Nietzsche,

> The body is the inscribed surface of events (traced by language and dissolved by ideas). The locus of a dissociated Self (adopting the illusion of a substantial unity), and a volume in perpetual disintegration. Genealogy, as an analysis of descent, is thus situated within the articulation of the body and history. Its task is to expose a body totally imprinted by history and the process of history's destruction of the body.[3]

The body is not the focal point for an originary history, a genesis that can be traced back to its founding level and the bearer of sedimentations. The body is its agonies, and history is the scene of the deadly conflicts that dismember it and, at the same time, stifle its cries. But, nonetheless, the body bears the traces of its dismemberment. It is the body of Damien, drawn and quartered, transformed into the disciplined and confined body: the exterior dismemberment shared by the body politic, or the interior dismemberment that produces the soul.

Not history, in the singular, but histories. Not universal history, but general history.[4] *Madness and civilization* traces not one direct line of development but several, between leprosy and madness: linkage with animality, the line that extends from passion and delirium to dream and dazzlement, from techniques of the cure to the moral perception of madness, and from the fear of the contagion of madness to the fear inhabiting madness itself. The language of madness arises from the conjunctures of those transitions and their interplay. In them madness is constituted as madness, the language of delirium, and a language of madness takes shape as an objectifying language, as the subjection through guilt of a moralized subjectivity.

In *The History of Sexuality*, the hypothesis of repression covers multiple avenues leading toward the development of the discourse of sexuality and the deployment of sexuality in power over life. The ancient penitentials, confession, pedegogy, scientific discourse, class relations, demography, eugenics: the affective mechanism of the discourse of sexuality that produces the sexed body is at the end of many histories. Finally, as do all the discourses that arise from these multiple histories, the deployment of sexuality incorporates death. From the hollow skull symbolizing madness, through the cadaver, to a sexuality governed by the ability to wield death in the name of life, history appears within the disintegration of the body.

Foucault sees the will to knowledge as degeneration. The will to know is the will to die, the will to put to death: it is not the will to live, the solidarity of bodies and pleasures and the resistance of the plebs to the pulverizations of power. The reference to bodies and pleasures shares with Nietzsche the epistemological perspective of a hierarchy of the affects and instincts, and the priority of the physiological. But it is impossible to absolutely decouple knowledge and power; decadence is an essential element in the struggle of life (WP,38-45,24-28). The body is not an object beyond or beneath history: genealogy is not a commentary upon the body, in which the agonies of the body are the deep meaning of the surface events of history. The body is surface: the violence of knowledge consists in rendering it completely surface, either through dismemberment in which power resides in the reversal of the inside and the outside (quartering, disembowelment, public manifestation, or autopsy). The secrets of the body are, in *The History of Sexuality*, the effects of the discourse on sexuality. The constitution of the within and the without, of depth and surface, is a function of a discourse that objectifies and institutionalizes.

In describing the emergence of self-consciousness in the discourse of sexuality that positions sexual desire in the body, Foucault has clearly revealed another facet of the analysis of the power/knowledge couple: the discourse of affects. In *Madness and Civilization*, madness is isolated from unreason as a disease through the transformation of the fear of contagion into the fear and guilt felt by those confined in the asylum.[5] In *The Birth of the Clinic*, palpation and the stethescope are deployed in a space governed by modesty, transgression, and a *libido sciendi*. The semio-techniques of *Discipline and Punish* mobilize against the body its own kinesthetic awareness, auto-affectivity. And, finally, *The History of Sexuality* analyses a *libido sciendi* that organizes sexual desire as the field for self-knowledge and self-consciousness.

The multiple histories that converge upon the events in which modern self-consciousness appears – the history of the founding subject and of sexual consciousness – are the various spaces in which desire, fear, revenge, sadism, voyeurism – in effect all the particular figures of affectivity – are configured as particular, delimited, historical conflicts and struggles. "The body," Foucault writes apropos Nietzsche again, "manifests the stigmata of past experience and also gives rise to desire, failings, and errors. These elements may join in a body where they achieve a sudden expression, but as often, their encounter is an engagement in which they efface each other, where the body becomes the pretext of their insurmountable conflict."[6] Affectivity reveals for Foucault its historical dimension in the conflict between warring antagonisms. In the context of Foucauldian genealogy, affectivity is not an intentionality directed toward objects, it is not a consciousness that serves as the principle for the analysis of a priori values, but the struggle of effects, instincts, values, and intentions among themselves. The coupling of power and knowledge on the level of analysis manifests a coupling of power and pleasure, spirals of power and pleasure. Sexuality is constituted as the coupling of power and knowledge in the discourse of sexuality. Desire arises to consciousness in pleasure. The discourse of sexuality gives pleasure. That is its function. It gives pleasure by creating multiple bonds between social institutions: "medical examination, psychiatric investigation, the pedagogical report, and family controls" function as a "mechanism" of power and pleasure. The attention paid to sexuality in the medicalization of the sexually peculiar objectified the evocation of pleasure in response to the gaze that embraces it. Confession feeds curiosity; the detected pleasure reinforces the power of the gaze circumscribing it. In that way, pleasure is bound to the power of the gaze and the power of the gaze is tied to the evocation of pleasure. And from that mutual coupling, the individual nuances of pleasure emerge; its individuality, delicacy, differentiation, and insistence.[7] In the discourse that implanted perversion as an object of medical discourse within sexual relations, the power of the gaze and pleasure were bound together into a new reciprocity that defines pleasure and intensifies the gaze.

The analysis of power and knowledge as political anatomy, political economy, semio-techniques, and biopower reveals a connection between discourse and affectivity that only emerges in the historical event. The attempt, hallowed by phenomenological preoccupation with intentionality, to focus upon the relationship between affects and objects surpressed the strategic field of affects: the relation betwen pleasure and gaze; palpation and *libido sciendi*; fear and the isolation of disease; and confession and self-consciousness. The strategic field of affects is the arena of the agonies of the body, in which the body is twisted into contortions of fear, isolation, military alterness, or sexual desire. Affects emerge, not through the fascination of objects, but through the first step in their evocation: the action of other affects, affects as the effects of affects; instincts at war with one another; values struggling for domination. This area is the body at war with itself, involuted, turned against itself, an immanence in imminent flight and dissolution, the erection of barriers against an internal void.

The will to truth/power is, then, not an intentionality; it does not pursue a purpose secreted by the perpetual pregnance of consciousness. The will to truth/power emerges from the conflict inscribed into the perpetually inscribed body, in which the trajectories of history are imprinted in the scars left by the rendering of its presumptously solid surface. There is no solid surface, there is only disintegration: the constant ebb and flow of instincts and drives at war with each other. Foucault writes,

> In itself the exercise of power is not violence: nor is it a consent which, implicitly, is renewable. It is a total structure of action brought to bear upon possible actions: it incites, it induces, it seduces, it makes easier or more difficult; in the extreme, it constrains or forbids absolutely; it is, nevertheless, always a way of acting upon an acting subject or acting subjects by virtue of their acting or being capable of action. A set of actions upon other actions.[8]

The affective dimensions of power is the bond created between action and action resulting from their implacement in a field of desire, in a field of strategic operations in which the individuality of pleasure is delimited and in which the inversion of pleasure upon itself arises through the gaze that embraces it. Affectivity involves spirals of power and pleasure, because the gaze and the pleasure rising to its caress are a doubling and inversion. They build upon one another, resulting in an inextricable linkage that defines the deployment of a specific discourse: the discourse of sexuality. The linkage of gaze and pleasure in ascending spirals of power and pleasure does not commit Foucault to a theory of the intentional or constitutional relation between knowledge and pleasure. It only commits him to a will to truth/power arising from the emergence of a specific desire deployed through the discourse that brings into play the sexual body: a body whose desires are inscribed by an affective mechanism brought into play by the discourse of sexuality, a *libido sciendi* liberating men and women from sexual repression. The will to truth/power for Foucault is a question of a dominant historical individuality arising through the emergence of a desire that, transgressing its own myth of repression, gains power over the body by giving a specific affective shape to its pleasures. But there are still bodies and pleasures. A will to truth/power is not *the* will to power. Historical discourse does not transcend the event, neither does it evade it.

The question, then, must be put to Foucault. Is not the discourse of *The History of Sexuality* part of the discourse of sexuality? Is it not the confession of reflective thought about its own involvement in the transgressions upon the sexual body part of the discourse of sexuality? To disclose the illusion of the hypotheses of repression, is that not also to be implicated in liberating sexual desire from repression, but this time from the hypotheses of repression itself in the liberation of desire from sexuality? What is this desire, this *libido sciendi*, that (implicated in the discourse of sexuality) raises the question of desire in terms, not of its unity as a philosophical theme, but in terms of its multiplicity?

Clearly, philosophical discourse as part of modern self-consciousness emerges in its particular historical reality on the basis of the discourse of sexuality. In the question of philosophy, the question of a desire that can transgress its own limits signifies a reflective desire that can call into question the values that dominate it, that can reflect upon its own morality and produce its own antagonisms. It is a desire at war with itself, so structured into a discourse that it can pit itself against itself, and can seek to know in the very act of transgression and only in the act of transgression. This is indeed, Foucault points out, the language of modernity. The language of infinity, that writes and speaks its limits, is a space without an absolute. It signifies itself within the limits of its own particularity by transgressing those limits.

Is this not the desire for pure language, the desire to be a language without referential supports, a language without limits because it chooses to be its limits? What self-desire is this: a desire that delights in transgression, a desire whose pleasures lie in eluding the gaze to which it is bound as the nomad is ground to the cycles of migration: an inscribed space, but inhering in no place? This is a language of the nowhere of desire: a desire that *wants to choose* its object, the desire for desire. If rationality has constructed the discourse of truth by twisting passions into forms of deceptions, thereby deluding itself, perhaps only the transgressions of desire can liberate reason.

Notes

1. Friedrich Nietzsche, *The Will to Power*, trans. Walter Kaufmann and R. J. Hollingdale, ed. Walter Kaufmann (New York: Random House, 1967), sect. 481, p. 267. (Henceforth cited as *WP*.)

2. Friedrich Nietzsche, *Thus Spoke Zarathustra*, Part II, "The Convalescent," 2, in *The Portable Nietzsche*, trans. Walter Kaufmann (New York: Viking Press, 1954), p. 329.

3. Michel Foucault, "Nietzsche, Genealogy, History," in *Language, Counter-Memory, Practice*, ed. Donald F. Bouchard (Ithaca, NY: Cornell University Press, 1977), p. 149.

4. Michel Foucault, *The Archeology of Knowledge*, trans. Sheridan Smith (New York: Random House, 1972), p. 9.

5. Michel Foucault, *Madness and Civilization*, trans. Richard Howard (New York: New American Library, 1967), p. 199.

6. Michel Foucault, "Nietzsche, Genealogy, History," p. 149.

7. Michel Foucault, *The History of Sexuality*, trans. Robert Hurley (New York: Random House, 1978), p. 45.

8. Michel Foucault, "The Subject and Power," in Hubert Dreyfus and Paul Rabinow, *Michel Foucault: Beyond Structuralism and Hermeneutics* (Chicago: University of Chicago Press, 1982), p. 220. For additional material, see Charles C. Lemert and Garth Gillan, *Michel Foucault: Social Theory and Transgression* (New York: Columbia University Press, 1982).

Part V.
Rewriting Patriarchy

11. Women Recovering Our Clothes, Perhaps

Iris Marion Young

Is This a Frame-Up?

In her monumental book, *Seeing Through Clothes*, Ann Hollander claims that the meaning of clothes is conditioned by pictorial images. Throughout the modern period, Western artists have depicted and sanctified clothing images, associating clothes with kinds of personages and situations. This representation of clothes freezes the conventional into the natural, and people measure their women in their clothes in relation to the natural aesthetic created by clothing images.[1]

For most of the modern period, this thesis about the relation of the experience of clothing to images of clothing applies only to those classes able to buy works of art or invited to places where they are displayed. As Ewen and Ewen discuss, however, the midnineteenth century witnessed a revolutionary proletarianization of the image with the invention of cheap methods of colored printing. By the early twentieth century it would seem that the experience of clothing, especially women's experience of clothing, is saturated with the experience of images of women in clothing – in advertising drawings and photographs, catalogs, and film.[2]

Hollander cites the historical specificity of twentieth century women's clothing standards and images and conditioned by cinema. The nineteenth century held an image of women's demeanor as statuesque, immobile, hiding, or hobbling the limbs. The twentieth century, by contrast, emphasizes the mobility of women in clothes – the exhibition of legs, skirts, and pants that do not so much inhibit movement. Images of clothes show women on the move – striding down the street, leaping with excitement, running on the sands, leaning over a desk. If she is standing still, her hair or skirt or scarf fly with the wind. Contemporary images of women's clothes capture a single movement in a narrative whose beginning and end lie outside the frame.[3]

In wearing clothes, Hollander suggests, we seek to fashion ourselves in the mode of the dominant pictorial aesthetic. In this project, the mirror provides us a means of representation. In the mirror, we see not the "bare facts," but a clothed image reverberating the dominant magazine and film images of us in our clothes. Contemporary urban life provides countless opportunities for us to see ourselves – in hotel and theater lobbies, in restaurants and powder rooms, in train stations and store windows.[4] I love to walk down a city street when I feel like I am well-dressed and catch sight of my moving image in a store window, trying not to see myself seeing myself. I imagine myself in a movie, freely swinging down the street in happy clothes, on my way. The mirror gives me pictures, and the pictures in magazines and catalogs give me reflections of identities, in untold but signified stories. And the feminist questions is: *Whose* imagination conjures up the pictures and their meanings?

Reflections on Snow White's Mirror

Our experience of clothes derives from film in more than a merely associative way, Maureen Turim suggests, but also through producing the implicit narrative imagination of our clothes.

> Films not only expose new fashions to a mass audience, they not only provide the fashion industry with a glittering showcase; because we see those fashions within a narrative context, films also invest fashions with unconscious attachments, connotations. This process, the narration of fashion, means more than the association of a style with a given story or fiction. It is a process that fuses the unconscious effects of film experience with the very lines and colors of clothing designs.[5]

My question is: How can I describe a women's pleasure in clothes? If I live my identification with the clothing images through my experience of film narrative, then it may not be too wild to explore our pleasure in clothes through feminist film theory. Following a Lacanian framework, feminist film theorists have developed an account of a female experience of pleasure in the objectified female body within a patriarchal order. The story goes something like this.[6]

Subjectivity is crucially constituted by relations of looking. Through active looking, the subject acquires a sense of subject set off against objects. Through looking at an image of himself in the mirror, the subject gains a sense of narcissistic identification with a totalized motor being misrepresented as a unity. In the phallocratic order, however, this subject that takes pleasure in looking at objects other than himself and who takes pleasure in looking at totalized images of himself is a male subject. The phallocratic order splits looking into active and passive moments. The gaze is masculine and that upon which it gazes is feminine. Women are only lack, the other that shores up the phallic subject, the object that gives power and unified identity to their looking. If women are to achieve any subjectivity, it can only be through adopting this position of the male subject that takes pleasure in the objectification of women.

In film the activity of looking has two aspects: voyeuristic and fetishistic; and film positions women's bodies in relation to both sorts of looking. Voyeuristic looking takes a distance from the object of its gaze, from which it is absent and elsewhere. From this distance, the object of the gaze cannot return or reciprocate the gaze; the voyeur's look is judgmental, holding power over the guilty object of the gaze by offering punishment or forgiveness. In fetishistic looking, conversely, the subject finds his likeness in the object, re-presented as the unity of the phallus. In film, both voyeuristic and fetishistic looking deny the threatening difference of the female, either judging her lacking and guilty, or turning her body or parts of her body into an icon in which the subject finds himself, his phallus.

Women also watch films and enjoy them. What, on this account, makes women's pleasure in the films possible? Only identification with the male subject. I quote Ann Kaplan:

> Why do we find our objectification and surrender pleasurable? . . . Such pleasure is not surprising if we consider the shape of the girl's Oedipal crisis . . . . The girl is forced to turn away from the illusory unity with the Mother in the prelinguistic realm and has to enter the symbolic world which involves subject and object. Assigned the place of object (lack), she is the recipient of male desire, passively appearing rather than acting. Her sexual pleasure in this position can thus be constructed only around her own objectification. Furthermore, given the male structuring around sadism, the girl may adopt a corresponding masochism . . . . We could say that in locating herself in fantasy in the erotic, the woman places herself as either passive recipient of male

> desire or, at one remove, as *watching* a woman who is passive recipient of male desires and sexual actions.[7]

I cannot deny that these analyses apply to our experience of clothes, to our experience of images of women in clothes. The voyeuristic gaze is often implicit or explicit in magazine advertising for clothes, and it is easy to find the language of guilt and imperfection attached to the clothed woman.[8] Sandra Bartky describes how women internalize the objectifying gaze of what she calls the "fashion-beauty complex," a gaze that deprecates and evaluates a woman's body.

> I must exist perpetually at a distance from my physical self, fixed at this distance in a permanent posture of disapproval. Thus, insofar as the fashion-beauty complex shapes one of the introjected subjects for whom I exist as object, I sense myself as deficient. Nor am I able to control in any way those images which give rise to the criteria by which those deficiencies appear . . . . All the projections of the fashion beauty complex have this in common: they are images of *what I am not*.[9]

Good clothes, new clothes, this year's clothes, will cover up my flaws, straighten me out, measure me up to the approving eye.

Maureen Turim discusses how, within the matrix of film imagery, women's clothing fashions fetishize the female body. Through what she calls the "slit aesthetic," clothing cuts play fabric off against bare skin, turning the body or body parts into fetishes. Sweaters cut low in front or back, bathing suits and lingerie cut high on the hip, cut outs in midriff or cut off at the waist, skirt slits or short skirts, cut off pants, all pattern the clothing cut to focus on bare flesh, and frequently the cuts also direct attention to the fetishized neck, breasts, stomach, genitals, thighs, calves, and ankles.[10] The slit aesthetic creates the image of the sexy clothed body, an image of phallic female power. We women sometimes respond to this image with desire, the desire to be that sexy woman.

It's all true, I guess, at least I cannot deny it: In clothes, I seek to find the approval of the transcending male gaze; in clothing, I seek to transform myself into a bewitching object that will capture his desire and identity. When I leaf through magazines and catalogs, I take my pleasure from imagining myself perfected and beautiful and sexual for the absent or mirrored male gaze. I take pleasure in these images of female bodies in their clothes because my own gaze occupies the position of the male gaze insofar as I am a subject at all. I will not deny it, but it leaves a hollowness in me. If I simply affirm this, I must admit for me no subjectivity exists that is not his, that no specifically female pleasure exists that I take in clothes.

But I remember the hours that Suzanne and I played with paper dolls, cutting, drawing, coloring, trading their clothes, stacks of their clothes, in shoe boxes. Suzanne and I talked about the clothes, and we dressed up the dolls for their activities – going to work or on vacation, visiting each other or going on shopping trips, yes, they went on dates too, although I do not remember any male paper dolls. I remember playing paper dolls with Suzanne, and I want to be loyal to her.

Through the Looking Glass

> When the/a woman touches herself, a whole touches itself because it is in-finite, because it has neither the knowledge nor the power to close up or to swell definitively to the extension of an infinite. This self-touching gives a woman a form that is in(de)finitely transformed without closing over her appropriation.[11]

My question is: How shall we describe women's pleasure in clothes? When I look at the other side of the picture, I find three pleasures for women in our clothes: touch, bonding, and fantasy.

Touch.

When I "see" myself in wool, it is partly the wool itself that attracts me, its heavy warmth and textured depth. Some of the pleasure of clothes is the pleasure of fabric, and the way the fabric hangs and falls around the body. Straight skirts with slits may give thigh for the eye, but the skirt in all its glory drapes in flowing folds that billow when one twirls. I lose myself in the cushioned feel of wool, wonder at the smoothness of silk. History documents the measurement of nobility and grace through fabric. Women have been imprisoned by this history, used as mannequins to display the trappings of wealth. But feminine experience also affords many of us a tactile imagination, the simple pleasure of losing ourselves in cloth. We wander through yard good stores stroking the drapery hanging from the bolts, pull them out to appraise the pattern, imagine how they might be best formed around the body, or the chair, or the windows.

Some of our clothes we love for their own sake: the wool blend pin striped elephant bottom pants that held a crease so well and flopped so happily around my ankles; the green herring bone wool blazer I made with my own hands, and after the lining fell apart I sadly gave it to my sister because the new lining was too small; the wine red print full-sleeved smooth rayon blouse gathered at the shoulders to drape lightly over my chest. Many of our clothes never attain this privileged status of the beloved, perhaps because our motives for having most are so extrinsic: to be in style, or give our face the most flattering color, to be cost-effective, or to please others. Some we loved with passion or tenderness, though, and we are sad or angry when beloved clothing becomes damaged or goes out of fashion.

Bonding.

The dedication for Diane Keury's marvelous movie, *Peppermint Soda*, about two teenage sisters in a Paris lycée, reads: "To my sister, who still hasn't given me back my orange sweater."

Clothes often serve for women in this society as threads in the bonds of sisterhood. Girls and roommates raid each other's closets, sometimes unpermitted; daughters' feet clomp around in their mother's shoes. I love my sweater, and by letting you wear it, you wear an aspect of me, but I do not possess it since you can wear it. As the clothes flow among us, so do our identities; we do not keep hold of ourselves but share.

Women often establish rapport with one another by remarking on their clothes, and doing so often introduces a touch of intimacy or lightness in a serious or impersonal situation. When we are relaxing with one another, letting down our guard or just chatting, we often talk about clothes: what we like and what we can't stand, how difficult it is to get this size or that fabric, how we feel when we wear certain kinds of clothes or why we do not wear others, and the anxieties we sometimes have about what to wear. Such female conversations are strangely safe, enclosed.[12]

Fantasy.

Women take pleasure in clothes, not just wearing clothes, but looking at clothes and looking at images of women in clothes, because they encourage fantasies of transport and transformation. We experience our clothes, if Hollander is right, in the context of the images of clothes from magazines, film, television, that draw us into situations and personalities at which we can play.

Implicitly feminist critics of media images of women have tended to assimilate all images of women in advertising into the pornographic: that such images position women as the object of a male gaze. Clothing ads are split, however, between positioning women as object and women as subject. Clothing images are not always the authoritative mirror that tells "who's the fairest of them all," but the entrance to a wonderland of characters and situations.

Roland Barthes analyzes the rhetoric of fashion magazines to show how they evoke such fantasy. In using Barthes's idea to describe women's experience of clothes, I no doubt will tear them from their systematic fabric. Only a man, I think, would presume to present *The Fashion System* between two covers. Barthes is a self-conscious theoretician of ideology, aware that no theoretician transcends the ideology he analyzes. At the close of *The Fashion System* he writes:

> There remains a word to be said about the situation of the analyst confronted with, or rather, *within* the systematic universe he has just dealt with; not only because it would be akin to bad faith to consider the analyst as alien to this universe, but also because the semiological project provides the analyst with the formal means to incorporate himself into the system he reconstitutes (FS,292).

Here is the sensitive theoretician, withdrawing from the authority of the transhistorical gaze precisely in relation to a universe from which he *is* alien, which speaks a rhetoric not addressed to him. For all his reflexive attention to history and social context, Barthes never remarks on the position of the fashion analyst as a man.

I don't know that this surprising silence makes his analysis unsatisfactory, or more unsatisfactory than it would otherwise be. He offers wonderfully evocative discussions of the meaning of the rhetoric of fashion magazines that I think express the pleasure of fantasy that clothes can have for women. Fashion, he says, offers women a double dream of identity and play, indeed the invitation to play with identities (FS,255–56).

The fantasies I have as I leaf through the magazine or click the hangers on the rack, or put on the outfit in the dressing room, may be fleeting and multiple possibilities of who I might be, character types I try on, situations in which I place myself imaginatively. I see myself in wool, but in the mode of another, or several others, in transforming possibilities, all without the real life anxiety of having to decide who I am:

> Yet, in the vision of Fashion, the ludic motif does not involve what might be called the vertigo effect: it multiplies the person without any risk of her losing herself, insofar as, for Fashion, clothing is not play but the *sign* of play (FS,256–57, cf. 260–61).

This fantasy of multiple and changing identities without the anxiety of losing oneself is possible because fashion creates unreal identities in utopian places. In our clothing fantasies, we are not the voyeuristic gaze before whom the narrative reel unfolds, because the pictures come to us only with the feeling of a narrative, not with narrative itself. Clothing ads, catalogs, music videos, and the like present images of situations, clips of possible narratives, but without any thread and temporality. "The doing involved in fashion is, as it were, abortive: its subject is torn by a representation of essences at the moment of acting: to display the being of doing, without assuming its reality" (FS,249, cf. 253,262,266). Fashion images are vague, open – a woman walking on a street, sitting on a patio, leaning on a bed, climbing up a rock – the variables in the formulae can be filled in with any number of concrete narrative values, and our pleasure in fantasy of clothes is partly imagining ourselves in those possible stories, entering unreality.

A certain freedom is involved in our relation to clothes, an active subjectivity not represented in the male gaze theory. Here I draw on Sartre, but not his gaze theory. In *The Psychology of Imagination*, Sartre proposes imaginary consciousness as a modality of freedom.[13] An image is consciousness of an unreal object. In imagining, I am aware of an unreal object and aware that the object is unreal. The pleasure of imagining derives from just this unreality: for the unreal object has no facticity, no givenness that constrains, no brute physicality with which freedom must deal or face the consequences. The unreal object has no aspects not presented to me in the image, no "other side" that transcends my apprehension, as does the perceived object. The image gives the affective dimensions of a person or situation, what it feels like to be or see them, without their material contexts and consequences. The freedom of the imaginary object lies in the fact that nothing is in the object that has not been put there by imaginary consciousness.

Part of the pleasure of clothes for many of us consists in allowing ourselves to fantasize with images of women in clothes and in desiring to become an image, unreal, to enter an intransitive, playful utopia. There are ways of looking at oneself in the mirror that do not appraise oneself before the objectifying gaze, but rather desubstantialize oneself, turn oneself into a picture, an image, an unreal identity. In such fantasy, we do not seek to be somebody else; fantasizing is not wishing, hoping, or planning; it has no future. The clothing image provides the image of situations without any situatedness; there is an infinite before and after; thus, the images are open at both ends to an indefinite multitude of possible transformations. However much some of the content and consequences of these fantasies may be manipulated by patriarchal interests, the activity of the imagining is ours in a unique, and potentially subversive, experience of freedom.

Until, that is, we confront the sharp decree of fashion that these clothes are out, no longer in. But that episode lies outside this series of frames.

Notes

1. Ann Hollander, *Seeing Through Clothes* (New York: Viking Press, 1978).

2. Stuart Ewen and Elizabeth Ewen, *Channels of Desire: Mass Images and the Shaping of American Consciousness* (New York: McGraw-Hill, 1982).

3. Ann Hollander, *Seeing Through Clothes*, pp. 345–52.

4. *Ibid.*, pp. 391–416.

5. Maureen Turim, "Fashion Shapes: Film, the Fashion Industry and the Image of Women," *Socialist Review*, no. 17, vol. 13, (September 1983), p. 86.

6. I derive my account of the male gaze and film from the following authors: Turim (cited above); Laura Mulvey, "Visual Pleasure and Narrative Cinema," *Screen*, vol. 16, no. 3 (Autumn 1975); Annette Kuhn, *Women's Pictures: Feminism and Cinema* (London: Routledge and Kegan Paul, 1982) pp. 47–65; E. Ann Kaplan, *Women and Film: Both Sides of the Camera* (New York: Methuen, 1983), pp. 23–35.

7. *Ibid.*, p. 26.

8. Sandra Bartky, "Narcissism, Femininity and Alienation," *Social Theory and Practice*, vol. 8, no. 2 (Summer 1982), p. 136.

9. *Ibid.*

10. Maureen Turim, "Fashion Shapes . . . ," pp. 86–89.

11. Luce Irigaray, *The Speculum of the Other Woman*, trans. Gillian G. Gill (Ithaca, NY: Cornell University Press, 1985), p. 233.

12. Logic and Patriarchy

Craig R. Vasey

In this essay, I examine the meaning of several closely associated terms and themes of one line of the new French feminism. In particular, I want to focus on the claim that logic is patriarchal, phallocentric, or masculine. To do this, I briefly discuss the questions of sexual difference and what is meant by the ideas of masculine and feminine languages. I propose an account of logic and its relationship to patriarchy that shows both why one might be inclined to think that logic is patriarchal and why this is, in fact, false. Finally, I examine the term "phallogocentrism," and suggest a distinction between it and "logocentrism," which I think is constructive for feminism.

My discussion of these issues is primarily based upon the work of Luce Irigaray, for she seems to be of the opinion that logic is patriarchal, that masculine language is paradigmatically logical, that part of feminist strategy must involve the creation or evolution of feminine language, and that feminine language is a powerful and perhaps essential weapon for the subversion of patriarchy.

Irigaray maintains that an irreducible difference exists between the sexes, a difference of a kind that has never been acknowledged, and which, in fact, patriarchy cannot afford to acknowledge, for in her view, the subordination of woman is really rooted in the denial and repression of, and the horror at, this difference. This difference or otherness of woman is such that she is not representable or sayable in the only kinds of languages we have had, masculine languages, or languages based on the principles of logic – noncontradiction, identity, clarity, and univocity. She speaks of this in an interview:

> It can be shown that all Western discourse presents a certain isomorphism with the masculine sex: the privilege of unity, form of the self,

> of the visible, of the erection . . . . Female sexuality cannot articulate itself within an Aristotelean type of logic.[1]

and:

> For I do not think that language is universal or neutral with regard to the difference between the sexes. In the face of language constructed and maintained by men only, I raise the question of the specificity of a feminine language: of a language which would be adequate for the body, sex, and imaginary of the woman.[2]

Irigaray speaks of the difference in languages and of the phallocratic nature of logic in terms of an account of the different genital morphology and sexual sensitivity of males and females. Evaluating the theory such as she expresses it is not my concern, for I have no problem accepting the claim that there is genuinely a radical difference between male and female sexuality and that this difference will matter in the construction of the unconscious, yielding significant and real differences between the typical male and female unconscious. It seems to me that this difference can be adequately accounted for only if one includes attention to social relations, such as the impact on children of interaction with exclusively female child-caretakers under sexist and heterosexual conditions, but it is not entirely clear that this would be excluded by Irigaray. I take her emphasis upon gential morphology as an emphasis upon what one makes of one's body in the unconscious, and how that relationship to one's body is acknowledged or denigrated in one's culture.

However, I want to show that we can accept the idea of an irreducible sexual difference without being committed to any of the following claims: First, that logic is patriarchal, masculine, or phallocentric; second, that the languages we know are masculinist, if by this one means that women's interests cannot be represented or promoted through them. (The refutation of the charge that our language or discourse is masculinist is not tantamount to saying that no legitimate and important functions exist to what she calls feminine language, nor that that function might not be primarily in women's interests; it implies only that not all of women's interests are included in the project of being able to articulate their body, sex, and imaginary.) The third claim is that the principle features of feminine language are absent from masculine language or from phallocratic ideology. (Irigaray does not, in fact, make this claim, but I think that many expect this to be true.) The final claim is that feminine language is an efficacious tool for the subversion of patriarchy.

I begin by examining the isomorphism Irigaray points out between male sexuality and logical or masculine discourse. The relevant features of masculine language that she identifies are noncontradiction, identity, clarity, and univocity, all of which indicate a certain rigidity; she sees these features as expressing specifically male or masculine values (*i.e.*, values implicit in the male body, male sexuality, and the male unconscious), and rendering impossible that specifically female or feminine values express themselves. This masculine language silences woman even as she speaks it. According to Irigaray, woman is exiled from herself because the language she speaks and the order in which she lives repress, deny, and cover up the values which define her sexuality and her unconscious.

Feminine language, she feels, would be characterized in terms of nonunity, ambiguity, fluidity, and the contradictory, described as follows:

> For a feminine language would undo the unique meaning, the proper meaning of words, of nouns, which still regulates all discourse. In order for there to be proper meaning, there must indeed be a unity somewhere. But if a feminine language cannot be brought back to any unity, it cannot be simply described or defined: there is no feminine metalanguage.[3]

As is well known, this feminine language is thought of as a powerfully subversive tool, since it functions as a maddening unsaying and is disturbing of what the order of coherent discourse says and requires; it baffles clear thinking and plays games with the ordinary logical mode of thought. However, I think it is somewhat misleading to call this "feminine *language*," for it is impossible for anything to be asserted if no proper meaning exists. All one can do in feminine language is undermine what has already been said in discourse. This implies, for one thing, that feminine language requires masculine language and is impossible without it, *i.e.*, it is parasitic upon, and marginal and relative to, masculine language. The other, central point, is that feminine language cannot be the language within which one could claim that anything was true or false, politically wise or foolish, fair or unfair, etc. Rather, feminist thought still must adhere to or follow the rules of masculine language, even in order to be a thinking against patriarchy. This provides a first reason to dispute the claim that logic or logical language is masculine or patriarchal. Either the expression "masculine language" is meant to convey the claim that the interest of women cannot be articulated within the order of coherent discourse (because they are such that they cannot be represented at all without being distorted), in which case it appears that what is called "feminist theory" is not really feminist precisely because it *is* theory, or else the label "masculine" does not mean the same thing as "patriarchal," in which case it is doubtful that feminine language is at all essential to feminism as the promotion of women's interests *qua* women's interests, *i.e.*, as the struggle against patriarchy. In saying this, I am not saying that logical discourse is necessarily adequate to the articulation of all of women's interests (or to all of men's interests either), but I am emphasizing that feminism has required logic, theory, critical analysis, and coherent discourse in order to constitute itself as a movement in the interests of women.

Another point should be considered regarding the usefulness of feminine language: the defining virtue of feminine language is ambiguity irreducible to univocity, however, this is an important political tool that patriarchal ideology uses against woman, and it is quite central in so-called masculine languages. Two examples, both from French, come to mind. First, the word for "women," "femme," which certain French feminists have rejected as irredeemable (*e.g.*, Monique Wittig)[4] because it means so many things at once and is irreducibly ambiguous. "Femme" means woman, wife, female human being, and feminine human being. These are not identical meanings, but they are all rolled together into one. The second example helps to explain why, although I listed four meanings for "femme," a speaker of French would be likely to list only three: only one word in French, "le sexe," corresponds to two English words, "sex" and "gender." Consequently, finding biological determinism intuitively plausible from the perspective of the French language is easier; or, stated differently, making the distinction between maleness and masculinity or femaleness and femininity is more difficult for the French speaker. This is evident in the writings of Irigaray in fact, for she tends to emphasize the body – the sexual difference – to such a degree, that one gets the impression she might think that an essence of masculinity and femininity exists beyond the reach of culture. Regardless, my point is that the insistence upon clarity and univocity that typifies what she calls "masculine language" is quite able to serve the interests of women against patriarchy, while the defining virtue of "feminine language" (irreducible ambiguity) can be a powerful tool for the mystification of consciousness.

Of the points mentioned earlier, I have considered the two minor ones: first, that within logical discourse it is impossible for women's interests to be expressed *qua* women's interests, and second, that feminine language's features are either entirely absent from phallocratic ideology or entirely in the service of women's interests. The major issues still remain: the relation between logic and patriarchy and the implications that should and should not be read into the expression "phallogocentrism" and into the portrait of patriarchy as phallogocentrism.

The approach I use to consider the relation between logic and patriarchy, and which should help identify the nature of that relation precisely, is suggested by Irigaray's idea that not only the order of logical discourse, but also the order of society, is intrinsically patriarchal. In *This Sex Which Is Not One*, she writes that if the goal of women "is to reverse the existing order – even if that were possible – history would simply repeat itself and return to phallocratism.[5] (I interpret this to indicate that, in her view, the real task feminists must face is the undermining of logic and masculine language; without this, no change in gender of those who direct society will eliminate the oppressive nature of society, its phallocratic nature, *i.e.*, that logical order renders woman exiled from her own body, sex, and imaginary.) I believe Irigaray's reasons for this view derive ultimately from her conception of the teleological (or goal-oriented) nature of male sexuality and the male unconscious. For if, as she contends, the penis is a tool, something that must be manipulated and controlled and that becomes "useless" once its purpose is achieved, and if, conversely, female sexuality exhibits no such rigidly structured goal-orientedness, then there would be reason to expect that a stance of manipulation, control, mastery, and establishing and maintaining order, etc., could come to be deeply inscribed in the male unconscious, but not in the female unconscious. Goal-oriented activity can be described as coherent, intentional, and logical, exhibiting the values of clarity, unity, and identity; therefore, if logic is patriarchal, and such activity is a prerequisite for establishing and maintaining social order, social order is patriarchal by nature.

I find several objections to such reasoning, but I will mention only two. First, whether all social order is necessarily repressive is questionable, but this does appear to be what Irigaray maintains when she says that even if women reversed the existing order it would return to phallocratism. Second, however, I feel that attributing the adjective "masculine" to goal-oriented activity as such is a serious mistake, for all human beings (and not only human) depend upon activity that is goal-oriented in order to preserve their existence. Yet, clearly, goal-oriented action is characterized by certain regularities – especially the regularity that to aim at one goal precludes aiming at the opposite goal – and that a basic principle (such as the law of noncontradiction) is an expression of this feature of all goal-orientation. Goal-oriented activity and thinking are spontaneously logical in that they manifest certain requirements for successful interaction with the environment, which at another level, are expressed as rules, at the level of Logic, the discipline or science. What is "Logic" in comparison to the spontaneously logical nature of goal-oriented activity? First, I think it is the awareness and appreciation of the fact that goal-oriented activity is successful and predictably successful when it is not inconsistent or incoherent, when it is persistent, and when it is methodical, *i.e.*, when it pursues only those intermediate goals consistent with the final goal. It is first the statement of the criteria that distinguishes goal-oriented activity from activity that is not goal-oriented. Having discerned that adherence to these criteria increases the chances of success and decreases the need for luck, Logic is, then, the further study of connections and rules of procedure, thanks to which success can be most often and most efficiently achieved. The knowledge afforded by this study and appreciation of the defining criteria of successful goal-oriented activity is clearly an empowering knowledge; it serves the interests that humans have in efficient and successful action that will satisfy needs and intentions. Logic thus expresses a basic human interest, and to that degree, it is misleadingly described as neutral or free from interests or interestedness. But Logic *is* neutral in the sense that adherence to its advice will maximize success whether the goal is ultimately to promote one's own self-interest at the expense of the interests of others, or whether one's goal is to promote the interests of others even at one's own expense. Inferring that because Logic is not entirely independent of human interestedness, it is therefore necessarily a tool of selfishness or oppression, or that all activity adhering to the rules of Logic is at the expense of others is a mistake. Recall that Martin Luther cursed Reason and called it a whore, on the grounds that it would serve any master; he was right that it can serve a wide variety of interests, and he was wrong to think it something immoral on those grounds.

Thus, the logical nature of goal-oriented action ought not to be called "masculine," least of all by a feminist, since in addition to this being false, it is a mainstay of traditional patriarchal ideology. I suggest that Logic be looked upon as being basically the refinement and study of the basic features of goal-oriented activity or praxis, which is something essentially human, not peculiarly male. This still leaves another question, however: whether some reason exists to think that in the gap between the basically logical nature of human praxis and Logic as the self-awareness of this nature constituted as an authoritative system of statements, anything intervenes that would help determine whether *Logic such as it has developed in the West* is intrinsically masculine, or whether and how Logic might be seen to be contingently masculine, *i.e.*, masculine for reasons that are foreign to the nature of Logic.

Let me build on the assumption that a teleological orientation is equally natural and necessary to both female and male human beings in so far as each is a self-aware being interacting with an environment within which it is continuously in the process of creating its life. Whatever differences may exist in the female and male unconscious will not alter this basic fact about our being-in-the-world. However, under specific social circumstances, namely, those within which males have power over females and relate to one another competitively and with basic hostility, the relationship of the male to his teleologically structured sexuality (including the fact that his tool is also a weapon and the symbol of his higher social status) can easily be expected to be characterized by a kind of anxiety. Of course, I suggest here that patriarchy should be invoked to explain the hostile, dominating masculinist unconscious of the male rather than the reverse. I think this makes perfect sense: all my suggestion needs in order to have plausibility is that we agree that social relations, cultural values, and anxieties about our status in the eyes of others mediate our relationships to our bodies. I think Irigaray will grant this, for she says at one point that men have become *culturally* distanced from their bodies.[6]

A relationship of anxiety to his teleologically structured sexuality is part of a man's anxiety about control of his body, about competence; and control of his body is a prerequisite to his social position of control and mastery over his possessions and his females. Anxiety over his competence will naturally enough explain an inclination to consolidate this competence, and that is one of the gifts that Logic and a capacity for theory bring. But I must emphasize that Logic would be equally empowering to any self-aware, competent active being, female or male. The conditions of competition, hostility, and anxiety go some way toward explaining an *obsession* with competence (and hence, Logic) in the patriarchal male, which one would not equally expect in the female living in a patriarchal society.

At this rate, nothing intrinsically male or masculine about Logic or theory is found, even though it has developed under patriarchal conditions. The male has been defining itself, in its theoretical but still defensive praxis, with greater and greater intensity, as obsessed with Logic as a consequence of the obsession with competence. Hence, it may well be that the typical male under patriarchy can be characterized in terms of a paranoic, defensive, logic-obsessed unconscious, complemented by an estrangement from the pleasure for pleasure's sake that being flesh offers. What I have described, however, is how Logic could have come to overlay the teleologically structured male sexuality as a result of the anxiety about this sexuality and about his competence and autonomy generally, as a possible account of the basic level of the complicity of Logic with patriarchy. This account would exonerate Logic as such from the charge of being intrinsically patriarchal, without entailing that the traditional epistemological claims about the neutrality of the acting or knowing subject with respect to power or sex are thereby in the slightest exonerated from that or any other charge. (Clearly,the critique of such claims about neutrality is as fully dependent upon adherence to the principles of Logic as is traditional epistemology, *i.e.*, logical coherent discourse is as well used *against* those who claim that their use of Logic places them in a privileged and neutral space.)

Thus, I can grant truth to the claim that Logic is masculine or patriarchal, only in the sense that the contemporary dominant form of typical masculine selfhood can be characterized in terms of an obsession with being logical, while insisting that once one sees *why* this is true, why it has come to be true, one will also see that it is only contingently so. In my view, with regard to the political problem of Logic, feminism is rebellion against patriarchy and against what patriarchy has done *with* Logic, but if feminism is to succeed in changing the world, it must also be rebellion against what patriarchy has done *to* Logic, rather than rebellion against Logic.

The essence of what is called masculinity can be said to lie in defensive separateness, competitiveness, hostility towards others, and anxiety about one's autonomy, one's reality, and one's competence. Logic is a basic tool of empowerment that has been appropriated by the masculine being in his project of overcoming this fundamental, obsessive, anxiety-ridden insecurity. This project cannot possibly succeed, for it only increases and aggravates the condition it seeks to overcome. The appropriation of tools of empowerment to the project of overcoming an insecurity that derives from a social condition of hostility and competitiveness through increasing one's defensiveness, will no more result in the end of insecurity than will arming oneself with bigger and bigger weapons against one's foes. It does nothing to alter the fundamental insecurity and anxiety, which only the cessation of the condition of hostility can bring about. What masculinity needs, in order to overcome its condition of anxiety, is to overcome masculinity, *i.e.*, the condition of being a self in terms of opposition and hostility towards others (both masculine and feminine others). Logic cannot possibly, by itself, accomplish that, for Logic has been incorporated *into* this condition. A different stance from that of hostility is needed. This would be a different stance on the Other, and would require a different relation to Logic. On the danger of technology, Heidegger suggested two possible choices: either take a stance that will still allow one to be free from it even as it is used or to allow one's self to be dominated by it and fall into bondage to it. This same kind of reasoning can be applied to Logic: a basic form of human praxis which has become, with logocentrism, a dominating alien force – not due to its intrinsic nature, but to the fact that an attitude of domination and hostility of self to other has for so long been the definitive attitude of human social life. I agree with feminists like Rubin, Flax, and Hartsock, who suspect that the roots of this attitude lie in the very emphasis upon the differences between the sexes that a rigid sexual division of labor institutionalizes when that division of labor is in the service of the unequal distribution of power between groups or individuals.[7]

This need not imply, however, a denial that some truly irreducible differences exist between the sexes, for example, between female and male sexuality and how that sexuality gets lived through the unconscious. What is needed is to establish the legitimacy of both, which means not defining the difference in terms of hierarchy or otherness-relative-to-a-norm. Similarly, in attempting to differentiate between Logic and patriarchy, and exonerating Logic itself from the charge of phallocratism, allowing the return of the traditional defensive and hostile claim that Logic offers the only legitimate stance or method for knowing the world, ourselves and others, or that other stances are necessarily less legitimate must be avoided. Opposition to the *primacy* of Logic is not the same thing, simply, as opposition to Logic. The encounter with the world offered by Logic is of value, but it is not of exclusive value, and reintroducing hierarchies and saying it is of highest value must be avoided.

It is not differences between the sexes that should be denied, but rather the framework within which all assertions of difference are translated into hierarchies, into evaluations of superior and inferior, into power-relevant differences. The real goal should be the elimination of power as an issue, by eliminating real power imbalances. Freeing ourselves from hostility, competitiveness, and domination as basic ways to be human would free us from translating sexual difference into differential distribution of power. Two things are required: first, having the tools of empowerment equally in the hands or domain of all, and second, eliminating the conditions that render one *obsessed* with the tools of empowerment, viz., the variety of anxieties about one's own reality, legitimacy, and autonomy which motivate one to try to overcome anxieties in ways that feed them. I think the analyses of gender differentiation in terms of social relations and the exclusively female role in childcare under conditions of obsessive heterosexuality and patriarchy help to identify those conditions, and to convince us that one of those conditions – the construction of the typical masculine self as a hostile, threatened, anxious self – is the root of the appropriation of Logic into domination strategies, which then deny that they are domination strategies by invoking the fact that they employ a method which in itself is neutral with respect to the distribution of power. Now it is apparent that the problem does not lie in Logic, but in traditional Western metaphysical and epistemological doctrines expressing the anxieties of masculinity and in the social task to which Logic has been appropriated.

I now come to the question of what "phallogocentrism" should properly be taken to mean, and what dangers it poses to feminism if taken in the wrong sense. "Phallogocentrism" clearly refers to the alliance between Logic and patriarchy. Given what I have already said, the possibility of undermining this alliance is quite real, but it should not be conceived as the undermining of Logic. Rather, it should include the aim of freeing Logic from phallocentrism and from obsessively anxious selfhood. Destroying Logic (the understanding of the criteria of successful goal-oriented activity) without destroying patriarchy seems possible, for I see no reason why patriarchy could not exist as a mere matter of brute force, as it probably was originally. Patriarchy might be weakened by the destruction of Logic without being itself destroyed; and I expect (in my version of Irigaray's prediction) if the conditions that made patriarchy appropriate Logic before are not eliminated (viz., anxiety about one's autonomy in a climate of hostility), this appropriation will be repeated.

I propose that phallogocentrism be seen as the alliance of phallocentrism with Logic such that *logocentrism* came into being. By "logocentrism" in this context, I mean the view that the perspective of Logic is the only legitimate perspective. (Part of this view is the claim that there *is* such a thing as the perspective of Logic, namely a neutral and disinterested perspective, which has no presuppositions to it, and that, in short, is aperspectival. Such a dream of an aperspectival perspective is itself consistent with the anxiety of the masculine unconscious. Logocentrism would be the view that Logic provides the only criteria by which anything can be judged worthwhile, valid, important, useful, or good. Logocentrism is the promotion of Logic to the first rank; it is the fiction of presuppositionlessness deriving from fascination with the empowering nature of method. But Logic is not the same thing as logocentrism, and should not be made to bear the blame for the sin of logocentrism.

If phallocentrism generated logocentrism out of Logic, constituting itself as phallogocentrism, then destroying logocentrism without destroying phallocentrism is possible: But destroying phallocentrism without destroying logocentrism, *i.e.*, without undermining the foundation of the edifice, is not possible. Furthermore (in addition to this merely logical consideration), what is it that undermines phallocentrism except a feminist femininity, *i.e.*, a self-conscious opposition to the obsessively anxious form of selfhood called masculinity? ("Feminist femininity" is opposed to patriarchal or masculinist femininity; the latter is femininity that accepts, and adapts to, masculinist anxiety, and even defines itself in terms of the task of taking care of masculinist anxiety, of helping it to be borne, of soothing it, whereas feminist femininity aims at overcoming masculinity.) In destroying phallocentrism, this healthy (feminist) form of selfhood comes into possession of a tool of empowerment; but as it does not seize that tool in response to anxiety over its own reality and competence, it does not put it to defensive uses.

One of the most crippling effects of patriarchy and logocentrism has undoubtedly been – to the detriment of males as well as females – that the anxious obsession with one's autonomy, which triggered the appropriation of Logic into the service of phallocentrism, has meant the devaluation, denigration, and denial of nonlogical ways of encountering self, others, and world. And yet, there seems to be some reason to hope for a happy ending, for those devalued and denigrated modes of being, and of encountering self, others, and world, historically have been women's domain, both by their being excluded from the realm of power and by their being chosen in response to the recognition of the evils of that power. Thus, they have not been eliminated or lost; they have become feminine. Hence, the fate of Western culture, as it faces the future and turns deconstructively in circles at the end of metaphysics, lies with feminism, which is in a position to show a way out of the century's nihilism.

The prospects for a *constructive* way out of this nihilism are increased if, as I suggest, feminism can avoid logocentrism and yet appropriate Logic, as a nonprivileged mode – one among others – of encountering self, others, and world. There is then the possibility that something like Irigaray's feminine language, language that is not governed by the logocentric tradition, can exist in its own right, without being confined to the marginality it currently enjoys.

Notes

1. Luce Irigaray, "Women's Exile: Interview with Luce Irigaray," *Ideology and Consciousness* 1 (May 1977), p. 64.

2. *Ibid.*, p. 62.

3. *Ibid.*, pp. 64–65.

4. Monique Wittig, "The Straight Mind," *Feminist Issues* I, 1 (1980), pp. 103–12.

5. Luce Irigaray, "This Sex Which Is Not One," in *New French Feminisms*, eds. Elaine Marks and Isabelle de Courtivron (New York: Schocken Books, 1981), p. 106.

6. Luce Irigaray, "Women's Exile: Interview with Luce Irigaray," p. 76.

7. Gayle Rubin, "The Traffic In Women: Notes on the 'Political Economy' of Sex," in *Toward An Anthropology of Women*, ed. Rayna R. Reiter (New York: Monthly Review Press, 1975), pp. 157–210, and Nancy C. Hartsock, "The Feminist Standpoint: Developing the Ground for a Specifically Feminist Historical Materialism," in *Discovering Reality*, eds. Sandra Harding and Merrill B. Hintikka (Boston: Reidel, 1983), pp. 283–310.

13. (Re)writing Patriarchial Texts: *The Symposium*

Barbara Freeman

During the summer of 1984, a course entitled "The Philosophy of Sexuality" was offered by the philosophy department of a major United States university. Nothing unusual took place: the professor was male; the required texts – Plato, Augustine, Freud, Ellis – were written by men; more important, the view of sexuality put forward was so thoroughly masculine that, although two-thirds of the students were women, sexual difference did not enter the classroom. Everything about the course illustrated Luce Irigaray's precept that "sexuality is never defined with respect to any sex but the masculine."[1] When, for example, looking at a centerfold in Playboy magazine was taken as a paradigm of sexual arousal, no one questioned whose experience was being described; when orgasm, following the Platonic/Freudian model of pleasure as the cessation of tension, was equated with ejaculation and assumed to be the end of sexual activity, no one asked for whom this assertion was true. Woman's absence was so total that no one noticed it.

This particular philosophy class should be taken as a microcosm of woman's position in Western philosophy: the omission of sexual difference has been so massive that until recently, it has gone unremarked. Such theorists of the feminine as Irigaray, among others, have taught us that classrooms today propagate the theory of sexuality proposed by Plato. If Western thought since Plato constitutes what Derrida has called the epoch of the metaphysics of presence, that era, marked by indifference if not antagonism to the very possibility of sexual difference, is also one in which woman does not exist. Woman's exclusion is the condition for and marks the borders of Western philosophy: within its confines she has not, perhaps cannot, be thought. Or taught. Contemporary theories of sexuality too often reproduce the Platonic model which successfully, if unconsciously, continues to omit any question of feminine difference.

But what, one wonders, might have occurred if *woman* had participated in that class on sexuality – that is, if sexual difference had been included as a subject in philosophy, rather than omitted and repressed? A more graphic way of posing this question is: What might have been said if a woman had spoken at the most influential philosophy class the West has known, namely, at *The Symposium*, the pedagogic scene at which the Western theorization of erotic love was first established? How might sexual difference be thought if it had not, in Irigaray's words, "always been conceptualized on the basis of masculine parameters?" (TS,23).

I address these questions by grafting excerpts from Irigaray's *This Sex Which Is Not One* onto a reading of *The Symposium* in hopes of inscribing sexual difference where none was previously seen to exist – at the heart of one of Western philosophy's founding texts. My main concern, however, is not to produce a correct or corrected reading of *The Symposium*, but rather to employ the text as leverage in a feminist wager. The gambit will be to allow Irigaray to *rewrite* or *reenvision* the text in such a way as to make a space for feminine sexual difference within philosophy – a tactical infidelity that might deliberately misread or mistranslate the "master text" it departs from, works out of, or in relation to. Additionally, to complicate what might otherwise be construed solely as a rereading of *The Symposium* and focus attention on the issue of revising patriarchal texts in a feminine context, I occasionally interrupt this narrative with comments and citations that stray from the subject of *The Symposium* even as they (re)mark upon it.

Irigaray enters the symposium, the philosophy classroom, or scene of a conference on philosophy, in order to examine what follows from the fact that "the feminine has never been defined except as the inverse, indeed the underside, of the masculine" (TS,159) and to demonstrate what it means to write about femininity, or write philosophy, from a nonmasculine perspective. The title of her book *The Sex Which Is Not One*, yields a critique of woman's position within the metaphysics of presence (she is the sex which does not have one) and a revaluation of femininity (she is the sex which, always both more and less than one, calls the One and its privilege into question). According to Irigaray, *woman* has been defined only as the sex which lacks what man has; her sex organs, which "are neither one nor two but plural" (TS,102), are counted as no sex organ: she is the creature without a penis who is essentially defined by that lack. Thus, what is called "the feminine" has simply meant man's inverse or opposite; and woman, as the possibility of a genuine difference rather than one term in a binarism, does not exist in Western thought. Consequently, when the philosophy of erotic love is formulated, as in *The Symposium*, one cannot assume that woman is included or that the discourse is addressed to or necessarily true for women. The philosophic speaker is a male who desires other men; the audience for whom the statements are destined, the *destinataires* for whom these statements are true, are likewise male homosexuals.[2] Woman can be a symbol of truth or wisdom, like Diotima, as long as those doing the actual desiring or truth-seeking are men.

"We've never been dealing with more than one, after all. A unity divided in halves. More, or less. Identifiable, or not. Whose possibilities of pleasure have not even been exhausted . . . .

Because we're aproaching the borders of its field, of its present frame, however, the affair is growing acrimonious. Subsequent events attest to an increasing exacerbation. But we can't be sure that it won't all end up in a sort of regression. With all parties retreating to their positions" (TS,19).

The Symposium may be read as an allegory of the position of woman in Western philosophy: she is present either as a crucial, initiatory absence – for example, as the flute-girl who is asked to leave the room before the symposium proper can begin, or as the image of plenitude personified by Diotima, guardian of and spokesperson for Platonic truth. The alliance the text establishes between Alcibiades and the flute-girl and between Socrates and Diotima merits examination in some detail. I discuss Diotima first because it is her speech that, within the context of the Symposium, firmly establishes the Platonic account of love.

When Socrates speaks as a philosopher in *The Symposium*, rather than as a character in the drama it narrates, he does so in drag, disguised by a woman's body and dressed in a woman's clothes. Everything Diotima says supports his interests by establishing the opposition that is indispensable to the idealist view of love: that between matter and form, between body and soul. It is she who makes the distinction, so crucial to the dialogue, between the procreancy of the soul and that of the body. Hers is the speech in which the material, which she aligns with the maternal, is put in opposition to the spiritual, or paternal, which supersedes the maternal and becomes, as John Brenkman has pointed out, "the name for spiritual as opposed to biological reproduction."[3] Love may then be understood as the motive for sublimation: it is "a longing for immortality" (TS,207) that is fulfilled by the propagation of the beautiful on the part of the male lover. The feminine, initially associated with the maternal function, "has nothing to do with the highest form of sexual desire – the relation between two men – and by the end of the speech is excluded from spiritual love altogether."[4] Metaphors of materiality and corporeal procreation are summoned in order to banish the maternal. Just as "the beauties of the body are as nothing to the beauties of the soul"[5] (*Symp.*,212b), so the children of the spirit are superior to those of the flesh. Diotima's speech thus adds more weight to the valuation of the spirit, which has become synonymous with and valorized as male, as though it were a ruse whereby sexual difference, now absorbed by the paternal function, completely disappears.

The flute-girl is the only member of the female sex ever to actually enter the Symposium, but it is as if her presence is contrived so that her absence can be requested. Eryximachus, establishing rules for the discourse in praise of love, first proposes that each member drink only as much wine as he feels inclined to drink, and then suggests that "we should send away the flute-girl who has just come in – let her play to herself or, if she likes, to the women of the household – and entertain ourselves today with conversation" (*Symp.*,176e). The flute-girl's absence marks and can even be seen to occasion the dialogue proper: her removal from the scene of the discourse officially inaugurates it and she will return only when Alcibiades enters; that is, when the disruption of the conversation commences. The text thus allies Alcibiades and the flute-girl, for her return coincides with his appearance. Women, the music of flutes, and wine – elements associated with Dionysus as well as Alcibiades – are linked together, made contiguous. What each element shares is a relationship to an opening on the bodies' surface: wine enters the body through the mouth; music, here produced by the lips' suction, is received through the aural cavities; and the vagina, an opening in the center of the woman's body, marks the feminine sex. Elements associated with femininity are banished so that the dialogue can begin. It can conclude, however, only when the repressed returns, when Alcibiades theatrically enters (and when Dionysian theatricality enters). Loud knocking at the street door, which sounds like a party of drunks, announces his presence; one can immediately hear the sound of a flute; and a drunken Alcibiades is helped into the room by the heretofore exiled flute-girl. The entrance of Alcibiades coupled with the return of the repressed – sound, wine, flute, girl – signals the end of philosophical dialogue on the nature of love, just as her absence had initiated it. It is as if the traces of openings, of banished femininity, encircle philosophy: they become the borders that mark the beginning and end of the theorization of Platonic love.

The mistake dramatised by *The Symposium, "monumentally obvious yet so deeply inscribed in our culture as to be invisible, is in its premise that for both sexes desire is phallic."*[6]

Platonic desire constitutes itself as a lack to be filled and hence, abolished. As such, it reveals an animosity toward, a dislike of, desire. Desire is monstrous: it distorts the bodies' boundaries, involves the opening and moistening of its orifices, displaces its limits by swelling and extending them, and implies a deviation from the (masculine) body's unique, proper form. Perhaps for this reason to feel sexual desire is understood as a defilement.

Desire, thus, should be extinguished as quickly and efficiently as possible – sublated or sublimated – so that the integrity of bodily form can be restored and the body can return to its "normal" state.

Irigaray's initiative: To allege that the West's definition of desire, despite its pretension to be gender-free, might after all be thoroughly male.

Her domain is precisely with what occurs only on the borders and along the margins of Platonic thought: she brings sexual difference and the specificity of feminine desire into the forefront of the symposium and explicitly raises the question of how they might be represented. In so doing, she offers an alternative to Plato's view that love is by necessity the love of something lacking. For Plato, "everything longs for what it lacks, and nothing longs for what it does not lack" (*Symp.*,211b); therefore, desire's fulfillment consists in its abolition: the aim of desire is to extinguish itself, that is, to remove the lack inherent in it. In the place of love as an indispensable lack that permits the activity of desiring, Irigaray posits a mode of loving that lacks lack and a concept of fulfillment that has nothing to do with eradication. Whereas Platonic love cannot conceive of a desiring relation that fulfills itself without its simultaneous extinction, fulfillment for Irigaray implies the repetition of desire because the specificity of feminine desire is that it desires more and not less of it/"self" – a self which, simultaneously constructed, undermined, and multiplied by desire, also is not one. Whereas fulfillment for Plato means primarily the absence of the irritating lack desire excites, to think desire otherwise, in the feminine, necessitates rethinking the very notions of closure or an "end": fulfillment produces a certain relation between excitation and gratification such that the abolition of the one instills the reproduction of the other.

This Sex Which Is Not One demonstrates that it is possible to think, and write, love otherwise. Irigaray inscribes a nonrestrictive psychic and corporeal economy of fluids, a multiple economy not organized around the primacy of the One, be it sexual (the phallus), logical (the self-identical), linguistic (the law of the copula), or political (the law of the father). Emphasizing woman's unique auto-erotic economy and the specificity of her self-affection, she revalues feminine sexuality by writing the woman's body, particularly her sex organs, as the locus of difference and not the site of lack. The specificity of feminine sexuality, according to Irigaray, is the desire for "the proximate rather than for (the) proper/ty" (TS,79). Woman cannot touch. "Indeed, she touches herself all the time and moreover no one can forbid her to do so, for her genitals are formed by two lips in continuous contact. Thus, within herself, she is already two – but not divisible into one(s) – that caress each other" (TS,24). Speech and sex are not, as for Plato, two distinct and separate entities, but wrapped up in, part and parcel of, each other. Just as woman's sexuality is bound up with touch, so words for women are ways of binding. The distinguishing feature of women's statements "is one of contiguity. They touch upon" (TS,104). Sex and speech are contiguous: words join in the same way as do muscles and joints.[7]

Irigaray's anatomical metaphor, or way of metaphorizing anatomy, yields an almost Heraclitean notion of identity as a continuous flux or stream of mobile energies, and a way of thinking the terms of an opposition simultaneously and nondualistically. What is unique about the feminine body is that "woman does not have *a* sex organ. She has at least two of them, but they are not identifiable as ones" (TS,228). Woman's sexuality cannot be reduced to any singular numerical value, nor can her identity be conceptualized in terms of a model of meaning based upon the notion of the self-identical. Although within herself she is already two, the "contact of at least two lips (which) keep woman in touch with herself," means precisely that "she cannot be identified either as one person or as two" (TS,126). Irigaray's dynamics of the near rather than the proper yields a notion of the one, or the self, as a fluid identity which, both one and many, provides an alternative to the Platonic concept of identity as a necessarily fixed and autonomous unit.

Interestingly enough, Heraclitus makes a brief appearance at the Symposium, albeit within quotation marks. Eryximachus, the doctor who is particularly sensitive to the combined threats of wine, flute-music, women, and the aphorisms of pre-Socratic philosophers, cites Heraclitus's fragment on the relationship between conflict and harmony, "the one in conflict with itself is held together, like the harmony of the bow and of the lyre" (TS,187), as an example of a philosophically absurd position, and so as to provide his listeners with a moment of comic relief. For Eryximachus, harmony and conflict cannot coexist because the very presence of the one annuls the possibility of the other. Commenting on the quotation, Eryximachus says,

> Of course, it is absurd to speak of harmony as being in conflict, or as arising out of elements which are still conflicting, but perhaps he meant that the art of music was to create harmony by resolving the discord between the treble and the bass. There can be no harmony of treble and bass while they are still in conflict, for harmony is concord and concord is a kind of sympathy and sympathy between things which are in conflict is impossible as long as that conflict lasts (*Symp.*,187b).

Just as Plato conceives of fulfillment – or concord – as the removal of a lack, and of beauty as "perfect harmony" *Symp.*,206b), so Eryximachus, Socrates's spokesman, can conceive of harmony only as the eradication of tension, or in his words, as "the resolution of discord." For Eryximachus, harmony means by definition the absence of conflict; for Heraclitus, harmony consists in a certain relationship between conflicting forces – such as discord and concord – which involves and may even be heightened by tension.

The body, in the form of Aristophanes's uncontrollable attack of hiccups, interrupts the symposium by forcing a change in the order of the speeches. Since Aristophanes is too hiccup-ridden to talk, Eryximachus has first to proscribe a treatment for his ailment and then to speak in his place. The treatment – to tickle his nostrils three or four times and sneeze until the hiccups have stopped – focuses attention on the orificial (curing what erupts through the mouth by entering the nostrils) and mocks the notion of harmony Eryximachus has just proposed. The series of sneezes which finally eliminates his hiccups, described by Aristophanes as "an appalling union of noise and irritation" (185e), dramatizes the difference between Heraclitus's notion of harmony as a relationship between conflicting elements and that of Eryximachus's as the elimination of tension. What cures the hiccups is precisely the union of discordant elements Eryximachus has just called ridiculous.

"To play with mimesis is thus, for woman, to try to recover the place of her exploitation by discourse, without allowing herself to be simply reduced to it. It means to resubmit herself to ideas, in particular to ideas about herself, that are elaborated in/by a masculine logic, so as to make 'visible,' by an effect of playful repetition, what was supposed to remain invisible: the cover-up of a possible operation of the feminine in language" (TS,76). "To play with mimesis" might mean, in this instance, to shake up

The Symposium's *order, displace its philosophical ground, through a repetition which does and does not reproduce it.*

(By interrupting the reading of The Symposium *at this point, my text* mimes *Aristophanes' body: this fragment breaks into my commentary the same way Aristophanes's hiccups disrupt the narrative sequence. The effect in both cases is to bring about a change in the temporal order and a change of mood. Reading* The Symposium *one expects Aristophanes's contribution to the discussion of the nature of love and instead finds a physical intervention that makes discourse impossible; here the reader perhaps expected more analysis of the text and instead finds a parenthesis that reflects upon the status of interruptions.)*

Heraclitus's view of harmony has an affinity with Irigaray's emphasis on the desire for touch in a feminine affective economy. For both, conflict may have a positive function: rather than something to be eradicated, it binds or "holds together," and is thus, like touch, a source of connection and contiguity. This view – intimacy as a harmonious relation that might heighten rather than abolish tension – is profoundly at odds with that of Eriximachus and the other speakers at *The Symposium* who, following Socrates, need to abolish conflict in favor of a static notion of concord and harmony. Nonetheless, the inscription of the Heraclitean fragment within the confines of the Symposium might be understood provisionally as an instance of difference, of a repressed feminine element appearing momentarily within a phallogocentric or metaphysical economy, if only so as to provoke derision. A certain logic links Irigaray and Heraclitus, as if the name of woman and the pre-Socratic philosophers have in common the possibility of an alternative theory of desire in which "it is possible to secure a place for the feminine within sexual difference" (TS,159).

Agathon's vacuous but elegant speech in praise of Love's youth, beauty, and moral excellence for Socrates summons up the twin specters of rhetoric and female monstrosity. Socrates praises Agathon by remarking that his "flood of eloquence" which "held us all spellbound with the sheer beauty of his diction" (*Symp.*,198b) reminds him of Gorgias, the famous rhetoric teacher. Then, either because both names contain the same first syllable or he is supposed to speak next, Socrates recalls Odysseus's fantasy of being struck dumb by Medusa, a glimpse of whose snake-like hair and hideous "Gorgon's head" turned man or beast to stone. "Besides," says Socrates, "his speech reminded me so strongly of that master of rhetoric, Gorgias, that I couldn't help thinking of Odysseus, and his fear that Medusa would rise from the lower world among the ghosts, and I was afraid that when Agathon got near the end he would arm his speech against mine with the

Gorgon's head of Gorgias's eloquence and strike me as dumb as stone" (*Symp.*,198c). Gorgon/Gorgias?

Rhetoric and monstrosity are coupled in Socrates's imagination because Odysseus's fear of Medusa resembles his fear of eloquence: the two are alike in that both deviate from, and have no inherent relation to, the truth. In addition, both share a relation to death and the deadly: Medusa, as trace of repressed or buried femininity, can only survive in the underworld, among the ghosts, but when she emerges it is with murderous intent. Eloquence, which has the power to silence opposition whether or not it tells the truth, also has a deadly power, for as Jean-Paul Debaux points out, "to reduce to silence is to reduce to powerlessness; that is how the masculine will to castrate operates."[8] *And to castrate, at least in symbolic terms, is to kill.*

What is the effect of systematic fragmentation?

Medusa's trace reappears with Alcibiades. Demanding to see Agathon at once, he stands "in the doorway with a mass of ribbons and an enormous wreath of ivy and violets sprouting on his head" (*Symp.*,212e), decorations which make him resemble Medusa with her long, wavy hair. First he "crowns" Agathon by removing some of the ribbons and tying them to his head; next he transfers a share to Socrates so that both bear Medusa's emblem. Then, by putting an end to the philosophic discourse, he does to Socrates what Medusa had done to Odysseus (and what Socrates had feared, or fantasized, at the hands of Agathon): silences him.

Alcibiades from the outset threatens the oppositions upon which Socrates's theory of love depends by confounding the distance that divides its two terms. Indeed, the first sentence of his speech tampers with one of Socrates's most privileged distinctions: that between truth and rhetoric. Disjunction is immediately established between Alcibiades's alleged intention – "to tell the solemn truth" (*Symp.*,214e) about Socrates – and the styles in which he tells it. Insisting upon the impossibility of separating truth from figuration, he proposes to describe Socrates by a series of comparisons. Noting that he has chosen a particular simile "not because it's funny but because it's true," he first likens Socrates to the figure of "those little sileni that you see in the statuaries' stalls" and then to "Marysas the satyr" (TS,215). Alcibiades thus employs a trope, a rhetorical figure, in order to compare Socrates to a sculpture, another kind of figure; that is, he uses a simile to situate the figure of Socrates in the domain of the figurative. In so doing, Alcibiades effects an almost comic reversal, for he compares Socrates to the exact opposite of everything he represents himself to be: not only does he ally Socrates with rhetoric instead of philosophy, with beauty and not truth, but he uses a metaphor to link Socrates with Dionysus, or at least with his companions, for both the sileni and Marsyas are satyrs, fertility spirits and semidivine counterparts of Dionysus's male worshippers. Alcibiades's speech satyr/izes Socrates in more ways than one.

Alcibiades does not give arguments but instead tells stories; his speech is structured by a combination of analogy and autobiography: the detailed account of his attempt to seduce Socrates follows the comparison of Socrates to a satyr. He neither provides reasons for his beliefs nor tries to discern the true nature of love; his elaborate praise of Socrates is a ruse intended to win Agathon, the beautiful boy who is the object of Socrates's desire, for himself.

Just as it is essential to distinguish "femininity" – as one term in the masculine/feminine opposition – from sexual difference, so it is important to distinguish Agathon's function from that of Alcibiades's. Whereas Agathon's relation to Socrates supports and endorses the subordination of femininity to masculinity, Alcibiades's appearance calls the very functioning of the couple into question.

Alcibiades's intervention at the Symposium thwarts Socrates's seduction of Agathon and with it philosophy's appropriation and possession of the beautiful, for his intrusion not only interrupts Socrates's seduction but at the same time disrupts his philosophical speaking as such. Just as he displaces Socrates by sitting next to Agathon, forcing Socrates to change places, he places himself in between philosophy and poetry, truth and beauty. He thereby gets between the masculine/feminine couple and subverts Plato's ends by preventing a certain kind of appropriation or assimilation from taking place. Alcibiades may be said to act "in the name of woman" because he engenders the kind of difference that does not fit into and cannot be incorporated by the masculine/feminine (or Socratic/Agathonic) dialectic.

How candidly should I write about what I am doing with (or to) Alcibiades? Even if, in the technical sense, my interpretation of his intervention at The Symposium *is "wrong," perhaps I am still "right": just as important as finding the correct meaning is to show how Alcibiades abets Irigaray by inscribing a kind of desire that insists upon what Platonic philosophy excludes – which is precisely what's at stake in rereading the philosophical canon* as a woman.

Alcibiades does not use words to describe the truth but rather to produce affect and effect, not to ascertain what love is but to get the lover he wants. His speech obscures the distinction between passion and reason or between being a lover and a philosopher by enacting the ways in which the one cannot exist without the other. Alcibiades's performance shows the difference between a philosophy that must separate itself from the body in order to establish the superiority of form over matter and one which takes as its principal subject its relationship to the body.[9] The important difference here is not an opposition between philosophy as the search for the true versus philosophy as the scene of passion, but rather a deconstruction of the traditional formulation between reason and passion or form and matter.

Irigaray's realignment of the relationship of speech to sexuality in a feminine economy may be aligned with Alcibiades's performance at *The Symposium*, for her inscription of textual/sexual relations mimes or is mimed by his enactment of it. Just as Alcibiades conjoins in a scene of heterosexual intercourse, the very oppositions upon which the Platonic theory of love depends, so Irigaray's deconstruction of the relation between body and letter breaks out of the confines imposed by the conceptual scheme that structures *The Symposium*. If Alcibiades introduces the effect of the feminine into a discourse that denies femininity in order to obtain its philosophical coherence, Irigaray in turn makes explicit what can be enacted in the drama of the symposium on the condition that it remain philosophically unspeakable. The force of reading philosophical texts as a woman may be to locate the eruption of feminine difference in a text, thereby demonstrating that philosophy already includes within itself that which has the power to disrupt it. Just as Irigaray's insights open *The Symposium* to a reexamination of the ways in which sexual difference has always been implicit in and contained by it, so too rereading *The Symposium* has confirmed Irigaray's insights regarding the position of the feminine in Western thought since Plato. By aligning two kinds of lover's discourse – Alcibiades's outrageously rhetorical performance with Irigaray's subtle articulation of and insistence on women's speech and sexuality – I have tried to demonstrate that there is indeed room in *this* Symposium for a thoroughly feminine desire.

What kind of a method – or style – is appropriate to a "feminist" revision of a text that occupies a formative, constitutive role in the philosophical canon?

It should (have) address/ed the difficulty of articulating female meanings to a philosophical (that is, male) audience, the difficulty Annette Kolodny has called "the inaccessibility of female meaning to male interpretation."[10] *To have made the issue of reading or writing philosophy* in the feminine *part of the subject of the rereading.*

One goal might have been: to overturn an old story by retelling it.

" . . . it is indeed precisely philosophic discourse that we have to challenge, and *disrupt*, inasmuch as this discourse sets forth the law for all others, inasmuch as it constitutes the discourse on discourse" (TS,274).

Bedtime stories. Let a worn-out era rest.

Notes

1. Luce Irigaray, *This Sex Which Is Not One*, trans. Catherine Porter with Carolyn Burke (Ithaca, NY: Cornell University Press, 1985), p. 69. All citations of *This Sex Which Is Not One* are to this edition and are given in the text as: (TS,).

2. I wish to thank Judith Butler for her many astute comments, in particular for distinguishing a misogynistic "male homo-eroticism" from homosexual practices as such. It may well be the case that a certain male homosexuality, uniting homosexuals and feminists in resistance to a common opponent, may be on the side of, indeed articulate, an *other* sexuality. The object of Irigaray's critique is rather what Michel Foucault has called "virile Greek homosexuality," which he takes as paradigmatic of male homosexuality in the West. Foucault employs this term to describe a sexual economy in which there is never any question of the partner's pleasure, the subject is always either active or passive, penetrator or penetrated, and reciprocity of pleasure between male lovers is neither desirable nor even imaginable. See Michel Foucault "On the Genealogy of Ethics: An Overview of Work in Progress," Hubert L. Dreyfus and Paul Rabinow, *Michel Foucault: Beyond Structuralism and Hermeneutics*, 2nd ed., (Chicago: University of Chicago Press, 1983), p. 229–52. At stake for Irigaray is what Alice Jardine has described as "the potential for, the possibility of, new logic for radical heterosexuality, beyond the hetero-homo dualism." See Alice Jardine, "Death Sentences: Writing Couples and Ideology." *Poetics Today*, vol. 6, nos. 1–2 (1985):121.

3. John Brenkman, "The Other and the One: Psychoanalysis, Reading, *The Symposium*," *Yale French Studies*, No. 55–56 (1978):400.

4. *Ibid.*

5. All citations of *The Symposium* are from Michael Joyce's translation in *Plato: The Collected Dialogues*, ed. Edith Hamilton and Huntington Cairns (Princeton, NJ: Princeton University Press, 1963), pp. 527–74.

6. See the introduction to *The (M)other Tongue*, ed. S. N. Garner, C. Kahane, M. Sprengnethen (Ithaca, NY: Cornell University Press, 1985), p. 18.

7. The problem of writing the feminine body or "metaphorizing anatomy" so as to displace traditional oppositional modes of formulating mind/body (or textual/sexual) relations is as urgent as it is complex. Complete development of this issue is impossible here. I discuss it more fully in "*Plus corps donc plus écriture*: Hélène Cixous and the Mind-Body Problem"

(*Paragraph*, forthcoming). There, to summarize very briefly, I argue that, like Irigaray, Cixous's conception of the mind-body relation departs from the masculinist or metaphysical tradition in that the (woman's) body is understood neither as constructed in and by language (structuralism), nor as language's ground or other (phenomenology). Rather, to *metaphorize* the body means precisely that the one already inhabits and is inhabited by the other, for to say that the corporeal is always already linguistic means also that language is also always corporeal. It follows, then, that neither mind nor body, head nor sex, can be used as the basis of an hierarchical, ultimately patriarchal, opposition in which a (feminine) body is inevitably subordinated to a (masculine) mind. I submit that precisely this kind of reformulation is what is demanded by the project of inscribing a philosophically different, *i.e.*, feminine, body in, and as, text.

8. Jean-Paul Debaux, 1980, "Et voilà pourquoi votre femme est muette," in Christine Brooke-Rose, "Woman As A Semiotic Object," *Poetics Today*, nos. 1–2 (1985): p. 14.

9. More could be said about a feminist-deconstructive politics of grafting. Jane Gallop, for example, describes the strategic function of *infidelity* as "a feminist practice of undermining the Name-of-the-Father." According to Gallop, "the unfaithful reading strays from the author, the authorised, produces that which does not hold as a reproduction, as a representation. Infidelity is *not* outside the system of marriage, the symbolic, patriarchy, but hollows it out, ruins it, from within." Jane Gallop, *The Daughter's Seduction: Feminism and Psychoanalysis* (Ithaca, NY: Cornell University Press, 1982), p. 48.

10. Annette Kolodny, "A Map for Rereading; Or, Gender and the Interpretation of Literary Texts," in *The (M)other Tongue*, p. 257.

Part VI.
Archaeology of Deconstruction

14. Rereading Deconstruction (Today?)

Christie V. McDonald

My perplexity at the title of a philosophical conference, "Deconstruction and its Alternatives,"[1] led to the reformulation of my previous work on Saussure and Lévi-Strauss and the critique Jacques Derrida gives of semiology and anthropology in *Of Grammatology*.[2] What seemed curious about that title was the use of the word "alternative," which the *American Heritage Dictionary* defines as "two mutually exclusive possibilities," or "one of a number of things from which *one* must be chosen." Since the problem of exclusion, and of mutually exclusive systems, has been basic to the critique of Western metaphysics given to us through deconstruction, this paper addresses the thought of alternative, choice, and decision in order to understand how they play themselves out within specific instances of a deconstructive strategy.

I begin with a rather long quotation concerning the question of alternative in "The Ends of Man," in *Margins*:

> . . . the 'logic' of every relation to the outside is very complex and surprising. It is precisely the force and the efficiency of the system that regularly change transgresions into 'false exits.' Taking into account these effects of the system, one has nothing, from the inside where 'we are,' but the choice between two strategies:
>
> 1. To attempt an exit and deconstruction *without changing terrain*, by repeating what is implicit in the founding concepts and the original problematic, by using against the edifice the instrument or stones available in the house, that is, equally, in language. Here, one risks ceaselessly confirming, consolidating, *relifting [relever]*, at an always

more certain depth, that which one allegedly deconstructs. The continuous process of making explicit, moving toward an opening, risks sinking into the autism of closure.

2. To decide to *change terrain*, in a discontinuous and irruptive fashion, by brutally placing oneself outside, and by affirming an absolute break and difference. Without mentioning all the other forms of *trompe-l'oeil* perspective in which such a displacement can be caught, thereby inhabiting more naïvely and more strictly than ever the inside one declares one has deserted, the simple practice of language ceaselessly reinstates the new terrain on the oldest ground. The effects of such a reinstatement or of such a blindness could be shown in numerous precise instances.

It goes without saying that these effects do not suffice to annul the necessity for a "change of terrain." It also goes without saying that the choice between these two forms of deconstruction cannot be simple and unique. A new writing must weave and interlace these two motifs of deconstruction . . . .[3]

Derrida then points out that if the style of the first deconstruction was mostly that of the Heideggerian questions, and the other was mostly that of the France of 1968, what is needed perhaps (now as then) is, as Nietzsche has said, "a change of 'style.'" But such a style must be "plural."[4]

In *Of Grammatology*, published in 1967, Jacques Derrida wrote: "Because we are beginning to write, to write differently, we must reread differently."[5]

In 1979, during a colloquium now published under the title, "The Ear of the Other,"[6] he reflected that he had used the term "deconstruction" at first very little in his writing, and the paradox was now history: from what was one word out of many, situated within a system it did not at all command, deconstruction had become the much disputed catchword for a series of philosophical, literary, and pedagogical questions. In its constitutive phase within Derrida's early works, the term designated a dismantling of systems for the purpose of analyzing structures; Derrida then set about undoing the structural levels within the writing of major thinkers from Plato to our time. Although there may have been nothing "new" methodologically about scrutinizing the way systems structure and destructure themselves, what became important through this term was the radical questioning of classical ontology and the tradition of metaphysics.

Deconstruction, as it was first worked out and then properly named, contained within its general strategy a double edged, doubly bound move or operation, designed to displace the notion of truth *per se*; therefore, no single position could be attributed to it or simply maintained. To look at what one might call *one* of deconstruction's constitutive moments (a strategy learned from Derrida) is then to review it as more than a critical operation. And this is so because, as he suggests elsewhere, deconstruction always bears, at one moment or another, on the confidence given the critical, critico-theoretical, that is to say, "deciding authority."

Within the founding discourses of semiology (in Ferdinand de Saussure's *Course on General Linguistics*) and structural anthropology (in the works of Claude Lévi-Strauss), it became possible to identify specific resistances, in the reassessments of limits, which were then to mark out the shifting domain of deconstruction. In the first instance, *hierarchy* would be maintained such that the "determined fields of science, its formal objects or material" submit to philosophical jurisdiction, as a question preliminary to the constitution of a "rigorous" and systematic theoretical discourse. In the second, an *envelopment* exists in which the "movement of the whole is remarked in the partial determinations of the system."[7]

The question asked then was "what is writing?" But second generation grammatologists, students (as it were) of the letter, know that it is not simply a matter of where and when writing begins. In a system without origin or end, it is rather a problem of how one re-marks the question for us here and now.

What follows is an attempt fo reread briefly two of the arguments in *Of Grammatology* – as the text in which Derrida massively introduced the term deconstruction.

When Saussure maintained in no uncertain terms that language and writing were distinct systems in which the second, that is to say the written, only existed to represent the first, he vituperated in a remarkably moralistic tone, referring to the "tyranny of writing" as "depraved" in its effects and "pathological" in its mistakes. What was at stake in such a statement was the delimitation and establishment of the boundaries of linguistics, in the primacy accorded both to spoken language and the internal system of *langue*, henceforth set off from everything external to it.

In one of his key analyses, Derrida demonstrates that the binary opposition that separates speech from writing, as the inside from the outside, depends upon a restrictive definition of phonetic writing, and it is this localized definition that is then expanded by Saussure to reject writing in general. The question then is

> Why does a project of *general* linguistics, concerning the internal system of language in general, outline the limits of its field by excluding, as *exteriority in general*, a *particular* system of writing, however important it might be, even were it to be in fact universal? A particular system which has precisely for its *principle* or at least for its declared project to be exterior to spoken language.[8]

In his interrogation of the assumptions upon which semiology was founded, Derrida aims at those moments in the *Course on Linguistics* when contradictions occur within the binary pairing: value as an economic metaphor for a function, for example, is countered by the motif of language as difference. This means that two currents in Saussure's thought about the sign emerge, the first of which maintains the differentiation between the signifier and signified, as a source of linguistic value, one indeed which privileges the phonic. The second shows language to be based purely on difference. At stake, is the contradiction between value within a hierarchy and the sense that no hierarchy is possible within a differential system. If that is so, then language is engendered by an infinite series of differences, each term having no other present value than a trace, a trace of all others that are absent. If, for modern linguistics, the signifier is a trace, and the signified thinkable meaning given to intuitive consciousness, the function of the trace can be none other than the enacting of such an opposition. That is, before representation of the spoken word in writing, there is a preliminary kind of writing, one that harbors an originary violence. And this means that for Saussure, as for others, the presuppositions that are most firmly anchored within the tradition of logocentrism co-habit and co-exist with critical motifs: just as the distinction between spoken and written language collapses as a binary opposition, so too the signifier may be shown to be already contained within the signified. The operation of the trace within the continual play of signifiers will be then to constitute itself as the absolute origin of meaning in general. And this suggests quite literally, the paradoxes notwithstanding, that there is no absolute origin of meaning in general.

As the new sense of writing emerged in the displacement from semiology to grammatology, it no longer hinged upon exclusion within binary opposition. Henceforth, denying any forms of security, "deconstruction" became associated with the movement of writing in which nothing anywhere – or ever – is either simply present or simply absent.

Such a move precluded choice in that, if one could no longer subscribe to the description given of the sign, in a tradition where an unbroken chain linked the phonê to presence, one could never abandon the concept of the sign either, as the basis upon which semiology would henceforth be built. The lesson of the various scenes of writing is, therefore, that (as Freud suggested) one never really renounces anything. Writing does not replace speech, as one system replaces another. It comes to inhabit it otherwise. Here is how Derrida describes it in *Of Grammatology*:

> The movements of deconstruction do not destroy structures from the outside. They are not possible and effective, nor can they take accurate aim, except by inhabiting those structures. In habiting them in a *certain way*, because one always inhabits, and all the more when one does not suspect it. Operating necessarily from the outside, borrowing all the strategic and economic resources of subversion without being able to isolate their elements and atoms, the enterprise of deconstruction would always in a certain way fall prey to its own work . . . . No exercise is more widespread today and one should be able to formalize its rules.[9]

This meant that one would never simply turn the page of philosophy, as book, nor for that matter any other discipline or venture. It would become a question of the inscription of a new form of writing in the movement of a constant *rereading*.

How then does deconstruction become prey to its own work in the writing of a rereading? Or must one be resigned to the thought that, between chance and necessity, what is mandatory and impossible in deconstruction accounts at all moments for its own rhetorical mode, as Paul De Man has suggested for Rousseau's texts in his essay on *Of Grammatology*?[10] For De Man also states that "the necessary correlative of the rhetorical nature of literary language" dictates that a "degree of blindness is part of the specificity of all literature."

Put another way, how can one hear/understand (*entendre*) Derrida literarily speaking? To answer such a question, one must look briefly at the argument in *Of Grammatology* concerning Lévi-Strauss. As the founder of structuralism, and Rousseau's avowed modern disciple, Lévi-Strauss accepted without reserve a certain aspect of thought inherited from the epoch of Rousseau (as Derrida calls it) specifically regarding the written word: while writing is seen as a disruption, a kind of violence, it stands "outside" a more "pure" state of society and language. What Derrida suggests is that Lévi-Strauss, in this respect like Saussure, strains at the limts of a conceptuality which is at times uncritical yet at others skirts the edges of an enclosed system (logocentrism) and works toward its deconstruction; thus, structuralism as a nascent science remained anchored within logocentrism. He takes aim specifically at the inconsistencies within Lévi-Strauss's argument: as a theoretical study of myths, structural anthropology sought to reveal an intelligible system whose object was to be those relations elaborated by speculative thought; but interpreting through models, as logical constructions, it would raise without solving the problem of relating the model to empirical reality. What happens then when ethnology begins to unhinge European culture, as the culture of reference, is that a critical relationship to language can only emerge out of the very tradition that it purports to contest. That is why Lévi-Strauss opposes, as a kind of discourse on method, the *bricoleur* (as the one who uses whatever is at hand to work) to the engineer whose totalizing (and ultimately Theological) project makes of him the absolute origin of his construction. In thus conserving as an instrument of analysis the very opposition whose truth value he criticizes, Lévi-Strauss raises the important questions: How does one alter a system? What are the means for an intellectual system to change?

Consider the traditional opposition between nature and culture in which the first term traditionally presides over the second as that which is essential or universal; the second designates societal norms (laws, institutions, art, technology, etc.) that may vary from one society to another. Lévi-Strauss himself comments upon the opposition, advocating maintenance of the all-important distinction between nature and culture on methodological grounds while he refuses at the same time to credit it with truth-value. In distinguishing thus between truth and method, he destines his own venture to a series of compelling contradictions. For whatever may be said of the method and its imperatives, Lévi-Strauss never ceases to long for a culture (existing somewhere sometime) that is "intact." His search for origins is indeed more than a theory; it is more than a hypothesis, although it is both of these; it is a vocation. Whence comes the sense of filiation and affiliation to Rousseau:

> . . . Rousseau . . . has been so maligned, . . . is more misunderstood now than ever before and is preposterously accused of having glorified the state of nature . . . . When in fact he said exactly the opposite and is the only thinker who can show us how to escape from the contradictions in which we are still floundering in the wake of his opponents; Rousseau, the most anthropological of the *philosophes* . . . Rousseau our master and brother, to whom we have behaved with such ingratitude but to whom every page of this book could have been dedicated, had the homage been worthy of his great memory . . . . It was he who taught

> us that, after demolishing all forms of social organisation, we can still discover the principles which allow us to construct a new form.[11]

It is by reading a scene (entitled "The Scene of Writing") from *Tristes tropiques* that Derrida shows how, through the perpetuation of binarity, Lévi-Strauss's thought remains caught – at perhaps its most productive level – in the grip of metaphysics. In this scene, writing is viewed as an evil that comes to impose itself, through the agent of the ethnographer, on a society "that one easily might take – although wrongly – for the childhood of humanity." It is presumably his presence in the midst of the Nambikwara tribe that "causes" this people "without writing" to initiate through imitation what are taken to be their first acts of writing. Another constitutive moment, if you will.

Here is the scene from *Tristes Tropiques*:

> It is unnecessary to point out that the Nambikwara have no written language, but they do not know how to draw either, apart from making a few dotted lines or zigzags on their gourds. Nevertheless, . . . I handed out sheets of paper and pencils. At first they did nothing with them, then one day I saw that they were all just drawing wavy, horizontal lines. I wondered what they were trying to do, then it was suddenly borne upon me that they were writing or, to be more accurate, were trying to use their pencils in the same way I did mine . . . . The majority did this and no more, but the chief had further ambitions. No doubt he was the only one who had grasped the purpose of writing. So he asked me for a writing pad, and when we both had one, and were working together, if I asked for information on a given point, he did not supply it verbally but drew wavy lines on his paper and presented them to me, as if I could read his reply. He was half taken in by his own make-believe; each time he completed a line, he examined it anxiously as if expecting the meaning to leap from the page, and the same look of disappointment came over his face. But he never admitted this, and there was a tacit understanding between us to the effect that his unintelligible scribbling had a meaning which I pretended to decipher . . . .[12]

Understanding in these newly learned gestures is not what is at stake; rather, a form of communication takes place here through writing that constitutes a political act: one of domination, exploitation, and enslavement. What is at stake in the description of this scene is the line of demarcation between a society *with* and a society *without* writing, an opposition or exclusion that depends upon the generalization of a restricted sense of writing. In this instance, the passage, as Derrida demonstrates, is less one from the spoken to the written word than a passage operating within writing in the general, more inclusive sense of the term; the zigzags scratched by the Nambikwara on gourds attest to a nonphonetic form of writing that Lévi-Strauss "neglects" to recognize for what it is.

Derrida's analysis depends upon the juxtaposition of what is said in the thesis that Lévi-Strauss devoted to the Nambikwara (1948), as a theoretical statement, and what he transmits in this more empirical rendition from *Tristes tropiques*, as an autobiographical text. Derrida reads the lapses of a theoretical discourse which is at once transgressed and maintained in the portrayal of a people – both innocent and good – that Lévi-Strauss scratches into a notebook by flashlight. Perhaps the most significant moment in this reading comes with the scene Derrida has entitled "The Battle of the Proper Names." Here again the presence of the ethnographer seems to invite destruction as it incites a group of youngsters to divulge what is strictly forbidden within their world: the proper name – not only their own but that of the adult as well.

> Although the Nambikwara were easygoing and unperturbed by the presence of the anthropologist with his notebook and camera, the work was complicated by linguistic difficulties. In the first place, the use of proper names is taboo; in order to identify individuals, we had to follow the custom adopted by the telegraph works, that is, come to an agreement with the natives about arbitrary appellations such as Portuguese names – Julio, José-Maria, Luiza, etc. – or nicknames like *Lebre* (hare) or *Assucar* (sugar) . . . .
>
> One day, when I was playing with a group of children, a little girl who had been struck by one of her playmates took refuge by my side and, with a very mysterious air, began to whisper something in my ear . . . . After some hesitation and questioning, the meaning of the incident became clear. Out of revenge, the first little girl had come to tell me the name of her enemy, and the latter, on becoming aware of this, had retaliated by confiding to me the other's name. From then on, it was very easy, although rather unscrupulous, to incite the children against each oher and get to know all their names. After which . . . I had little difficulty in getting them to tell me the names of the adults.[13]

What is at issue in this scene is not only what it is that links violence to writing and the way such violence becomes equivalent to the operation of the trace (although it is both of these); rather, the analysis by which one locates the different levels at which this description works. Let me add, however, that the term *level* has a functional value that then permits the dismantling of the system.

Locating three "levels" of violence, Lévi-Strauss's reading is relegated to the third and, in a sense, more superficial level. The first of these so-called levels is the originary violence of language in which one must think of the impossibility of uniqueness within the system; the second brings with it a protective, moral dictate that effaces the proper name "from the very beginning"; the third is empirical, that which makes possible the emergence of local, conscious transgressions. What this means is that any "war" provoked among the young children is not situated – as Lévi-Strauss would have it – at the empirical level but has always already begun at other levels within language and society. It is because the name has never been more than a function within a classification, and within a system of differences, that its prohibition becomes possible – and so, too, its transgression.

The position of the ethnographer is, then, explicitly the following:

> In the ethnolographic experience, the observer takes himself as his own instrument of observation; it is evident that he must learn to know himself, to obtain an evaluation from a *self* that reveals itself as *other* to the self it is enacting, and which will become an integral part of other selves.
>
> Does the ethnologist write anything but confessions? First, in his own name . . . since it is the driving power of his vocation and work; and within this work, he speaks in the name of his society, which – with the ethnologist as its representative, its emissary – chooses other societies and civilizations for him.[14]

The inscription of a superimposed origin (within society, within the self as subject) is then its inscription within a system of which it is no more than a place and a function. Derrida shows that not only does the 'other' society become that by which to measure the state of degradation of European society, but that the critique of ethnocentrism has as its real goal the constitution of the other, through choice, into a model of original goodness destined to humiliate the self. If then the problem rests on the passage from an *a priori* to the delimitation of experience within Lévi-Strauss's critique of ethnocentrism, then this passage signals the inability of theroetical language to account for what is unique.

What then can be said to be the deciding factors in a deconstructive strategy? What are the choices and how are they made? At the end of "Structure, Sign and Play in the Discourse of the Human Sciences," Derrida suggests that nothing fortuitous exists in the contemporaneity of this critique of ethnocentrism and the deconstruction of metaphysics. That is, because ethnology – in this respect like any science – comes about within the element of discourse, "the ethnologists accepts into his discourse the premises of ethnocentrism at the very moment when he denounces them . . . . And this, Derrida continues, does not depend on a decision on his part: "At the same time, there is nevertheless a 'declared choice,' a 'certain doctrine' elaborated by Lévi-Strauss in a more or less explicit manner."[15] In the text on Rousseau, Derrida reads what Rousseau wanted to say, in showing a pure origin in man and nature, and what he was compelled to say, as he played out the impossibility of such a project within his writing. Therefore, with respect to the two kinds of interpretation (the first of which deciphers the truth of an origin, the other which moves affirmatively into a kind of play), there is no "question of choosing," because, on the one hand, choice takes place at perhaps the most superficial level (the historical or empirical), and on the other, it is necessary to conceive of the common ground, the *differance* of the irreducible differences.

Because deconstructive discourse, like the discourse on myths, must "have the form of that of which it speaks," the alternatives are largely determined. That is, in order to gain access to another text, the text of another, it is necessary to assume its faults and moves in a very rigorous manner: by assuming the "weaknesses" of the other, one confronts what "one could not confront, thereby allowing it to become manifest."[16] It is with this determination in mind that I read, and reread, a sentence (and a few of its corollaries) in order to see if one might not be able to establish, through resistance, a tactic of interpretation.

Derrida writes of bricolage: "If we wanted to pose the problem of empiricism and bricolage in depth, we would probably end up very quickly with a number of absolutely contradictory presuppositions concerning the status of discourse in structural anthropology."[17] For a writer whose model of writing, and interpretation, comes out of readings based on a non-dialectical economy of contradiction, such a comment seems curious, and all the more so because the "weakness" of bricolage, which is seen as "irremediable," is "a total inability to justify itself in its own discourse."[18] Thus, empiricism is "the matrix of all faults menacing a discourse which continues, as with Lévi-Strauss in particular, to consider itself scientific."[19]

I am neither building a case nor writing an apology for empiricism.[20] Rather, I am asking whether Derrida's reading in *Of Grammatology* suggested that Saussure in some sense *wanted* to show the exclusion of two systems (the spoken and the written) as alternatives;

if he was then compelled to show something quite different; why the Derridian argument excludes Lévi-Strauss's inclusion of empirical evidence into his argument?

Such questioning might lead us to reread a passage, one already quoted, by substituting terms (as Derrida's precedent allows in the displacement within a sentence first written by Saussure, and then rewritten by Derrida in which grammatology comes to replace semiology):

> Why does a project of *general* deconstruction, based on an economy of *internal contraction in general within the movement of writing in general,* outline the limits of its field by excluding, as *exteriority in general,* a *particular* view of the empirical, however important it might be, even were it to be in fact universal? A particular system which has precisely for its *principle* or at least for its declared project the critique of ethnocentrism.[21]

Derrida questions the specific resistance of philosophical discourse to deconstruction. In so doing, as hierarchy and envelopment come to be the identifiable regions of that reisistance, he played out their operation within the moves of deconstruction. Indeed, as it has unfolded and refolded, the program of deconstruction was – as stated in *Positions* – a two-phase program (*phase* being understood as a structural rather than a chronological term). In the first phase, a reversal was to take place in which opposed terms would be inverted; in this case, for example, one might dictate those choices that are conscious and those that are not in order to privilege the latter. Yet, because the simple inversion of terms could not suffice for any real change in reading or writing to occur (because reversal only repeats the traditional scheme in which the hierarchy of duality is reconstituted), change only begins to take place through the "second" and more radical phase of deconstruction in which the new sense of writing would be forged simultaneously. Perhaps what one is, in some sense, "left" with in the rereading of deconstruction is the call of an interminable two-step – a rigorously choreographed program in which writers write in language about language on the conditions of possibility of all literature and philosophy. In it, I think, is our chance: of plurality.

Notes

1. The first version of this essay was presented in a session entitled "Deconstruction Today" at an International Association for Philosophy and

Literature (IAPL) conference, held at the State University of New York at Stony Brook (May 1983).

2. See Christie V. McDonald, *The Dialogue of Writing* (Waterloo: The Wilfred Laurier Press, 1984).

3. Jacques Derrida, "The Ends of Man," in *Margins of Philosophy*, trans. Alan Bass (Chicago: University of Chicago Press, 1982), p. 135.

4. *Ibid.*

5. Jacques Derrida, *Of Grammatology*, trans. G. C. Spivak (Baltimore, MD: John Hopkins University Press, 1976), p. 000.

6. *The Ear of the Other: Otobiography, Transference, Translation*, ed. Christie V. McDonald, trans. Peggy Kamuf (New York: Schocken, 1985).

7. Jacques Derrida, "Tympan," in *Margins*, pp. XIX, XX.

8. Jacques Derrida, *Of Grammatology*, p. 39.

9. *Ibid.*, p. 29.

10. See Paul De Man, "The Rhetoric of Blindness: Jacques Derrida's Reading of Rousseau," in *Blindness and Insight* (Oxford: Oxford University Press, 1971), pp. 102–42.

11. Claude Lévi-Strauss, *Tristes tropiques* (New York: Atheneum, 1975), p. 390.

12. *Ibid.*, p. 296.

13. *Ibid.*, p. 278–79.

14. Claude Lévi-Strauss, "Jean-Jacques Rousseau, fondateur des sciences de l'homme," in *Jean-Jacques Rousseau* (Neuchâtel: La Baconnière, 1962), p. 241.

15. Jacques Derrida, "Structure, Sign, and Play in the Discourse of the Human Sciences," in *Writing and Difference* (Chicago: University of Chicago Press, 1978).

16. See Jacques Derrida, "Pas," *Gramma*, 3/4 ("Lire Blanchot"):111–27.

17. Jacques Derrida, "Structure, Sign, and Play," p. 288.

18. *Ibid.*, p. 138.

19. Jacques Derrida, *Writing and Difference*, p. 288.

20. On the question of empiricism see Marion Hobson, "Deconstruction, Empiricism, and the Postal Services," *French Studies*, vol. XXXVI, no. 3 (July 1982): 290–314.

21. "I shall call it (grammatology) . . . . Since the science does not yet exist, no one can say what it would be; but it has a right to existence, a place staked

out in advance. Linguistics is only a part of that general science . . . , the laws discovered by (grammatology) will be applicable to linguistics." [Jacques Derrida, *Of Grammatology*, p. 51.]

15. Genealogy and/as Deconstruction: Nietzsche, Derrida and Foucault on Philosophy as Critique

Alan D. Schrift

> This is not the censorship but the *criticism* of reason, whereby not its present *bounds* but its determinate [and necessary] *limits*, not its ignorance on this or that point but its ignorance in regard to all possible questions of a certain kind, are demonstrated from principles, and not merely arrived at by way of conjecture.
>
> – Kant

Gilles Deleuze writes in *Nietzsche and Philosophy* that "Philosophy is at its most positive as critique."[1] In what follows, I examine a few strategies of critical philosophy and, in so doing, attempt to demonstrate that the method known as "deconstruction" can be traced to certain forerunners within what might be called mainstream Continental philosophy. Specifically, I show the way a certain critical strategy found in the works of Jacques Derrida has a precursor in Nietzsche's method of genealogical analysis. This strategy involves a rejection of the binary logic both Derrida and Nietzsche view as a mainstay of the philosophical tradition. I suggest, finally, that Derrida and Nietzsche are engaged in a similar critical project, and the particular attacks they advance should be understood in the context of a general critique of authority. To this end, I begin with Derrida's characterization of the strategy of deconstructing binary oppositions, examine a prefiguration of this strategy in Nietzsche's method of genealogical analysis, introduce Foucault into the discussion and explore an example of a related strategy in his critique of the subject, and conclude with a sketch of a general critique of authority in which each of these three thinkers is engaged.

Derrida reads the history of philosophy as a history of certain classical philosophical oppositions: intelligible/sensible, truth/error, speech/writing, literal/figurative, presence/absence, etc. What he finds is that these oppositions do not peacefully coexist. Rather, one side of each binary opposition has been privileged and the other side has been devalued. That is to say, a "violent hierarchy" and "order of subordination" has been established within these oppositions, and truth has come to be valued over error, presence has come to be valued over absence, etc. Derrida takes as his task the dismantling or deconstruction of these binary oppositions. In *Positions*, the following disclosure of Derrida's critical strategy is found:

> I try to keep myself at the *limit* of philosophical discourse. . . . the limit, on the basis of which philosophy became possible, defined itself as the *episteme*, functioning within a system of fundamental constraints, conceptual oppositions outside of which philosophy becomes impracticable. . . . To "deconstruct" philosophy, thus, would be to think – in the most faithful, interior way – the structured genealogy of philosophy's concepts, but at the same time to determine – from a certain exterior that is unqualifiable or unnameable by philosophy – what this history has been able to dissimulate or forbid, making itself into a history by means of this somewhere motivated repression.[2]

In practice, the deconstruction of these oppositions involves a biphasic movement Derrida calls "double writing" or "double science." The first phase initiates an overturning of the hierarchy. A certain reading of Derrida, which focuses only on this phase, finds him valorizing those poles traditionally subordinated by the history of philosophy. Derrida's text is thus read as privileging, for example, writing over speech, signifier over signified, or the figurative over the literal. Such a reading appears overly simplistic; Derrida, like Heidegger before him, realizes that in overturning a metaphysical hierarchy, care must be taken to avoid reappropriating the same hierarchical structure.[3] The hierarchical oppositional structure itself is metaphysical; to remain within the binary logic of metaphysical thinking is to reestablish and confirm the closed field of these oppositions.

To rest at the view of deconstruction as a simple inversion of these classical philosophical oppositions omits the second phase of deconstruction's "double writing": "we must also mark the interval between inversion, which brings low what was high, and the irruptive emergence of a new 'concept,' a concept that can no longer be, and never could be, included in the previous regime."[4] These new "concepts" are the Derridean "undecidables" (e.g., "differance," "trace," "*pharmakon*," "supplement," "spacing," "hymen,"): marks that in one way or another resist the formal structure imposed by the binary logic of philosophical opposition. Much of Derrida's early work involves elucidating the play of these undecidables: the play of the trace, which is both present and absent; the play of the *pharmakon*, which is both poison and cure; the play of the supplement, which is both surplus and lack.

When marking the interval between philosophy's classical hierarchical oppositions and the undecidables, Derrida marks the limits of the binary logic that has guided the history of metaphysics. In so doing, he displays another sort of logic which he calls the "logic of supplementarity."[5] This "other" logic has been repressed and excluded by the history of philosophy. Whereas binary logic operates within the limits of an "either . . . or . . .," Derrida's undecidable logic of supplementarity is a logic of "both . . . and . . ." that resists and disorganizes classical binary thinking. The fundamental laws of binary logic are the principles of identity (A = A) and noncontradiction (not [A and not-A]). The movement of the undecidables exhibits a different principle: *both* A *and* not-A. The *pharmakon*, for example, "acts as both remedy and poison . . . . [It] can be – alternatively or simultaneously – beneficent or maleficent."[6] "*Pharmakon*" plays between the poles of remedy and poison, and to render *pharmakon* as either "remedy" or "poison," as the binary thinking of the history of metaphysics is prone to do, cancels out the resources of signification reserved in that sign. Thus, when Socrates drinks the *pharmakon* at the conclusion of the *Phaedo*, the metaphysical tradition is quick to translate this *pharmakon* as "poison." In so doing, the tradition must repress Socrates's final speech in the *Apology*, where he claims we have reason to hope that death is a good which a virtuous man need not fear, while it forces us to interpret as *ironic* his last words concerning the debt his death will incur with Asclepius. This overdetermination of the meaning of *pharmakon* (= poison) is, for Derrida, paradigmatic, and his focus on the movement of the *pharmakon* exposes the limits of metaphysical thinking: because *pharmakon* is *both* remedy *and* poison, both a remedial poison and a poisonous remedy, its movement cannot be thought in the binary fashion that characterizes the metaphysical tradition. Derrida refuses to determine a univocal meaning for the *pharmakon* or the other undecidables; instead he emphasizes the tension and oscillating play which guides their use. His point, I must stress, is not to reify these terms nor to privilege them as foundational. Rather, he marks these terms in a way which inscribes his writing in the tradition of critical philosophy called for by Kant,[7] emphasizing the "determinate and necessary limits" of this binary logic while indicating "its ignorance in regard to all questions of a certain kind."[8]

Although Derrida does not follow Kant's move toward a transcendental philosophy, the structural similarities concerning their projects of philosophical *critique* should not be overlooked. Also in Kant there is a rejection of binary thinking. When discussing the antinomies of pure reason, Kant locates a moment of undecidability in the choice between the dogmatic and sceptical solutions to the antinomies:

> [S]ince the arguments on both sides are equally clear, it is *impossible to decide between them*. . . . There can therefore be no way of settling it once and for all and to the satisfaction of both sides, save by their becoming convinced that the very fact of their being able so admirably to refute one another is evidence that they are really quarrelling about nothing.[9]

It was, according to Kant, the task of critical philosophy to convince the two sides that it is not their solutions which are flawed; rather, the error lies in the nature of the questions which elicit their respective conclusions. The "critical solution" will thus "not consider the question objectively," but it will proceed "in relation to the foundation of the knowledge upon which the question is based."[10]

When Derrida resorts to the "logic of paleonymy," to the provisional and strategic *conservation* of the old names of the Western philosophical tradition, his aim is not far removed from this goal of Kantian critique. In other words, by using the tradition against itself, Derrida seeks both to expose the foundational choices of the philosophical tradition and to bring into view that which the tradition has repressed, excluded, or, in Derridean terminology, marginalized. Deconstruction cannot, he writes,

> proceed immediately to a neutralization: it must, by means of a double gesture, a double science, a double writing, practice an *overturning* of the classical opposition *and* a general *displacement* of the system. It is only on this condition that deconstruction will provide itself the means with which to *intervene* in the field of oppositions that it criticizes. . . .[11]

Derrida maintains both that no complete escape from the closure of metaphysics is possible and that philosophy itself provides the condition for the possibility of its own deconstruction.[12] The strategy of marginal, double writing thus permits the deconstructionist critique to circumvent the border between what is within the philosophical tradition and what is external to that tradition. By seizing concepts within the tradition and marking a movement of these concepts that the tradition both authorizes and excludes, deconstruction succeeds in inhabiting the closed field of metaphysics's binary oppositions without at the same time confirming that field. In so doing, it displays those choices, neither made explicit nor explicitly made, by means of which the tradition constitutes itself *as* a tradition.

An example may be helpful here, and I return to the use Derrida makes of the *pharmakon*, this time in terms of the remark in the *Phaedrus* that writing is a *pharmakon* (229d, 274e–275a). Again the polysemy of *pharmakon* (writing as a remedy for the weakness of memory and as a poison which infects the purity of speech) is overdetermined, as the tradition affirms Socrates' condemnation of writing as inferior to and derivative upon speech. Derrida highlights this overdetermination to show how the privileging of the spoken word over the written word follows from the determination of metaphysics as the metaphysics of presence. The immediate presence of meaning in the spoken word is the ideal of Western metaphysics, which must then devalue the written word as a secondary, derivative *re*-presentation of speech. By engaging in the strategy of double writing, Derrida first uses the *pharmakon* to question the privileging of speech over writing, and then proceeds to question the assumptions of the metaphysics of presence which make the binary opposition of speech/writing possible. In other words, after he shows that the primacy of speech over writing is itself grounded on the oppositions of presence over absence and immediacy over representation, he can demonstrate that the spoken word, which is itself a phonic signifier of a mental signified, is no more immediate a presentation of meaning than the written word. This demonstration makes possible his substitution of the notion of the "trace," always differing and deferring, for the concept of the sign, and it is a typical example of Derrida's strategy of using the binary concepts of the metaphysical tradition in order to intervene in and deconstruct that tradition.

The method of critique utilized both by Kant and Derrida in their resistance to traditional metaphysical thinking appears also in the writings of Nietzsche. It takes the form in Nietzsche's text, as in Derrida's, of a rejection of the binary logic of classical philosophy. The "typical prejudice" and "fundamental faith" that gives away the metaphysicians of all ages, he writes, "is *the faith in opposite values*."[13] Throughout his critique of morality, philosophy, and religion, Nietzsche attempts to deconstruct such oppositional hierarchies as good/evil, truth/error, being/becoming. *Genealogy* is the name Nietzsche gives to his method of critical analysis, and it will be instructive to spend a few moments examining this analytic method.

As a method of analysis, genealogy is by no means limited to the genealogy of morality and the ascetic ideal found in his 1886 text entitled *On the Genealogy of Morals*. Instead, a careful reading of Nietzsche's writing reveals numerous examples of genealogical analysis in his examination of various phenomena. In a few pages of *The Gay Science*, for instance, we find Nietzsche inquiring into the origins of morality, scholars, religion, consciousness, and knowledge,[14] and as early as the notes for *We Philologists* (1875), he wrote of the examination of antiquity as a search for the origins of "contemporary wrong-headedness."[15]

In these genealogical inquiries into the origins of contemporary values and beliefs, Nietzsche is by no means seeking an origin to serve as the foundation for these values and beliefs.[16] In fact, he explicitly distinguishes his genealogical method from the misguided glorification of origins that he finds exhibited in the observations of historians.[17] He regards this glorification of origins as a "metaphysical after-shoot" [*metaphysische Nachtrieb*] of the historical contemplation that "makes us imagine that *in the beginning* of things lies all that is most valuable and essential."[18] This quest for the origin as the true locus of significance and value is quite different from Nietzsche's genealogical inquiry. In a section from *Daybreak* entitled "Order of Rank," Nietzsche distinguishes four types of thinkers and, in so doing, he makes clear the difference in value between the historical *quest* for the origin as a path to salvation and the genealogical *questioning* of the origin as a moment of critique:

> There are, first of all, superficial thinkers [*oberflächliche Denker*]; secondly, deep thinkers [*tiefe Denker*] – those who go down into the depths of a thing; thirdly, thorough thinkers [*gründliche Denker*], who thoroughly explore the grounds of a thing – which is worth very much more than merely going down into its depths! – finally, those who stick their heads into the swamp: which ought not to be a sign either of depth or thoroughness! They are the dear departed underground [*Untergründlichen*].[19]

These "underground thinkers" are not genealogists, for in their search for "the origin of things, they always believed they would discover something of incalculable significance [*Bedeutung*] for all later action and judgment, . . . they always *presupposed*, indeed, that the *salvation* of man must depend on *insight into the origin* of things."[20]

What the foundational inquiry into origins fails to recognize is what Nietzsche sometimes refers to as the "psychological" aspect of genealogy. This is to say, genealogical analysis seeks not only the origins of modern convictions but also the reasons and justifications which the proponents of these convictions have given in asserting their hegemony. For example, regarding the errors of metaphysics, Nietzsche remarks that mere recognition of these errors *as* errors is not sufficient for overcoming them. In addition, a "*retrogressive movement* [*rückläufige Bewegung*] is necessary: [one] must comprehend the historical as well as the psychological justification in such representations . . . ."[21] The same requirement holds for epistemological errors: "What I noticed was rather that no epistemological skepticism or dogmatism had ever risen free from ulterior motives – that it has a value of the second rank as soon as one has considered *what* it was that *compelled* the adoption of this position."[22] In pursuing a genealogical inquiry into the history of origins, Nietzsche produces something quite different from a simple history of particular systems of belief. Instead, what is discovered is "the *hidden* history of philosophy, the psychology of its great names,"[23] that is, the hidden *values for life* at work behind the explicit affirmation of certain values as ideal. Nietzsche's call for *psycho-genealogical* inquiry is thus a call to reflect upon what was ultimately willed in the positing of certain values as valuable. It is in this sense that psychology will be the "queen of the sciences [and] path to the fundamental problems."[24] Psychology, if it is to discern the worth of these originary values, must "descend into the depths" and investigate the morphology and development of the will to power as manifested in those values which have been posited. In this way, "*psychological genesis*" will discover what these ideals "genuinely mean,"[25] not in the epistemological sense of uncovering the true referent or the accurate description of a state of affairs, but rather in the psycho-genealogical sense of deciphering the significance these ideals hold as a symptom of the health or disease of the will to power that has posited them *as ideal*.

This view of psychology makes clear that the aim of the genealogical search for origins is not the discernment of truth but the deciphering of value. Genealogy, thus, functions in the Nietzschean text primarily as a method of critique which uncovers the significance of the affirmation of certain values within social praxis rather than as a tool for the acquisition of knowledge or the discovery of true descriptions regarding states of affairs. In other words, genealogical inquiry involves a critical rereading and reinterpretation of the history of various phenomena from the perspective of the values inscribed *at their origin* in an attempt to trace the evolution of the reinscription of these values through the course of their historical development. My recourse here to the metaphors of reading and inscription are carefully chosen, but the allusion in this case is not so much to Derridean deconstruction as to Nietzschean genealogy itself. In the preface to *On the Genealogy of Morals*, Nietzsche writes that the color gray is vital for a genealogist of morals: "*gray*, that is, what is documented, what can actually be confirmed and has actually existed, in short the entire long hieroglyphic record, so hard to decipher, of the moral past of mankind."[26] In the context of a discussion of genealogy, "gray" is a metaphor serving a twofold function. First, it alludes to language and brings to bear Nietzsche's critique of language as an imperfect tool for the acquisition of knowledge. Given the metaphorical and anthropomorphic origin of concepts, the genealogist must be attentive to the implicit values which have been fixed within (linguistic) concepts.[27] Rather than accepting these concepts as a gift from tradition, Nietzsche advises that "what is needed above all is an absolute skepticism toward all inherited concepts."[28] In addition to the allusion to language, "gray" implicates the process of interpretation. What is gray is neither black nor white, neither true nor false; gray is *in between* and it is within the realm of the gray that the interpretive play of values will unfold.

Returning now to the question of truth, it is clear that Truth is not the *telos* of genealogical inquiry. The "will to truth" is itself to be "investigated psychologically."[29] In part, the task of Nietzsche's *Genealogy of Morals* was to undertake this investigation: "the value of truth must for once be experimentally *called into question*."[30] The *Genealogy of Morals* emerges as an example of the psychological investigation called for in *The Will to Power* and *Beyond Good and Evil*:[31] it descends into the depths of morality and the ascetic ideal to genealogically uncover the morphology of decadent will to power that manifests itself there as the "will to truth." Because the assessment of the *value* of the will to power, as "the force that forms, simplifies, shapes, invents," is more significant for genealogical inquiry than ascertaining the "truth" of what is formed, simplified, etc.,[32] Nietzsche's *Genealogy of Morals* thus concerns itself with the life-negating origins and consequences of the ascetic ideal, its *Woher* and *Wohin*, rather than with an inquiry into the "truth" of that ideal.

In descending to the psychological depths of morality and the ascetic ideal, the *Genealogy of Morals* exhibits the critical function of all genealogical inquiry. As the work of "subterranean" men, genealogy both mines and undermines.[33] In seeking the origins of contemporary cultural convictions and assessing the value for life of those convictions, Nietzsche resorts again and again to genealogical analysis as a critical tool. Returning now to the double movement of Derridean deconstruction, we can locate instances of just such a movement in Nietzsche's genealogical critique. For example, regarding the genealogy of the will to truth, Nietzsche overturns the traditional hierarchy of truth over falsity. Investigating the origin of the positive valuation of truth, Nietzsche finds that it is simply a moral prejudice affirming truth over error.[34] To this, he suggests that error might be *more* valuable than truth, that error might be a necessary condition of life. His analysis does not stop here, however, as Heidegger assumed when he accused Nietzsche of "completing" the history of metaphysics through a "mere inversion" of Platonism. In offering the doctrine of perspectivism, Nietzsche in effect displaces the truth/falsity opposition altogether. That is to say, the question is no longer whether a perspective is "true" or "false," as Nietzsche makes explicit when he writes, for example, in the epilogue to *The Case of Wagner*, that "the concepts 'true' and 'untrue' have . . . no meaning in optics." The sole question that interests the genealogist is whether or not a perspective enhances life.

In a similar fashion, in the famous chapter of *Twilight of the Idols* where Nietzsche traces the history of the belief in the "true world," he moves quickly from overturning the true/apparent world hierarchy to deconstructing the oppositional structure itself:

> The true world we have abolished: what world then remains? The apparent one perhaps? . . . But no! *with the true world we also abolished the apparent one*![35]

We have abolished the apparent world because it has come to be defined as "apparent" only in terms of its opposition to the "true" world. Without the "true world" to serve as a standard, the designation as "apparent" is rendered meaningless. That is to say, the traditional (de)valuation of "appearance" is wholly dependent on its being the negation of that which the tradition has affirmed as "truth." In deciphering one pole of the binary opposition (the "true world") as an illusion, the opposition itself loses its critical force.

Nietzsche, like Derrida, discovers a certain faith in binary thinking at the center of philosophical discourse. Whereas Derrida highlights the oscillation between undecidable opposites, Nietzsche shows the way these opposites merge into one another. That is to say, he genealogically uncovers the will to power whose imposition of a certain value gives rise to the two poles of that opposition. And in bringing to light this original imposition of value, genealogy obviates the force the opposition is believed to have. The clearest example of this strategy is his deconstruction of the good/evil opposition. Nietzsche moves *beyond* good and evil precisely by showing that both "good" and "evil" owe their meanings to a certain type of will to power – the slavish, reactive will to power of herd morality. To simply invert the values of slave morality, making "good" what the slave judges to be "evil," is no less reactive than the original imposition of value by the slave, who reactively judges all that is different from himself to be "evil" and defines the good in reactionary opposition to what is other than himself. A reading of Nietzsche as an "immoralist" or "nihilist" remains at this level of mere inversion. But a reading of Nietzsche as the "transvaluer of values" locates a second movement in the Nietzschean critique of morality. This second movement flows from the *active* imposition of new values arising from a healthy will to power that has displaced the hierarchy of good/evil altogether. In rejecting the binary structure of moral evaluation, Nietzsche's transvaluation calls forth a playful experimentation with values and multiplication of perspectives that he labels "active interpretation."[36] The affirmation of perspectival multiplicity emerges as the life-enhancing alternative for those with a will to power sufficient to go beyond the reactive decadence of binary morality.

A further similarity between Nietzsche's and Derrida's strategies concerns the relation between these binary oppositions and language. Regarding the origin of both our moral and epistemological values, Nietzsche writes:

> *language*, here as elsewhere, will not get over its awkwardness and will continue to talk of opposites where there are only degrees and many subtleties of gradation.[37]

For this reason, as Nietzsche puts it, "we really ought to free ourselves from the seduction of words."[38] The basic presuppositions of the metaphysics of language involve us in a "rude fetishism" that tends to dichotomize the world into truths and appearances, causes and effects, subjects and objects:

> The separation of the 'deed' from the 'doer,' of the event from someone who produces events, of the process from a something that is not process but enduring, substance, thing, body, soul, etc. – the attempt to comprehend an event as a sort of shifting and place-changing on the part of a 'being,' of something constant: this ancient mythology established

> the belief in 'cause and effect' after it had found a firm form in the functions of language and grammar.[39]

Because our language has seduced us to a faith in all sorts of metaphysical presuppositions, Nietzsche calls for a deconstruction of our grammatical habits. We must not forget that language is a "mere semiotic," a simplified, falsified, man-made sign system, and to this "semiotic" we must bring the critical tools of genealogy. That is to say, we must decipher linguistic concepts as a symptom of the forces that have achieved mastery by means of these "grammatical blunders." For this reason, an essential component in the transvaluation of values will be an extended critique of the philosophical articles of faith derived from our linguistic situation.

As such, overcoming the metaphysical presuppositions of language is intimately linked with another of Nietzsche's requirements for the project of transvaluation: the death of God.

> Indeed, what forces us at all to suppose that there is an essential opposition of 'true' and 'false?' Is it not sufficient to assume degrees of apparentness and, as it were, lighter and darker shadows and shades of appearance – different *valeurs* to use the language of painters? Why couldn't the world *that concerns us* – be a fiction? And if somebody asked, "but to a fiction there surely belongs an author?" – couldn't one simply answer: *why*? Doesn't this 'belongs' perhaps belong to the fiction too? Is it not permitted to be a bit ironical about the subject no less than the predicate and object? Shouldn't philosophers be permitted to rise above faith in grammar?[40]

God, the ultimate foundation of those values that will be revalued, is himself the product of a grammatical habit: God is the doer added to the deed of the world; he is the great author to whom philosophers faithfully attribute responsibility for the creation of that cosmological text we call "world." And as long as we continue to believe in grammar, in the metaphysical and epistemological presuppositions concealed within language, we will continue to believe in God.[41] The death of God and deconstruction of divine authority are prerequisites for the overman's transvaluation of all values. So, too, faith in the authority of language must be suspended if a transvaluation is to be possible.

It is important to note that Nietzsche, in resorting to the language of life-affirmation and life-negation or healthy and decadent will to power, appears himself to be offering another privileged binary opposition. I suggest, however, that this appearance is because Nietzsche remains, to some extent, caught in the metaphysical snares of grammar and the oppositional structures inherent in language. His analysis, however, suggests a means of avoiding these binary structures; that is, an interpretation of healthy and decadent will to power in a non-oppositional sense is possible in terms of viewing "health versus disease" or "affirmation versus negation" as two poles of a single continuum which is will to power. Such an interpretation does not posit two mutually exclusive alternatives which call for some choice, as is the case with the classical binary oppositions. Instead, the affirmation and negation of life are the normative limits of an open-ended continuum of will to power which admits only of "degrees of gradation." This continuum is appraised in terms of the degree to which an *active* imposition of creative force is manifested. Nietzsche indicates such an interpretation when he speaks of the will to power as the procreative force which *is* life. This will to power can be increased or decreased, but no binary opposition is involved – only will to power.[42]

Within Nietzsche's critique of divine and linguistic authority, an important strand in the critical project of Michel Foucault is found. That is, Foucault inscribes his early project of a critique of philosophical subjectivity within the space opened by Nietzsche's thinking on the relations between the subject, power, authority, and language. The modern *episteme* privileges the human subject as the master of language and discursive authority; therefore, Foucault finds a central question, first raised by Nietzsche, confronting modernity: "Who is speaking?"[43] Foucault raises this question on two occasions and his answer picks up a thread already woven into the Nietzschean text. It appears first in *The Order of Things* in the context of Foucault's crediting Nietzsche for again displaying language as "an enigmatic multiplicity that must be mastered." Foucault writes:

> For Nietzsche, it was not a matter of knowing what good and evil were in themselves, but of who was being designated, or rather *who was speaking* when one said *Agathos* to designate oneself or *Deilos* to designate others. For it is there, in the *holder* of the discourse and, more profoundly still, in the *possessor* of the word, that language is gathered together in its entirety.[44]

An outline of Foucault's response to this Nietzschean question of the subject of discourse is previewed in the following remark from Nietzsche's *Nachlass*:

> We see: an authority speaks – who speaks? – one may forgive human pride if it sought to make this authority as high as possible in order to feel as little humiliated as possible under it. Therefore – God speaks!

> One needed God as an unconditional sanction, with no court of appeal, as a 'categorical imperator' – or, if one believed in the authority of reason, one needed a metaphysic of unity, by virtue of which this was logical.
>
> Now suppose that belief in God has vanished: the question presents itself anew: 'who speaks?' – my answer, taken not from metaphysics but from animal physiology: *the herd instinct speaks*. It wants to be master: hence its '*thou shalt*!' – it will allow value to the individual only from the point of view of the whole, for the sake of the whole, it hates those who detach themselves – it turns the hatred of all individuals against them.[45]

We find in Nietzsche's remark that *authority* speaks, first the authority of God and then the authority of the herd. Nietzsche's overman, who heralds the demise of God and the last/herd man, will be subject to no authority and, inasmuch as both divine and human subjectivity function within a network of relations of power, authority and submission, the overman will not be a subject at all.

Foucault picks up this link between the subject and subjection when, in a late essay, he writes: "It is a form of power which makes individuals subjects. There are two meanings of the word *subject*: subject to someone else by control and dependence, and tied to his own identity by a conscience or self-knowledge. Both meanings suggest a form of power which subjugates and makes subject to."[46] The subject appears to Foucault as an ideological product, a functional principle of discourse rather than its privileged origin. This is not to say that the subject is entirely abandoned, but that its relations to and with authority must be deconstructed. It is a matter of depriving the subject of its role as originator and analyzing the subject as a variable and complex function of discourse and power:

> We should suspend the typical questions: how does a free subject penetrate the density of things and endow them with meaning; how does it accomplish its design by animating the rules of discourse from within? Rather, we should ask: under what conditions and through what forms can an entity like the subject appear in the order of discourse; what position does it occupy; what functions does it exhibit; and what rules does it follow in each type of discourse?[47]

Foucault here returns to a suggestion he made five years earlier at the Royaumont Colloquium on Nietzsche. In his concluding remarks on the obligation of interpretation to interpret itself to infinity, he notes that

> interpretation will be henceforth always interpretation by the 'who?'; one does not interpret what there is in the signified, but one fundamentally interprets: *who* has posed the interpretation. The principle of interpretation is nothing other than the interpreter, and this is perhaps the meaning that Nietzsche gave to the word 'psychology.'[48]

To ask "*Who* interprets?" or "*Who* speaks?" is not to be answered with the name of a subject, as Foucault makes clear at the conclusion of his essay "What is an Author?" when he claims that the question "Who is speaking?" must give way to the question "What difference does it make who is speaking?" Rather, the question "Who?" is inscribed within "psychology," understood by Nietzsche in *Beyond Good and Evil* as "morphology and *the doctrine of the development of the will to power*."[49] It is the will to power that speaks and interprets, not a "subject," and the question "Who?" calls for a genealogical inquiry into the type of force that manifests itself in speech or interpretation. The subject, according to Nietzsche, is itself an interpretation, a created entity, a "simplification with the object of defining the force which posits, invents, thinks."[50] Inasmuch as something is defined to make it more *manageable*, Nietzsche, like Foucault, recognizes the oppressive use that can be made of the principle of subjectivity as a principle of domination. As Nietzsche makes clear, for example in his tracing the genealogy of "free will" to the "hangman's metaphysics" of Christianity, individuality and subjectivity can and have been used for the purposes of subjection to the will or law or authority of another. The overman will not be, strictly speaking, a subject at all. He will be a conglomeration of forces, an amalgam of will to power. He will not exercise authority, nor will he be appealed to as an authority.[51]

In raising the question of authority, Nietzsche opens a passageway toward the space in which both his, Foucault's, and Derrida's critiques will play. While Foucault is primarily interested in the sociopolitical domination that has accompanied the classical and modern concepts of the subject, Derrida has addressed "literary" restrictions which have followed the privileging of meaning as a transcendental signified. Although these differences between their projects are significant, they have a common ground in the critique of authority. And insofar as these critiques of socio-political and literary authority can be traced back to their respective readings of Nietzsche, I suggest that the difference between them is best viewed in terms of a difference in regional application rather than a fundamental distinction in philosophical orientation. That is, a central issue in the work of Foucault and Derrida is, as it was for Nietzsche, the question of authority and its legitimation. For Nietzsche, this question of authority is posed in terms of moral authority:

> [I]n the presence of morality, as in the face of any authority, one is not *allowed* to think, far less to express an opinion: here one has to *obey*! As long as the world has existed no authority has yet been willing to let itself become the object of critique . . .[52]

Because authority demands obedience, a philosophy of the future will necessitate a critique of authority. If values are to be transvalued, obedience to the previous values must be undermined. The whole Nietzschean project of genealogy is directed toward deconstructing the foundations of the dominant values of modernity, which is to say that Nietzsche's project of a transvaluation of values presupposes a delegitimation of the existing (moral) authority.

Derrida, too, is engaged in a project of delegitimizing authority, whether in the form of the author's domination of the text[53] or the authority of the tradition's reading of the history of philosophy. Derrida characterizes this project of delegitimation as a deconstruction of the authority of meaning and he describes his early texts (*Speech and Phenomena, Writing and Difference, Of Grammatology*) in these terms, as an attempt "to systematize a deconstructive critique precisely against the authority of meaning, as the *transcendental signified* or as *telos*, . . ."[54]

The deconstruction of the authority of meaning and the supplementing of binary logic with undecidability emerge as complementary motifs in Derrida's reading of Nietzsche. In *Spurs*, Nietzsche is cited for inaugurating the "epochal regime of quotation marks which is to be enforced for every concept belonging to the system of philosophical decidability."[55] This regime, which for Derrida disqualifies the hermeneutic project of deciphering the true sense of the text, frees reading from the categories of meaning, truth, being, and presence. It also frees reading from the authority of the author and, in so doing, it opens the text to an infinite play of interpretation. In *Spurs*, Derrida displays this epochal regime in his discussion of the forgotten umbrella. Set between quotation marks in one of Nietzsche's unpublished notebooks, "I have forgotten my umbrella" stands without *arche* or *telos*, intention or context. What is perhaps most interesting about Derrida's play with this "text" is his remark (near the end of *Spurs*): "the hypothesis that the totality of Nietzsche's text, in some monstrous way, might well be of the type 'I have forgotten my umbrella' cannot be denied."[56] This hypothesis is precisely what attracts Derrida to Nietzsche's text. As a master of masks and dissimulation, we can never be certain of the identity of the author of "Nietzsche's" aphorisms. Nietzsche can lie, can refuse to mean what he writes. These are always possibilities, and Derrida uses Nietzsche's "umbrella" to pierce the assured horizon of the hermeneutic quest for deciphering the authoritative, decidable meaning, as Nietzsche attempted to perforate the projects of all the ontotheological *Schleier-machers*.[57]

In appealing to Nietzsche and the free play of interpretive forces, Derrida indicates a means of escape from the closure of authority by adopting a style of writing that affirms multiplicity, free play, and difference rather than the traditional logocentric values of subjectivity, univocity, autonomy, and self-identity. The similarity of style in their respective critiques betokens a basic similarity in their opposition to authority. Nietzsche opposes the "tyranny of the true,"[58] and he expresses concern that his writings take the appearance of proclamations of truth.[59] Likewise, Derrida is sensitive to the tendency of his undecidables to be privileged and reified into the foundations of a new philosophical system. For this reason, he moves from one to another, utilizing each for a particular, *strategic* purpose and then leaving them behind. These undecidables have the power to subvert, but they lack the power to command and they can exercise no authority.[60]

In light of Derrida's increasingly overt attention to the workings of institutional authority, his earlier attempts at deconstruction take on a new significance. To those who recognize "politics" only by the most familiar signs, Derrida's play with Rousseau or Plato seems harmless enough. But taken in terms of a strategy that is still unfolding, they emerge as stages in the deconstruction of authority itself, be it the authority of the author, of the history of philosophy, of the institutions governing academic discourse, or of social and political institutions. Derrida's deconstruction of the authority of meaning has made it very difficult for the philosopher or literary critic to proceed with business as usual. If we follow the movement of this deconstructive critique, will the legitimation of social and political authority appear any more secure than the self-authorizing discourses of Freud, Plato, Heidegger, or Rousseau have appeared under Derrida's critical gaze? This question remains to be answered. I have only suggested that Derrida's critical strategy is neither as unprecedented and eccentric as some believe, nor as "harmless" as believed by others.

Notes

1. Gilles Deleuze, *Nietzsche and Philosophy*, trans. Hugh Tomlinson (New York: Columbia University Press, 1983), p. 106.

2. Jacques Derrida, *Positions*, trans. Alan Bass (Chicago: University of Chicago Press, 1981), p. 6.

3. See, for example, Heidegger's discussion of Nietzsche's inversion of Platonism in *Nietzsche. Vol. One. The Will to Power as Art*, trans. David F. Krell (San Francisco, CA: Harper and Row, Publishers, Inc., 1978), pp. 200–20.

4. Derrida, *Positions*, p. 42; see also *Margins of Philosophy*, trans. Alan Bass (Chicago: University of Chicago Press, 1982), p. 329.

5. Cf. Jacques Derrida, *Of Grammatology*, trans. Gayatri C. Spivak (Baltimore, MD: Johns Hopkins University Press, 1974), pp. 179, 215.

6. Jacques Derrida, *Dissemination*, trans. Barbara Johnson (Chicago: University of Chicago Press, 1981), p. 70.

7. In what follows, I do not mean to imply that Kant is a deconstructionist or that Derrida is a Kantian. I only want to bring out a similarity between one aspect of Kant's project of "critical philosophy" and Derrida's strategy of deconstruction. Both Kant and Derrida endeavor to show the *limits* of a certain type of philosophical discourse. In so doing, they each disclose an area of inquiry about which the traditional discourse of philosophy is silent. I would not want to claim that the "areas" disclosed in Kant and Derrida's texts are the same, nor would I claim that their respective projects are limited only to this disclosure. Nevertheless, the structural similarities between their respective critiques should not pass unnoticed.

8. Immanuel Kant, *Critique of Pure Reason*, trans. Norman Kemp Smith (New York: St. Martin's Press, 1965), A 761, B 789.

9. *Ibid.*, A 502, B 530. (Emphasis added.)

10. *Ibid.*, A 484, B 512.

11. Jacques Derrida, *Margins*, p. 329.

12. See, for example, Jacques Derrida, *The Archeology of the Frivolous*, trans. John P. Leavey, Jr. (Pittsburgh, PA: Duquesne University Press, 1980), p. 132: "Philosophy deviates from itself and gives rise to the blows that will strike it nonetheless from the outside."

13. Friedrich Nietzsche, *Beyond Good and Evil*, sect. 2. While I have made

use of all existing translations of Nietzsche's texts, the responsibility for the translations appearing here is my own.

14. See Friedrich Nietzsche, *The Gay Science*, sects. 345–55.

15. See Friedrich Nietzsche, *Werke. Kritische Gesamtausgabe*, ed. G. Colli and M. Montinari (Berlin: Walter de Gruyter, 1967ff), Abt. IV, Bd. 1:3[52].

16. Michel Foucault develops this point in an essay entitled "Nietzsche, Genealogy, History" in *Language, Counter-Memory, Practice*, trans. Donald F. Bouchard and Sherry Simon (Ithaca, NY: Cornell University Press, 1977), pp. 139–64. In this essay, which is in part directed toward disclosing a conception of "*wirkliche Historie*" in Nietzsche's genealogy, Foucault makes some important points regarding the different sorts of origins (*e.g.*, *Ursprung* [origin], *Herkunft* [descent], *Entstehung* [emergence], *Geburt* [birth], *Anfang* [beginning], *Abkunft* [lineage]) that Nietzsche investigates and the different genealogical practices resulting from these different "origins." What is perhaps most interesting in this essay are the parallels that emerge between his analysis of Nietzsche's genealogy and Foucault's own method of archaeology (*logos* of the *arche*). Foucault's archaeological method, like Nietzsche's genealogical method, engages in a critical rereading of history, but from the perspective of the discursive rules and structures that were sanctioned at the origin rather than the Nietzschean perspective of the life-affirming or life-negating instincts of those who did the original sanctioning. See, in this regard, Foucault's discussion of archaeology in *The Archaeology of Knowledge*, trans. Alan M. Sheridan-Smith (New York: Harper and Row, 1972), especially pp. 131–48. For an interesting discussion of the use of both genealogy and archaeology in Foucault, see Hubert L. Dreyfus and Paul Rabinow, *Michel Foucault: Beyond Structuralism and Hermeneutics* (Chicago: University of Chicago Press, 1982), pp. 104–25.

17. See, for example, Friedrich Nietzsche, *Twilight of the Idols*, "Maxims and Arrows" sect. 23.

18. Friedrich Nietzsche, *The Wanderer and His Shadow*, sect. 3.

19. Friedrich Nietzsche, *Daybreak*, sect. 446.

20. *Ibid.*, section 44.

21. Friedrich Nietzsche, *Human, All-too-Human*, sect. 20.

22. Friedrich Nietzsche, *The Will to Power*, sect. 410.

23. Friedrich Nietzsche, *Ecce Homo*, preface 3.

24. Friedrich Nietzsche, *Beyond Good and Evil*, sect. 23.

25. Friedrich Nietzsche, *Kritische Gesamtausgabe*, Abt. VIII, Bd. 1:7[35].

26. Friedrich Nietzsche, *On the Genealogy of Morals*, preface 7.

27. I have discussed Nietzsche's critique of language elsewhere. See "Language, Metaphor, Rhetoric: Nietzsche's Deconstruction of Epistemology," *The Journal of the History of Philosophy*, vol. xxiii, no. 3 (July, 1985), pp. 371–95.

28. Friedrich Nietzsche, *The Will to Power*, sect. 409.

29. Friedrich Nietzsche, *The Will to Power*, sect. 583C.

30. Friedrich Nietzsche, *On the Genealogy of Morals* III 24; see also preface 6.

31. See Friedrich Nietzsche, *The Will to Power*, sect. 583C and *Beyond Good and Evil*, sect. 23.

32. See Friedrich Nietzsche, *The Will to Power*, sects. 602, 605.

33. See Friedrich Nietzsche, *Daybreak*, preface 1.

34. Friedrich Nietzsche, *Beyond Good and Evil*, sect. 34.

35. Friedrich Nietzsche, *Twilight of the Idols*, "How the 'True World' Finally Became a Fable."

36. See Friedrich Nietzsche, *The Will to Power*, sects. 600, 604, 605. Derrida has also used the term "active interpretation" to distinguish deconstructionist reading from the textual doubling of commentary. See *Of Grammatology*, pp. 157–64.

37. Friedrich Nietzsche, *Beyond Good and Evil*, sect. 24.

38. *Ibid.*, sect. 16.

39. Friedrich Nietzsche, *The Will to Power* sect. 631.

40. Friedrich Nietzsche, *Beyond Good and Evil*, sect. 34.

41. Cf. Friedrich Nietzsche, *Twilight of the Idols*, "'Reason in Philosophy'" sect. 5: "I fear we are not getting rid of God because we still believe in grammar."

42. This strategy of recasting the choice between binary opposites as a continuum appears in the works of many contemporary French thinkers. As Jean-François Lyotard has put it, "oppositional thinking . . . is out of step with the most vital modes of postmodern knowledge." (Jean-François Lyotard, *The Postmodern Condition*, trans. Geoff Bennington and Brian Massumi [Minneapolis: University of Minnesota Press, 1983], p. 14.) I suggest that we situate Derrida's discussion of "writing" (set between the limits of speech and "writing in the narrow sense"), Deleuze's discussion of "desire" (between the limits of repression and production), Bourdieu's discussion of "*doxa*" (between the limits of orthodoxy and heterodoxy), and Foucault's discussion of "power" (between the limits of domination and subordination) among these "most vital modes of postmodern knowledge." Each of these thinkers recasts the forced choice between binary opposites in terms of something akin to a "monistic" continuum: for Foucault, a continuum of power/knowledge; for Deleuze, of

desiring production; for Bourdieu, of *doxa* and *habitus*; and for Derrida, of writing and difference. I think Nietzsche was attempting something similar with his introduction of the will to power, recasting all substantialist differences in kind in terms of differences of degree of will to power. In this sense, Nietzsche emerges as an initiator of postmodern thinking, and to trace this particular genealogy back a little further, we may recall Nietzsche's own discovery of a precursor in Spinoza (Letter to Overbeck, July 31, 1881) and his affinity for the thought of Heraclitus.

43. Foucault addresses this question in *The Order of Things* (New York: Random House, 1973), p. 305; see also the conclusion of "What is an Author?" in *Language, Counter-Memory, Practice*, pp. 137–38.

44. Michel Foucault, *The Order of Things*, p. 305.

45. Friedrich Nietzsche, *The Will to Power*, sect. 275.

46. Michel Foucault, "Why Study Power: The Question of the Subject" in Dreyfus and Rabinow, *Michel Foucault: Beyond Structuralism and Hermeneutics*, p. 212.

47. Michel Foucault, "What is an Author?" p. 137–38.

48. Michel Foucault, "Nietzsche, Freud, Marx" in *Nietzsche: Cahiers du Royaumont*, Philosophie No. VI (Paris: Éditions de Minuit, 1967), pp. 191–92.

49. Friedrich Nietzsche, *Beyond Good and Evil*, sect. 23.

50. Friedrich Nietzsche, *The Will to Power*, sect. 556.

51. For a related discussion of the constitution of the subject, see Foucault's comments on the "genealogy of the modern 'soul'" in *Discipline and Punish*, trans. Alan Sheridan (New York: Random House, 1979), pp. 29–30. I should add before leaving Foucault's critique of subjectivity that in his later work, Foucault adopted a different strategy regarding the critique of the subject as he moved away from the provocative rhetoric of the "end of man" characteristic of his earlier discussion of subjectivity (see especially *The Order of Things*, chs. 9 and 10). Perhaps recognizing that he had become too caught up in the structuralist project of the "death of the subject," Foucault, in a 1981 essay, characterized the objective of his work of the last twenty years as an attempt "to create a history of the different modes by which, in our culture, human beings are made subjects" (Foucault, "Why Study Power: The Question of the Subject," p. 208). The "subject" is viewed here as a particular form of individuation, one which is a product of the power relations instituted in the modern Western state, and Foucault says of his present task that it is directed toward promoting "new forms of subjectivity through the refusal of this kind of individuality which has been imposed on us for several centuries" (Foucault, "Why Study Power: The Question of the Subject," p. 216).

52. Friedrich Nietzsche, *Daybreak*, preface 3.

53. Cf. Jacques Derrida, *The Archeology of the Frivolous*, p. 49.

54. Jacques Derrida, *Positions*, p. 49.

55. Jacques Derrida, *Spurs: Nietzsche's Styles*, trans. Barbara Harlow (Chicago: University of Chicago Press, 1979), p. 107.

56. *Ibid.*, p. 133.

57. Cf. Friedrich Nietzsche, *Ecce Homo*, "The Case of Wagner" sect. 3.

58. Friedrich Nietzsche, *Daybreak*, sect. 507.

59. See Friedrich Nietzsche, *Beyond Good and Evil*, sect. 296.

60. Cf. Jacques Derrida, *Margins*, p. 22.

16. Deconstructing, Fort/Derrida

John O'Neill

In the days when there was no writing and all texts had a single parent – due to His divinity rather than to the accidents of life – commentary involved honest work, like that of St. Joseph. Today's texts, like the rest of the world, are orphaned by their modernity. Texts no longer echo their paternity, and genre is as outmoded as family. Honored neither in their beginnings nor their ends, texts come into their own from the margins, float upon themselves, and proliferate with the least contact. Such is writing. What, then, of commentary? Upon what does it work? The text refuses to be the object of any steady craft such as commentary or illumination. Exulting in the freedom of its orphanage, writing runs away from the tutelage of commentary like a street kid fleeing from the flatfoot cop or social worker. Writing has no desire to be reflected in the father-text and is even less willing to look for its image in the mirror of commentary, however faithful.

This commentary should restrict itself to honest work and avoid any fancy of creation. It is beneath the copulation of writing and reading. The commentator's task is humbly to read and scarcely to write.* At best, a commentator reports upon the scene of writing/reading – as a dutiful voyeur, his place ensured by the order of things fulfilling its authority from behind the scene. By an order which I hereby return to its senders, in order to reassure them of the correspondence of our intentions, and in order to keep everything that here transpires as commentary within the bounds of philosophical propriety – I hereby produce my letters patent:

Codirector
SPEP Executive Committee
Department of Philosophy
Any University
Anywhere, U.S.A.

Dear Codirector:

Please accept this letter as a symposium proposal for the 1984 SPEP conference. The title of the session is "Towards an Archaeology of Deconstruction."

This session is motivated by a general dissatisfaction expressed by a number of members of SPEP regarding the way in which recent French philosophy has been received by many of the American practitioners of Continental philosophy, and the purpose of this session is to explore a number of prefigurations within what might be called mainstream Continental philosophy of the method *that has come to be called "deconstruction." The papers presented will not focus on any particular proponent of deconstruction. Instead, they will attempt to isolate certain methodolological procedures which emerge within the works of such figures as Foucault, Derrida, Deleuze, Lyotard, etc., with an eye toward disclosing the continuity between these figures and their philosophical predecessors (Nietzsche, Freud, Husserl, Heidegger, Levinas, Merleau-Ponty, Blanchot). The papers' intentions are not to usher deconstruction into what a "Rortyan" might call the "normal discourse" of Continental philosophy. Rather, the intention is to show that deconstruction, while radical, has precursors within the Continental tradition and as such, is deserving of serious consideration rather than the hostility and suspicion that it has to a large extent received thus far.*

Symposium participants will include the following persons:

Speakers:

Professor A. D. Script
Department of Philosophy
Any University
Any Town, U.S.A.

Professor I. E. Trace
Department of Philosophy
Any University
Any Town, U.S.A.

Professor C. Cry
Département de Philosophie
Any French University
Any French Town, Canada

Moderator/Commentator: *Professor John O'Neill*
Department of Sociology
Any University
Any Town, Canada

Professor John O'Neill has agreed to moderate the session and provide a summary/commentary on the three papers presented. He will isolate certain threads that run through the three individual discussions of the method of deconstruction as well as raise critical questions and/or suggestions for the three speakers regarding the intertextual connections emerging within their respective presentations and the Continental tradition. In so doing, Professor O'Neill will initiate a discussion of the pertinent issues and open the dialogue between the speakers and the audience.

I have requested that this session be considered as a symposium. The individual papers will not exceed twenty-five minutes; Professor O'Neill's comments will be limited to fifteen minutes. Given the discussions and questions which have followed past sessions addressing deconstruction in general and Derrida in particular, I believe that our session should have ample time (forty-five minutes) for comments and discussion with the audience. Inasmuch as I am unclear as to what formal distinctions, if any, exist regarding the differences between symposia, panels, and workshops, I would be pleased to be placed on the program under any heading that the SPEP Executive Committee feels would be appropriate.

I hope I have included all of the relevant information. If you have any questions or suggestions regarding this proposal, please do not hesitate to contact me.

Thank you for considering this proposal and I look forward to hearing from you.

Sincerely,

A. D. Script

I have presented my papers to show that we are committed to serious play in any of the sessions of a philosophical meeting. Our texts are from the very beginning ruled by an "outer text" ("*hors texte*"), which is oriented to the institution of philosophical authority, clarity, community, and concern for the tradition and the new.[1] Anyone of us might have made the submission (act of submission) presented here; anyone of us might have received it and in turn have endorsed it. It is, then, common practice. As such, it can be overlooked as a formality, an initial move, necessary to bring forward what is valuable in our work, but otherwise insignificant beyond its sheerly instrumental value. Such documents are not considered part of the philosophical archive. They reflect the bureaucratic practices of our universities and are the means by which we escape them for a few days to seek the convivial company of our truth-seeking colleagues. Even Socrates had to get down to the marketplace! Yet we do not have direct access to the site of philosophical encounter. Indeed, the site of philosophy is never outside our work. Rather, we have to internalize it in the rhetoric of our methods, our topics, our citations, and our invocation of the relevant tradition and respectable novelty which yields our philosophical vocation/vacation. There is, then, an act of submission, a prayer made before we begin our work. Admission to the practice of our philosophical rites requires that we formulate a certain *Credo* in which the institution of philosophy is recognized, the practices of its authorities are honored and its power to patent local proceedings conceded. Thus, the inseparability of philosophical form and content are organized in the pretexts that initiate our papers and are their necessary preface. To make this practice explicit is neither to ironize it nor to wish apart the form and content of philosophy, as though it could be unlike our other institutions. And, certainly, philosophy could not be above the committments of literary institution.[2] Rather, we argue as we do in order to see ourselves in and not through philosophy's mirror.

We may think of our "correspondence" as a device for specularizing the practice of philosophy, of matching its authority to our own authoriality within the limits of philosophy's discursive power. We write "on," or "about" philosophy's figures, *topoi*, and "aporia." We carry philosophy forward by restoring its future to its past; no problem is too difficult if it can contribute to this labor. On this occasion, our commentary labors under a triple Oedipalization, a triple submission to the authorities:

i. The Executive Committee of SPEP as presence/absence;

ii. Derrida as absence/presence; and

iii. O'Neill as moderator doubling the presence of Derrida and the absence of the Executive Committee of SPEP.

Thus, a subordinate sense of commentary exists, a topology structured like the discourse of enlightenment, divinely psychoanalytic. The scene erupts with the father-text, Derrida primal and iddish because he could not originate otherwise. The father-text, however, must constantly yield to the sense-making practices of its children, to the critical family invoking w/ego where there was only id. In-the-name-of-the-father-and-of-the-sons-and-daughters, the commentator adjudicates between the id-text and its w/ego-texts, charged with giving words their due, fixing the page, allowing and disallowing interpretation – super-w/ego of meaning from page to page. Thus, the commentator is authorized, and thereby foreswears his authorship, to find the sense by means of a line, in the triune papers, to set aside their individual errors, their wanderings, from the line, to discover in them the tradition. By means of such (im)pertinence, or permanence, the commentator sits to open a dialogue between the speakers, given their lines, and the audience, following the line. Beyond this, the moderator doubles as chronos, devouring the speakers a second time – his own alloted quarter of an hour completing their three quarters of an hour – with equal time to the audience guaranteeing the sacrificial dramaturgy of clarity and organization in the name of the philosophical community. A mass is as good as a miss.

Yet nothing in the scene of philosophy can prevent the irruption of its obscenities.[3] Despite our careful topology of authoritative discourses, and its insistence upon the serenity of interpretation and commentary in accordance with institutional practice, the copulation of thought and the fury of creativity fathering before the critical family cannot be prevented. Nothing prevents commentary from wandering across border lines, abandoning the coercion of super-w/ego, to turn prodigal id, and reaching toward writing – Derridean dereliction! But commentary should withhold itself from speech and writing. Like St. Joseph, its task is not to impregnate the text which has received the word from elsewhere. Such Christian commentary, of course, disavows all contamination, shrinks from any transgression of the scriptures that have chosen it. To do otherwise, makes commentary both master and servant of the scriptures, forever writing, displaced, Derridean commentary, breeding rabbis and poets[4].

Of course, in the ordinary way nothing prevents commentary from fulfilling its task. Indeed, everything serves it. The work of commentary presents itself under a rule of impartiality. It affects a self-effacing tone, so often discounting its own function that it is remarkable when commentary turns excessive and threatens to usurp the author-text, spilling unlimited ink where ordinarily a few remarks are sufficient to divide sense from nonsense.[5] Alternatively, where commentary adopts the voice of reason and justice, its complaints so proliferate that its own text risks outweighing the author-text, so that it were better the latter had never been born. Thus, one sees commentators at work busy with complaints about clarity, intentionality, priority, and the like. In the midst of such work, commentators record minor pleasures and satisfactions, subtracting their disappointments and dissatisfactions like accountants. Commentators, then, must struggle with themselves not to appear more than they are, not to take more than their due. If they do speak, it is not with their own voices. Their task is to apportion things, to restore sense, to point out pitfalls.

When we do catch the sounds of their voices, we despise commentators for being prescriptive in place of the creative, for promising a better life without being able to bring to life the passions that suffer learning and unlearning. Commentators are literary parasites, incapable of renewing the literary corpus that hosts their insatiable appetite for a text beyond the fall into language. By the same token, they are invited to all our table talks. In fact, commentators have a curious way of inviting themselves to our symposia. Thus, they constitute themselves around a sacrificial text or topic invoked to collect a membership whose interested concerns they claim to represent. The proposal that originated our own symposium on deconstruction is perfectly in order in this regard. Nothing we say is intended to fault its practice. Rather, we wish to make its practices more visible. Consider, therefore, our abstracts, offered to seduce the Executive Committee into authorizing the sacrificial refragmentation of the father-text into the tradition-text restored by the sons and daughters of criticism:

> *The papers that comprise this session (see enclosed abstracts) recognize the need to situate deconstruction within the context of Continental thought in a way that both acknowledges the continuity between this approach and the phenomenological/existential tradition, as well as marks the differences and contributions which deconstruction makes to Continental philosophy. In my paper, "Nietzsche between Foucault and Derrida: Genealogy as Deconstructive Technique," I show that both Foucault and Derrida have returned to Nietzsche's insight into the essentially critical function of philosophy. I trace the Derridean and Foucauldian rejections of philosophical binarism to Nietzsche's genealogical criticism of metaphysical hierarchization and I argue that just as Nietzsche's particular genealogical analyses are informed by his general project of a transvaluation of values, the particular turns of the Derridean and Foucauldian texts are informed by one and the same project — the deconstruction of authority.*
>
> *Trace, in "The Trace of the Trace: Derrida, Husserl, Levinas, and Freud," attempts to articulate the limits of the Derridean notion of the trace in relation to three precursors of this idea. Professor Trace addresses the Derridean critique of Husserl's notion of retention in his discussion of internal time-consciousness for not being radical enough in its attempt to "represent" the past. She goes on to show that, although Derrida borrows heavily from Levinas's discussion of the "trace of the other," he recasts the discussion of the trace in a way which seeks to avoid the ontotheological presuppositions of*

Levinas's metaphysics. She concludes by contrasting the Derridean trace with Freud's conception of the trace as "deferred effect," arguing that Freud has incorporated into the "trace" a metaphysics which Derrida cannot accept.

Cry will present a paper on tonality and the cry in Blanchot and Derrida. Although the details of Professor Cry's presentation are not definite at this time, he will extend his past discussion of the cry in Nietzsche's Birth of Tragedy *through Blanchot to the cry in Derrida as the excess of tone, an excess which moves language beyond meaning/*Sens.

Professor Script proposes to aim our criticism at "method," i.e., *at "deconstruction." Here he proposes to show that deconstructionism is neither to be reduced to a normal paradigm of criticism nor touted as a completely radical innovation, quite without precedent in the philosophical tradition.*

"Deconstruction" is neither fearsome nor familiar and so our Executive Committee ought, as it did, to find the will to sponsor us. However, to reassure our Executive Committee that it could reasonably "underwrite" our activities, the submission contains summaries of each of the proposed papers designed to render them comparably intelligible and motivated by the concern to bring deconstructionism within the tradition. To clinch matters, the Executive Committee is further assured that Professor O'Neill will "moderate" the session, provide further "summary/commentary" on the three papers, isolating common threads, and their intertextual ties with the continental tradition. Having predigested the papers in this way, they are then presented to the present collectivity (audience, readership) for final communion. Finally, the Executive Committee is assured that the various segments of the symposium will observe conventional time allotments. *Ite, missa est.*

We see, then, that we are gathered in "general dissatisfaction" with the reception of recent French philosophy by even its sympathetic American practitioners. At the same time, we are concerned to avoid *ad hominem* argument, presumably out of respect for our irreverent sense of the nonexistence of authors – or is it our murderous wishes towards the father that renders Derrida beyond presence?

Is it possible for commentary to remain within its prescribed boundaries, to keep the panoptical promise of self-surveillance? Perhaps as a philosophical or literary collectivity we are rendered righteous in our sense of the conformity of deconstructionist practices with the discipline and punishment of the literary body, reassuring our Executive Committee that we have bravely avoided the pleasures of the text.[6] Some such convenant is honored in Professor Script's paper. Derridean pharmacology may poison the inkwell but it remedies the text, opening it up to a double writing carried on within-and-without the tradition. Although it leaves behind the superficial, the deep, the thorough, and the underground thinkers on the question of origins, Derridean deconstruction has antecedents in Kant's practice of critique and in Nietzsche's genealogical inquiries into the fetishism of words and values. But does this make a respectable tradition? Shorn of the grammatical subject, respecting no kingdom of ends, and certainly no divinity, nor any authority, how are we to assure our Executive Committee of philosophy that our proceedings nevertheless observe the herd instincts of subjection to institutionalized discourse? Will the Committee not suspect the subversion of inverted commas, subjectless discourse, unauthorized texts motivated solely by the will-to-interpretation? Ought we to have made them any promises? Ought they to surrender philosophy to such scribble and not to dismiss us with shorter shrift, unshriven?

Professor Trace, although smuggling in quite a different paper than the one with which she solicited the Executive's interest in the restoration of the tradition, also takes her departure from Derrida via Kant. She does so, despite Kant's un-Derridean concern with the search for a key, or criteriology to the question of the limits of metaphysics. Kant nevertheless appears to be attractive as a rival father-text because of his intuition of a noumenal lack in the origins of reason. Thus in Trace's reading/writing, the Kantian critique labors to produce Nature as a ground of experience, to impregnate her with the transcendental categories of reason so as to have her bear particulars "roots and peculiarity." At the same time, Trace argues, Kant fears that reason is impotent with respect to the critical task – is all too metaphysical – unless Nature can seduce reason to see/sense/sign her to bring forth things. In short, Kant sees that desire must be at the heart of reason, that the very history of metaphysics betrays this complicity, and that the scandal of metaphysics as history rather than science is the very condition of its possibility. In other words, the *nature* of reason is neither inside nor outside of reason, neither metaphysical nor physical. Rather, the transcendence of reason consists in the play of reason with itself whereby it becomes its own child, discovering the particulars of nature in a world it has seeded through itself as language, logos, sign. It is in the play of language that reason achieves both unity and difference, that openness and closure, which are movements in the articulation of desire and reason in historical nature:

> For metaphysics in its fundamental features is placed in us by nature itself and cannot be considered the production of arbitrary choice or a

> casual enlargement in the progress of experience from which it is quite disparate.[7]

Here the Kantian critique, as Trace reconstructs it, approaches the very borders of deconstructionism but remains blocked for want of an adequate conception of the semiotic play at the heart of things. This seminal move would release us from Kant's impossible metaphysical demands for the completeness of reason and the satisfaction of desire. Or would it? Ought not we to ask for the seriousness of play? Might it not be the case that the divinity, the feminity of our play derives, overflows its limits, from the impossibility whose names are reason, God, desire, woman – all of which we pursue as the very condition of nature in us, that is, as embodied being, the conjecture of flesh, text, tissue? Perhaps Kant was, after all, married to such a conception of embodied reason and he may well have realized that in pursuing metaphysics he experienced himself as father/mother of his own experience and reflection:

> That the human mind will ever give up metaphysical research is as little to be expected as that we, to avoid inhaling impure air, should prefer to give up breathing altogether. There will, therefore, always be a metaphysics in the world; nay, everyone, especially every reflective man, will have it, and for want of a recognized standard, will shape it for himself after his own pattern.[8]

Kant, then, accepted the embodied condition of philosophy, its essentially human and historical nature, its yearning for an impossible unity that is the driving force in each of us who takes up metaphysics according to his or her "own pattern," that is, according to our own patterns of seduction, our transgressive, linguistic, and corporeal difference. If this were so, we might trace another genealogy from Montaigne, through Merleau-Ponty to Barthes, as I have done elsewhere,[9] according to my own pattern.

At this point, I must return to the margins, to correspond further with the natural history of our symposium:

> Dear Professor O'Neill:
>
> A problem has come up regarding our SPEP workshop in Atlanta. Professor Cry contacted me two days ago and said he would not be able to attend the meeting. I have been trying to get a replacement since then, and have invited Professor C. Supplement, who is now in the Department of Romance Languages at Another University. She has a paper on Derrida's resistance to empiricism which will fit nicely with Trace's paper on Kant and my paper on Nietzsche. However, she won't know until September 18 whether she can attend our meeting. She has

> another commitment in October, and the date of that commitment is still undecided. I told her it would be all right if she let us know on the 18th, since she was reasonably sure that her other commitment would not conflict with SPEP.

It turns out, then, that deconstructionists are substitutable and that for Professor Cry we can read Professor Supplement, between metonym and metaphor. Unfortunately, the proposed substitution of "The Cry and the Call in Derrida's Thought" by "Derrida's Resistance to Empiricism" did not meet the foolproof guarantees issued on its behalf. Thus, although I was prepared to read Supplement's paper in the light of either Cry's or Trace's paper, I was unable to read their papers in the light of Supplement's paper. So she was saved that impropriety – perhaps due to Canada Post's persistent purloining of the letters which regularly destroys ten percent of our mail – *hors texte*!

As a representative of the modest functions of commentary exercised on behalf of the Executive Committee's desire for order, clarity, and turnover, I have already exceeded my limits. I have done so to exemplify the claim that commentary that is or rather that is not simply translation cannot remain perched "on" what is offered for commentary. It necessarily falls into the "over" or "beyond" of the supplement of writing. It does so because, in the first place, Derrida refuses translation, or rather he makes writing difficult for those who live on by living off translation.[10] Now what is (who is) at stake here is Jacques Derrida who refuses to accept his death warrant; that is, the claim made for him by his critics that he is ready to be reconciled with the tradition – provided we can divide his radical desire between us – we Kantians, we Nietzscheans, we traditional radicals, we deconstructionists, we DJs of university philosophy. By their obsequent logic ye shall know them, these scribes who hide their belatedness in the celebration of the tradition they themselves wish to survive by living on deconstructionism once they have cleaned it from its impropriety; that is, from what they desire in J/D who must necessarily exceed them in order to go on living/writing.

The Executive Committee is asked to countenance a deed that the sons and daughters of criticism cannot face themselves. They look to the Executive Committee because they cannot face Jacques Derrida from whom they want deconstructionism without his radical signature. From all corners, they write on him, they imprint upon him in order to write him off in commentaries that are nothing but a series of death warrants – literal overkill. In this way, the Executive Committee is called to appoint its philosophical firing squads so that no one need know who killed J/D, supposing anyone hits the mark. Why are the critics so bent upon the mortification of Derrida? Why must they expropriate him in warrants bearing the collective signature of deconstructionism? I say (*J'ai dit*) it is to rid the Executive Committee of the scandal of J/D, to cleanse the community of philosophy driven by desire, to turn Derrida's self refusal (*je/u*) into a collective "yes" (*oui*) uttered by a first person plural (*we/nous*) in which no one can be heard for himself or herself – to enter safely the normal paradigm/paradise of kitchen criticism (*heil/heimlich*!).

The sons and daughters of criticism are, after all, capable of the deed, of the writ which prepares their own legacy as deconstructionists. They know how to celebrate the rituals, to organize the symposia, to collect anthologies in which the faded flowers of memory testify to the once living moment when desire could not survive death, when it could only live on love. But now the notice is out, the program printed, the warrants signed. The officers are in; the proceedings are official. The time has come for Jacques Derrida, tried in his absence, to separate himself from deconstructionism, to avail himself of the tradition, to take the ashes in his mouth – *memento mori*. The scribes will bear him away the better to honor his science. That is the way of institutional recognition. *Fort/Derrida*, the strength yielded through Derrida's absence from the group of deconstructionists, grows through the sacrifice of the presence of Derrida/*Da*, in unbearable love/hate. Such is the obsequious logic of institutions, as we know from Freud and ourselves. And so it is with philosophy and literature as institutions.

Now the commentator is in just as much difficulty as the translator whose troubles Derrida has self-consciously prepared. Both must proclaim fidelity in a world where nothing, and certainly not texts, honors such a notion, unless it be machines.[11] But commentators are not copyists – although much thinking aspires to little else. Yet if infidelity is no longer a textual virtue, it is just as empty to vaunt one's infidelity or even one's intertextual indecision. Perhaps, then, criticism and commentary are necessarily violent, murderous or incestuous designs upon the mother-text or father-text. Such anger broods upon itself given the fourfold sins of the parents against themselves, against their own accounts of their sins, against the style of their confessions, and against the penitential writing (*schrift*) through which their sins are redeemed in blindness and wandering without return. But then the father-text cannot be brought home to the tradition. Worse still, it cannot be broken and shared among its critical sons in castrated communication of the tradition. Only those are fathers who prefigure their misdeeds. Therefore, it is only in turn that sons become fathers but not through the father. This is the blind spot of criticism and commentary, still holding to an undeceived language, insane with the corrigibility of the absconding father to which sons are heir.

To come into its own, literary criticism must separate writing/reading from the body.[12] Criticism must dismember the original texts in commentary, separating their authors from the pleasures of their text, incorporating them in a collective history of dead names. Thereafter, literature keeps constant watch lest others repeat its improprieties – at least not without paying their dues! But, Jacques Derrida has already sent us a prepaid "check" to underwrite our festivities. I, too, must sign my debt – J/O – for what "I owe" him/you. This, therefore, will not have been a commentary.

Notes

*My text preserves as nearly as possible its play upon its own play as a commentary at the Workshop on Archaeology of Deconstruction. Twenty-third Annual Conference of the Society for Phenomenology and Existential Philosophy (SPEP), held at Georgia State University and Emory University, Atlanta, Georgia, October 18–20, 1984. I have removed personal details; I am concerned only to reproduce the conventions of philosophical practice as observed but unthematic features of the institution of philosophy within which we nevertheless strive to arouse philosophical desire. What follows, however, should alert readers to the liability of an apology for one's own practice.

1. John O'Neill, "The literary production of natural and social science inquiry: issues and applications in the social organization of science," *Canadian Journal of Sociology* 6 (2) 1981: 105–20; "A Realist Model of Knowledge: With a Phenomenological Deconstruction," *Philosophy of the Social Sciences*, vol. 16, no. 1 (March 1986).

2. John O'Neill *Essaying Montaigne: A Study of the Renaissance Institution of Writing and Reading* (London: Routledge and Kegan Paul, 1982).

3. Herman Rapaport, "Staging *Mont Blanc*," in *Displacement: Derrida and After*, ed. Mark Krupnik (Bloomington: Indiana University Press, 1983), pp. 59–73.

4. Susan Handleman, "Jacques Derrida and the Heretic Hermaneutic," in *Displacement*, pp. 98–129.

5. John R. Searle, "Reiterating the Differences: A Reply to Derrida," *Glyph 1* (1977): pp. 198–208; Jacques Derrida, "Limited Inc.," *Glyph 2* (1977): pp. 162–254.

6. John O-Neill, "Homotextuality:: Barthes on Barthes, Fragments (RB), with a Footnote," in *Hermeneutics: Questions and Prospects*, ed. Gary Shapiro and Alan Sica (Amherst: University of Massachusetts Press, 1984), pp. 165–82; "Breaking the Signs," in *The Structural Allegory: Reconstructive Encounters with the New French Thought*, ed. John Fekete (Minneapolis: University of Minnesota Press, 1984), pp. 183–200.

7. Immanuel Kant, *Prolegomena to Any Future Metaphysics*, trans. L. W. Beck (Indianapolis: The Bobbs-Merrill Company, 1950), p. 102.

8. *Ibid.*, p. 116.

9. See notes 2 and 6 above.

10. Jacques Derrida, "Living On," in *Deconstruction and Criticism* by Harold Bloom, Paul De Man, Jacques Derrida, Geoffrey H. Hartman, J. Hillis Miller (New York: The Seabury Press, 1979), pp. 75–176.

11. Barbara Johnson, "Taking Fidelity Philosophically," in *Difference in Translation*, ed. Joseph F. Graham (Ithaca: Cornell University Press, 1985), pp. 142–48.

12. Jacques Derrida, "Coming into One's Own," in *Psychoanalysis and the Question of the Text*, ed. Geoffrey H. Hartman (Baltimore, MD: Johns Hopkins University Press, 1978), pp. 114–47.

Part VII. The Future of Postmodernism

17. Postmodernism: It's Future Perfect

Andrew J. McKenna

It has become commonplace to observe that "postmodern" is a slippery term, that both from a historical and from an aesthetic point of view, both in terms of periodization and of formal production, postmodernism is not easily distinguished from what, with Eliot, Joyce, and Kafka, with Picasso and Duchamp, we have been calling modernism. That is as it should be, of course, once we recall, with John Updike as of just last month (*New Yorker*, September 10, 1984) the root meaning of modernism as referring to the present time, from the Latin: *modo*, "just now." If something called the postmodern is but the form of modernity, perhaps it only makes explicit the paradox which already informs the notion of modernism itself, which would apply to any self-consciously progressive or avant-garde cultural activity with respect to its own era. Consider for instance these remarks, which might have been culled from the pages of the *New York Review of Books* or the Times Literary Supplement or faculty memoranda on a recent candidate for tenure:

> Moreover, a new type of teaching has lately appeared, or rather a childish way of prating has gained inordinate popularity among certain men who hunt only for the leaves that cover up the fruit.
>
> Those who are busy teaching this way seem not to know and not to want others to know the things they pride themselves on teaching. Or perhaps they are anxious to be thought to teach new and bizarre things; I say this because by their weird and disgusting newness of terminology they do not fear to divulge what they hope.[1]

In fact, this is Robert of Melun inveighing against the *modernitas*, the *modo docendi*, emerging among Biblical scholars in the mid-twelfth century. So much then, perhaps, for the novelty of this conflict. It remains to be seen whether a notion like the postmodern harbors a deeper paradox, whether it has weightier implications for the present time, which it curiously designates as somehow or other past or "post." That is what I argue in this essay, with special reference to certain writings by Jacques Derrida and René Girard.

First Derrida, because he has done so much to render a sense of temporal presence, of being as presence, problematic, for which fact alone he might be deemed the philosopher of the postmodern. Furthermore, he is somewhat the philosopher of "what remains," of the marginal as both the liminal and the residual, as both originary and outlandish. This is exemplified by the first and last utterances of his *Glas*, which opens with this fragmentary question on Hegel, "quoi du reste aujourd'hui, pour nous, ici, maintenant, d'un Hegel?" and closes, in the column devoted to Genet, in such a way as to rethematize its own writing as a ruin, a wreck: *"Ce que j'avais redouté, naturellement, déjà, se réédite. Aujourd'hui, ici, maintenant le debris de."*[2]

Second Girard, because his sacrificial theory of culture lends both anthropological and epistemological reference to the issues raised by Derrida, most notably raised by Derrida's text on Shelley ("The Triumph of Life") and Blanchot ("La Folie du jour," "L'Arrêt de mort") entitled "Living On."[3] This is a translation from the French text, "Survivre," which is not available in French, in order doubtless that one might speculate more freely "On Living" as a matter of surviving. The question of the postmodern in its most far-reaching implications, which are nonetheless the most concrete, is the question of survival, of living on after the dead. A postmodern consciousness is indissociable, for demonstrable, concrete reasons bearing on the recent past as they affect the possibility of a future, from the consciousness of being a survivor, of living on. The consciousness of being as presence as being somehow or other belated, *nachträglich*, *après coup*, may be the consequence of our deconstructive activity. It is also, I argue, a matter of decisive historical consequence.

To acknowledge Derrida as the philosopher of the postmodern, is to acknowledge that we live, in the felicitous term of one of his commentators, in the "post-age."[4] We are post-structuralist in the (highly disputed) terrain of literary criticism and philosophy, postmodern in the (perhaps waning) field of literature and the fine arts, post-Christian in the domain of religion and (perhaps) of culture as a whole.

There are still other "posts" that we can add by which we mark our sense of belatedness, beginning with that very term, which for Harold Bloom describes the relation of virtually any poet as ephebe to a precursor with respect (or disrespect) to whose glory the ephebe stands in an anxious, fallen, rebellious state.[5] According to Richard Rorty, we are, or at least should be, post-Philosophical, to the extent that, precisely with Derrida, we are past the point where we can legitimately or convincingly distinguish between Philosophy and other kinds of writing.[6] We are in multiple senses post-postal: for the way telecommunications have supplanted and irrevocably altered our experience of communication-at-a-distance in the media age;[7] for the way, as already suggested, in which both our sense of historical periodization and of contemporaneity is transformed by our use and illustration of the term postmodern. According to Michel Serres, we are, finally and balefully, posthistorical: in the nuclear age, science has entered its definitive state, that of a thanatocracy, in which its most powerful impulses are working in service to the death instinct.[8]

It is in just this sense that I add that we are, finally and definitively, I mean historically and anthropologically, postwar. I mean that term in the narrowest and the broadest possible senses, in the sense in which historians speak of the period beginning in 1945, a period beginning unmistakably because so spectacularly and catastrophically with Hiroshima. Hiroshima marks (and indubitably mars) the end of World War II and the beginning of our era, the era characterized by the cold war because no one can afford the all-consuming, apocalyptic consequences of a hot one. And so we are postwar in the broadest sense, as Jonathan Schell makes plain in *The Fate of the Earth*, [9] where he shows that war conceived and waged with a view to palpable gains, territorial or ideological, is a thing of the past, that our age-old definition of war no longer applies to what we cannily dub nuclear holocaust in which all is lost, in which all are losers.

Holocaust, it is worth recalling, is a religious term, a properly sacrificial one, designating a wholly burnt offering – which all too humanly looms in our near future. In view of this imminent apocalypse, with which we are so familiar as to become frequently bored by the topic, I must ask, with René Girard, whether our violent culture is indeed pre- or post-Christian. For if, as Girard argues in *Des Choses cachées depuis la fondation du monde* and in *Le Bouc emissaire,*[10] Scripture consists in a critique of sacrificial practices, and if on the other hand our crisis is sacrificial, as our commonplace terms for it seem to suggest, then perhaps we need but to assume its message rather than relegate it to some "metaphysic of the book."

I am prompted to this remark by one of John Updike's observations on the postmodern. After quoting another critic who excludes from this category what he calls "secular news reports," meaning novels about everyday middle class life, Updike continues, "So whatever postmodern is, it is not secular news reports. Nor is it, one may hazard, sacred news reports."[11] But perhaps it is. I think it is; I think that we learn much from the media that suggests that it is; and I cite additional texts by some contemporary writers which further suggest the postmodern as "sacred news reports."

What news of the sacred? In a sense, we ever only have news of the sacred and never its full presence. It is just this notion of full presence, of parousia, that Derrida deconstructs as ontotheological, as theologocentric. Insted of presence, we have *differance*:

> *Differance* is what makes the movement of signification possible only if each element that is said to be "present," appearing on the stage of presence, is related to something other than itself but retains the mark of a past element and already lets itself be hollowed out by the mark of its relation to a future element. This trace relates no less to what is called the future than to what is called the past, and it constitutes what is called the present by this very relation to what it is not, to what it absolutely is not; that is, not even to a past or future considered as a modified present.[12]

The present is inscribed under erasure; it is but the mark, the trace of a relation to a future and a past which do not exist as modified presents (before or after) but only "divide the present in itself." Whence the relation between the poststructuralist critique of being as presence and the peculiar temporality of the postmodern, of the "just now" as the "after now," as mediation, spatialization, incarnate, as it were, in the "secondarity" of writing. To speak of the present as of what is always already past is to speak in the mode of the future with regard to it. The postmodern evokes a sense of the present as future and as past with respect to itself, never as present to itself.

If the (notion of the) postmodern has a grammatical tense, it is decidedly not the present, but the future past, the future perfect; as when I say, speaking of this essay at the present time, that this will have been a discourse on the postmodern; as when Derrida, disclaiming an "intention to *present*" the three essays composing *Dissemination*, says in "Hors Livre," "This (therefore) will not have been a book."[13] The future past is in fact the condition Jean Francois Lyotard lays down for identifying a properly postmodern work; it is not necessarily a text from any historical period, but one that testifies, without nostalgia, to *l'imprésentable*:

> A Postmodern writer or artist is in the situation of a philosopher: the text he writes, the work he accomplishes are not governed in principle by any rules already established, and they cannot be judged by means of a determining judgment, by the application to the text or the work of known categories. These rules and categories are what the work or the text are in search of. The artist and the writer work therefore without rules, and to establish the rules of what *will have been done*. Whence it is that the work and the text have the properties of an event, whence too that they always come too late for their author, or, much the same thing, that their *mise en oeuvre* always begins too soon. *Postmodern* would be understood according to the paradox of the future (*post*) anterior (*modo*).[14]

This is in fact a good description of what we find Derrida doing in "Hors Livre," where he interrogates – and practices – the aporetics of prefacing, "a necessary and ludicrous operation" as he describes it in Hegel. The preface is the future past of the system, a dangerous supplement to its integrity because – and although – its role is to announce that integrity. "Mais il faut choisir: vivre ou raconter," as Sartre's Roquentin observes in an archly postmodern moment of *La Nausée*, contesting alike false beginnings, false endings and the "total partiel" we make of them.[15]

It appears, then, that the future perfect, for Derrida and Lyotard, is the temporal modality, or at least the grammatical translation, of historical becoming in all its openness, in all its resistance to false totalization. It translates the present in its differance. Lyotard, for his part, is quite vehement in his opposition to the ideology of representation that informs efforts of totalization:

> That illusion is paid for at the price of terror. The nineteenth and twentieth centuries have given us our fill of terror. We have payed enough for the nostalgia of the all and the one, of the reconciliation of the concept with the sensible, of experience that is transparent and communicable. Beneath the general demand for relaxing and appeasement, we hear mumbling the desire to recommence the terror, to accomplish the fanaticism of embracing reality. The answer is: war on the all, bear witness to the unpresentable, activate the differends, save the honor of the name.[16]

However, the glaring symmetry of Lyotard's violent *re*sistance to what he deems terroristic *re*action is far too reminiscent of Victor

Hugo's patently rhetorical declaration of *Guerre à la rhetorique* (*Réponse à un acte d'accusation*) to serve as an alternative to the violence he ostensibly deplores. Rather, it conforms all too romantically to the model of human violence enunciated by Sartre's Franz von Gerlach at the conclusion of *The Condemned of Altona*:

> One and one make one – there's our mystery. The beast was hiding, and suddenly we surprised his look deep in the eyes of our neighbors. So we struck. Legitimate self-defense. I surprised a beast. I struck. A man fell, and in his dying eyes I saw the beast still living – myself. One and one make one – what a misunderstanding![17]

Franz has already committed suicide. His voice comes to us on a tape recorder, so that he addresses us as one who will have been killed. His voice remains, survives him – "après coup." Why the gimmick? Because violent reciprocity is not the rule of historical becoming but the rule of definitive historical closure:

> The thirtieth century no longer replies. Perhaps there will be no more centuries after ours. Perhaps a bomb will have blown out all the lights. Everything will be dead – eyes, judges, time. Night. Oh, tribunal of the night – you who were, who will be, and who are – I have been! I have been. I, Franz von Gerlach, here in this room, have taken the century upon my shoulders and have said: 'I will answer for it. This day and forever.' What do you say?[18]

The future perfect is necessarily employed to evoke this total violence, because, as Jonathan Schell reminds us, "extinction is a human future which can never become a human present." Schell's reflections on the peculiar temporality of the postwar era are instructive here:

> Like the thought 'I do not exist,' the thought 'Humanity is now extinct,' is an impossible one for a rational person, because as soon as *it* is, *we* are not. In imagining any other event, we look ahead to a moment that is still within the stream of human time, which is to say within a time in which other human beings will exist, and will be responding to whatever they see, looking back to present time and looking forward to future times that will themselves to be within the sequence of human time. But in imagining extinction, we gaze past everything human to a dead time that falls outside the human tenses of past, present and future.[19]

Such a future can never arrive; it is for the imagination alone, so that we can only speak of such a time now, and only in the tense of the future past, only as something that will have taken place. Our relation to the present is governed by the tense of the future past in an unprecedented manner.

But it is not only from Hiroshima, and the prospect of its planetary repetition, that we derive our sense of living on, of being survivors, of being as survival. Other events mark 1945 as the beginning of the postmodern; these are events, "on the Western front" so to speak, which Maurice Blanchot evokes in a highly allusive manner in "La Folie du jour":

> Shortly afterward, the madness of the world broke out. I was made to stand against the wall like many others. Why? For no reason. The guns did not go off. I said to myself, God, What are you doing? At that point I stopped being insane. The world hesitated, then regained its equilibrium.[20]

This is a work which, as Derrida shows in "Living On," contests the possibility of story, which frustrates what he calls "the demand for narrative," as instanced toward the end of Blanchot's text – which repeats its beginning:

> I had been asked: Tell us "*just* exactly" what happened. A Story? I began: I am not learned; I am not ignorant. I have known joys. That is saying too little. I told them the whole story and they listened, it seems to me, with interest, at least in the beginning. But the end was a surprise to all of us. "That was the beginning," they said. "Now get down to the facts." How so? The story was over![21]

The impossibility of story, however, to the extent it depends on a linear notion of time, of a selfsame present ever bounded by future and past (presents), is linked for Blanchot, as I have already suggested, to certain events, which he evokes explicitly in the recent essay appositely entitled *Aprés coup*: He cites Adorno's claim that there can be no "fictional narrative" of Auschwitz. Before pursuing his point, let us observe that it is a claim that Roland Barthes cites in Brecht and that is taken up at length by Lyotard as well, for whom Auschwitz is a "*clivage dans la pensée* de l'Occident," a "*fêlure dans le temps philosophique*."[22] Blanchot pursues:

> The necessity of bearing witness is the obligation of a testimony which only could be born, each in its singularity, by the impossible witnesses – witnesses of the impossible –; certain of them survived, but their living on [*sur-vie*] is no longer life, it is the rupture with the living affir-

> mation, it is the attestation that this good which life is (life which is not narcissistic, but for others) has undergone the decisive attack [*atteinte*] which leaves nothing intact any longer. From that point, it could be that all narration, nay all poetry, has lost the basis on which another language could raise itself, by the extinction of this happiness in speaking which is expected in the most mediocre silence. Doubtless forgetfulness does its work and allows for there still to be works. But to that forgetfulness, the forgetfulness of an event in which all possibility foundered, responds a memory which however failing and without recollection, the immemorial haunts in vain. Humanity was to have died [or had to die: *a eu à mourir*], in its entirety by the ordeal it underwent in some of its members (those who incarnate life itself, almost the totality of a people promised to a perpetual presence). That death is still going on. Whence the obligation to never again die only once, without its repetition being able to accustom us to the always capital end.[23]

It appears that for Blanchot all the living are survivors of Auschwitz, living, as it were, "après coup." For them, for us, nothing is left intact, everything is tainted. The living present is not conveniently, or plausibly, opposed to a dead past; rather the past lives on, irrevocably marking the present with its dead.

This, too, is the *structural* effect of Hiroshima, which as Robert Jay Lifton reminds us, was also "an end of the world," "a new dimension of death immersion" that, in the light of imminent catastrophe, "we all share." Lifton further observes, as if paraphrasing Blanchot on the problematic of representation, "impaired formulation is a central problem for survivors."[24] Impaired formulation is our postmodern condition, our postwar condition. It has ever been our condition of course, but now we have to acknowledge it, along with Derrida as its philosopher. The illusion, the nostalgia of unimpaired formulation is just what deconstruction reveals to us – as illusion, erasure, forgetfulness, ontotheology, logocentrism, phonocentrism: "la folie du jour," the madness of day, the madness of light, which, for Adorno, I submit, is the madness of (undialectical, undeconstructed) Enlightenment:

> After Auschwitz, our feelings resist any claim of the positivity of existence as sanctimonious, as wronging the victims; they balk at squeezing any kind of sense, however bleached, out of the victims' fate.

For Adorno, as well, all the living are survivors of Auschwitz:

> Our metaphysical faculty is paralyzed because actual events have shattered the basis on which speculative metaphysical thought could be

> reconciled with experience. Once again, the dialectical motif of quantity recoiling into quality scores an unspeakable triumph. The administrative murder of millions made of death a thing one had never yet to fear in just this fashion. There is no chance any more for death to come into the individual's empirical life as somehow comformable with the course of that life. The last, the poorest possession left to the individual is expropriated. That in the concentration camps it was no longer an individual who died, but a specimen – that is bound to affect the dying of those who escaped the administrative measure.[25]

Adorno locates the obstacle, the challenge, to our metaphysical faculty in the victim, in the massive and irreducible fact of victimage. This is the compelling interest of René Girard's sacrificial theory of culture, in which a mystified expulsion lies at "the foundation of the world." The victim is the term that provides Derrida's terminology – supplement, pharmakon, remnant-"restance," trace, differance itself – with both anthropological and historical reference.

In the beginning – this is Girard's anthropological hypothesis – was the victim, whose vulnerability is what singled it out for unanimous destruction by the group or horde in a melee of appropriate rivalry. With the disposition of projectiles or prosthetic devices to implement the kill (which, I submit, constitutes our formal continuity with more "primitive" ancestors), there are no instinctual brakes to intraspecific violence which characterize the animal world, as the ethological data on dominance patterns among animals demonstrates. Appropriation by any one group surrounding the victim now spells danger from each and every one of its other members. All share in this apprehension, indeed all mime it, all insinuate it to each other, so that there is a moment of noninstinctual attention bent on seizing the prey, but refraining from it out of self-preservation (out of an originary strategy of deterrence). Desire is born of this moment, as deferred appropriation of the object; out of a difference which constitutes an object as such; and so is the sacred, as that to which one defers infinitely rather than succumb to the mimetic violence that produced the victim; and so, consequently, is man, the infinitely desiring subject, the subject of infinite desires, of metaphysical desire, whose objects are ever only the symbols or signifiers of other objects in a chain leading out to the infinite but indissolubly linked nonetheless to the body, the remains of the victim, the first signifier:

> The signifier, that is the victim. The signified is all of the real and potential meaning that the community confers on that victim, and through its mediation, on all things.

> The sign is the reconciling victim. Because we understand without difficulty that men wish to remain reconciled once the crisis is over, we can also understand that they desire to reproduce the sign; that is, to employ the language of the sacred, substituting for the original victim in ritual new victims in order to insure the maintenance of this miraculous peace. The ritual imperative is one with the manipulation of the signs, with their multiplication and thus new possibilities of differentiation and cultural enrichment.[26]

Peace among men, it is important to note, is not the object of desire, not, one might add, by any stretch of the historical, political, or sociological imagination. Nothing unites a community, with all the good fellowship and cooperation one can imagine, like the external threat of a common enemy. But the threat is originally internal; it is the violent threat of all against all. (It is the annihilating threat of this internal difference, or differance, which we have rematerialized in the postwar, postmodern era: as Jonathan Schell observes, "With the world itself at stake, all differences would by definition be 'internal' differences."[27]

Peace then is not the object of desire, but its by-product as the calm to which the deferred appropriation of the victim gives rise. It is a calm attributed to the miraculous agency of the victim, thanks to whom for the first time something like a before and after, an inside and an outside is marked; marked, above all, as remarked, since its experience is necessarily mimetic and collective. Thus Girard's theory can accommodate a poststructuralist critique of origins without succumbing to infinite regression, to the aporetics of an origin "always already in search of itself,"[28] for it postulates that origin and violence are one.

Derrida's genial recapitulation, in "Plato's Pharmacy," of the violent origin of philosophy, as of representation itself, in terms of the sacrificial expulsion of writing and the phonologocentric erasure of its originary traces, follows the same scenario. The story of philosophy's violent rebirth in Descartes's *Meditations*, as recounted in "Cogito and the History of Madness," follows the same pattern, recapitulates the same structure: the mystified expulsion of madness as the originary other of reason.[29] The story of philosophy from Plato through Heidegger is ever the same story, the story of violent origins, of origin as violence.

I think it is a true story – indeed, in Derrida's words, although he uses them doubtless with an (un)certain measure of irony: "the truth on truth."[30] As the prospect of man's violent end repeats the dynamics of his violent beginnings, it appears probable that the very possibility of there any longer being anything like truth, positive truth upon which, despite all deconstructions and because of them as well, a science of man could be formulated and implemented – all that depends upon our understanding of that story, of its relevance, of its revelatory power, of its concrete, immediate, and verifiable reference to our postmodern condition, our postwar condition.[31] Truth is not before us, in the future, lying yet to be measured or mastered; it is not above us, in the empyrean, awaiting revelation, illumination or postsurvival representation; it is not behind us, either, in our past, awaiting Platonic recollection. Truth is not transcendental; if anything, it is transdescendental, for its lies beneath us, underfoot, in the victim. It appears probable – I mean provable – that no other notion or form of truth is salvageable from the wreckage of two and one-half millenia of truth-seeking, which Nietzsche, in the *Genealogy of Morals* (III, 27) hailed ambivalently as the work of Christianity[32] and of which deconstruction is the latest phase, perhaps the last phase. No other form or norm of truth is left remaining to us, or is desirable to us, because, among other things, our desire for truth is explained by our desire to escape victimization.

It is a true story then, which stands the test of deconstruction, above all that of undecidability: for between victim and persecutor, no one hesitates to decide the party of right without endangering his own right to decide anything. This is a story that satisfies the truth-seeking impulse of deconstruction itself, its demystifying fervor in the detection of occulted or mystified violence.

This, at the very least, is a bold enough claim to satisfy the demand for novelty, indeed for scandal, which we tend to expect when speaking of something called the postmodern.

The victim is the matrix of difference, and yes, the origin of différance, the play of differences: between signifier and signified, sacred and profane, violence and peace, chaos and community, whose presence to itself as *cum-unus* is mediated by the designation of the victim and the deferrals of violence which stem from that originary differance. Difference is the matrix of value, that is the epistemological conquest of our structuralism; and the victim is the matrix of the difference we value between good and bad and between true and false as well, which our critical, scientific spirit determines by the detection of natural or human causality behind allegedly supernatural causality. This is the thesis of *Le Bouc emissaire*, which articulates the epistemological conquest of our poststructural condition. This is the structural or matricial import of Auschwitz and Hiroshima, and if we are to believe Adorno, it is irreversible:

> A new categorical imperative has been imposed by Hitler upon unfree mankind: to arrange their thoughts and actions so that Auschwitz will not repeat itself, so that nothing similar will happen.[33]

For if we are not to believe Adorno, it can happen, and the difference between victim and persecutor will have been totally and definitively obliterated.

For all his apparent confusion about something like "unimpaired formulation," Robert Jay Lifton is right when he observes that truth is a matter of bearing witness:[34] witness against victimage, witness against death by administrative measure; witness against sacrifice, against holocaust, against scapegoating. For Lifton is more right than he knows when he remarks upon the "adaptive usefulness" of scapegoating:

> Yet a process at least bordering on scapegoating seems necessary to the formulation of any death immersion. It enters into the survivor's necessary theory of causation and his need to pass judgement on people and forces outside himself to avoid drowning in his own guilt and symbolic disorder.[35]

Scapegoating is the administration of death (as opposed to its advent by "natural" means), and the victim is witness against it. Scapegoating, as Girard has argued, is the origin of the symbolic order, and the victim is witness against its (structural) distortions. It is in the victim that our notion of causality originates, and it is the victim who testifies, in the *Psalms* (35: 19) and in John's Gospel, "They hated me without cause."

The truth, in sum, is the victim, and that condition is in our time universal. The post-age is the victim-age. The survivor who identifies with the victim, who adopts victimage as his truth, as his past and future, is a true survivor, a being in whom truth survives and through whom survival is a truth, a genuine human possibility, rather than a contingency, an alibi, an accident. Such a survivor is the antithesis to the sacrificial mechanisms of adaptation by which culture has waged its destiny, "from the foundations of the world" through its ensured sacrificial consummation, "a republic," as Jonathan Schell, along with numerous others, prognosticates, "of insects and grass." To restate the proposition in poststructural terms, the victim is the difference which makes for differance, then as now: by then, I mean at the violent origin our own species; by now, I mean any time now, any such time before man's future in victimization will have been perfected.

Notes

1. Quoted in M. D. Chenu, *Nature, Man and Society in the Twelfth Century,* trans. J. Taylor and L. Little (Chicago: University of Chicago Press, 1968), p. 311.

2. "What remains today, for us, here, now, of a Hegel?"; "What I had feared, naturally, already, is being reedited. Today, here, now, the ruin of." *Glas* (Paris: Galilée, 1974), pp. 7a, 291b.

3. In *Deconstruction and Criticism*, ed. Harold Bloom *et al.* (New York: Seabury, 1979).

4. Cf. Gregory Ulmer, "The Post-Age," *Diacritics*, II, 3 (Fall 1981) It is Ulmer's claim that Derrida seeks to "reassess the efficacy of the *prophet*" (p. 53) that I am somewhat exploring or calling to be explored here.

5. Harold Bloom, *The Anxiety of Influence* (New York: Oxford, 1973) and *Agon: A Theory of Revisionism* (New York: Oxford, 1982).

6. Richard Rorty, "Philosophy as a Kind of Writing: Jacques Derrida" in *Consequences of Pragmatism* (Minneapolis: University of Minnesota Press, 1982).

7. This is developed by Gregory Ulmer, "The Post-Age," who is reviewing Derrida's *La Carte Postale*, where communication-at-a-distance is explored at length.

8. Michel Serres, "Trahison: La Thanatocratie," *Hermes III: La Traduction* (Paris: Minuit, 1974), p. 77.

9. Jonathan Schell, *The Fate of the Earth* (New York: Knopf, 1982), esp. pp. 186–93.

10. René Girard, *Des Choses cachées depuis la fondation du monde* (Paris: Grasset, 1978) and *Le Bouc émissaire* (Paris: Grasset, 1982).

11. In "Modernist, Postmodernist, What Will They Think of Next" (*New Yorker*, September 10, 1984) p. 136, Updike cites this phrase: it originates with Richard Locke, as cited by John Barth in his now canonical essay, "The Literature of Replenishment: Postmodern Fiction," *Atlantic Monthly* (January 1980), p. 66. My readings in the "secular" theory of the postmodern are informed as well by Jean-François Lyotard, *La Condition postmoderne* (Paris: Minuit, 1979), by the essays in *The Anti-Esthetic: Essays on Postmodern Culture*, ed. Hal Foster (Port Townsend, WA: Bay Press, 1983) and by Stephen Watson, "Criticism and Closure of Modernism, *Sub-stance 42*, XIII, 1 (1984).

12. Jacques Derrida, "Differance," in *Speech and Phenomena and Other Essays on Husserl's Theory*, trans. David B. Allison (Evanston, IL: Northwestern University Press, 1973), pp. 142–43.

13. Jacques Derrida, "Hors Livre/Outwork" in *Dissemination*, trans. Barbara Johnson (Chicago: University of Chicago Press, 1981), p. 3.

14. Jean-François Lyotard, "Réponse à la question: Qu'est-ce que le postmoderne?" *Critique*, No. 419 (Apr. 1982), p. 367.

15. Jean-Paul Sartre, *La Nausée* (Paris: Livre de poche, n.d.) pp. 60-61. That this work performs a deconstruction of the novel, and very much in the mode prescribed by Lyotard, is not something which calls, in my view, for strenuous argument.

16. Jean-François Lyotard, "Réponse," p. 367.

17. Jean-Paul Sartre, *The Condemned of Altona*, trans. Sylvia and George Leeson (N. Y. Vintage 1960) pp. 177-178.

18. Ibid.

19. Jonathan Schell, *The Fate of the Earth*, p. 140.

20. Maurice Blanchot, *La Folie du jour/The Madness of the Day*, trans. Lydia Davis (New York: Station Hill, 1981), p. 6.

21. *Ibid.*, p. 18.

22. "Discussion, ou phraser après Auschwitz" in *Les Fins de l'homme: A partir du travail de Jacques Derrida* (Paris: Galilée, "Colloque de Cérisy," 1981), p. 289.

23. Maurice Blanchot, *Après Coup* (Paris: Minuit, 1983), pp. 98-99.

24. Robert Jay Lifton, *Death in Life: Survivors of Hiroshima* (New York: Random House, 1969), pp. 541–42, 526.

25. Theodor Adorno, *Negative Dialectics*, trans. E. B. Ashton (New York: Seabury Press, 1973), p. 362.

26. René Girard, *Des Choses cachées*, p. 112.

27. Jonathan Schell, *The Fate of the Earth*, p. 229.

28. Eric Gans, *The Origin of Language: A Formal Theory of Representation* (Berkeley: University of California Press, 1981), p. x. Gans's unduly neglected theory builds upon Girard's anthropological hypothesis, while according Derridean differance its due.

29. Jacques Derrida, "Plato's Pharmacy" in *Dissemination* and "Cogito and the History of Madness" in *Writing and Difference*, trans. Alan Bass (Chicago: University of Chicago Press, 1978).

30. Jacques Derrida, "Living On," *op. cit.*, p. 142, where Blanchot's "Arrêt de mort" is viewed as "the truth *about* truth, *on* truth, truth*less* truth *on* truth."

31. Cf. Eric Gans, "Scandal to the Jews, Folly to the Pagans," *Diacritics*, IX,3 (Fall, 1979) and "Le *logos* de René Girard" in *René Girard et le problème*

du mal, eds. Michel Deguy and Jean-Pierre Dupuy (Paris: Grasset, 1982), for the project in the human sciences which is opened up by Girard's hypothesis.

32. "After Christian truthfulness has drawn one inference after another, it must end by drawing its *most striking inference against* itself; this will happen, however, when it poses the question, '*what is the meaning of all will to truth?*'" Friedrich Nietzsche, *The Genealogy of Morals*, trans. Walter Kaufmann (New York: Vintage, 1967), p. 161.

33. Theodor Adorno, *Negative Dialectics*, p. 363.

34. Robert Jay Lifton, *Death in Life*, p. 528. Lifton is quoting another author, David Rawicz, on the Holocaust: "The only thing that matters, that *will* matter, is the integrity of witnesses."

35. *Ibid.*, p. 531.

18. Postmodernism's Short Letter, Philosophy's Long Farewell...

Wilhelm S. Wurzer

Heidegger's thinking marks the beginning of an 'ontological' exit from the logocentric apparatus of Western culture. This beginning evokes the speculative postmodernist mood of deconstruction, which emphasizes that a radical trembling can only come from the *outside*.[1] Postmodernist thinking, however, does not conceive the *outside* as the dialectic *other* of the inside. Its projective reading grants an attitude or tendency that breaks with the terrain of Hegel's idealistic and Adorno's neo-Marxist aesthetic dialectic. This essay focuses on postmodernist thinking with respect to the philosophic and cultural crisis of imagination.

The Western edifice of egocentrism is eroded when the *outside* is no longer employed as an infrastructural or superstructural model, that is, as an economic, political, or cultural phenomenon subjected to the reflexivity of a patriarchal impulse. Postmodernist thinking sketches the *outside* as a discontinuous image of contemporary culture which modern subjectivity is unable to illuminate. By inscribing the *outside* into the traces of *Ereignis*, *gram*, or *différance*, it begins to think in a manner that does not replicate the transcendental moorings of dialectics.

Derrida's deconstructive strategies, Foucault's genealogical discourse, Deleuze's schizo-analytic mode of thinking and Lyotard's concept of the postmodern condition (to mention a few of the postmodernist techniques) pave the way for a "plural style" of thinking that frees imagination from the anthropocentric legacy of metaphysics. Kant's desire to advance the freedom of reason by dislodging imagination from the spatial and temporal constraints of understanding is satisfied today by the narrative impulse to question representation radically. The marriage between philosophy and the transcendental ego in its a priori, a posteriori, transcendental, political, social, and economic manifestations has outlived its theoretical and practical usefulness. The individual subject who seems securely fastened to the conceptual "sitting-flesh" of the humanistic ideals of "excessive self-entanglement,"[2] is no more able to restore the voice of Descartes's *ego cogitans* to its pristine epistemic vitality than he seems willing to dwell poetically in the *city* of language for the price of losing what may already be lost – the self.

The displacement of subjectivity does not destroy the *inside* of being, not even the discursive representations of self-consciousness. Instead, deconstruction has all the characteristics of a *relève* (*eine Aufhebung*) of the *inside*, which is at the point of greatest proximity to *eine Lichtung* of the *outside*. What decentering rejects is precisely the dominance of oppositional philosophizing and dialectical ideologizing. It disrupts the continual logocentric spurning of subject against object, a spurning that purports to free subject from object but merely retains subject as object.

The intellectual audacity of deconstruction opens the field of thinking for a dialogical encounter between *inside* and *outside* and for a postmodernist dispersion of the self which does not correlate with the concealed transcendental relations of *Truth and Method*; rather, it points to a "change of terrain,"[3] notably a place where language lets thinking be and where thinking understands language in its openness. By pointing to a self that lies between *inside* and *outside*, language claims a "different" self, one that is not identical with the historically regional inside of self-consciousness.

The postmodernist mood, which affirms the negation of self-presence, recognizes the Kantian dilemma of "what to do with imagination" in the attempt to burst through the conceptual repressions of modern epistemology. It would be convenient to think that postmodernism in its speculative indeterminacy is free to escape from the ontotheological problems of philosophical discourse. In the attempt to be released from the epistemic constraints of transcendental apperception and the empirical overshadowing of objects (outside of appearances), imagination is still confined to *das freie Spiel* of subjective judgment. The subject may appear free from the cognitive operations of a transcendental analytic, but "it" is certainly not free from a subjective, dialectical state of knowledge even in the absence of the use of a concept. Imagination seems to find pleasure in what emerges as the aesthetic product of subjective judgment. The subject tends to dwell in a castle of subjectivity, free to glance at the open field of imagination, but not able to participate in *das Freie des Offenen*. This moderate freedom of imagination proclaims more of a critique of imagination than a critique of judgment. Imagination need not be guided by dialectic judgment; rather, aesthetic judgment need be inspired by a disseminating imagination in order to reinstate a mode of thinking that refuses to control *what* it is thinking.

Given this view, Kant's analysis of aesthetic taste deflects from the traditional method but not enough to question the legitimation of overseeing imagination from the egophanic perspectives of reflective judgment. The *Critique of Judgment* indicates that the Kantian turn of imagination (from the regional, transcendental sphere of understanding to the aesthetic space of reflective judgment) fails to reach the freedom of imagination conceived possible in imagination's own play of presence and absence. Instead, imagination extends itself to a supersensible, transcendental sphere in which a new limitation is determined for itself. This new limitation belongs to Kant's moral predilection and ineluctably supersedes the aesthetic project of freeing imagination from epistemic egocentrism. Kant's formal dialectic animated by a moral impulse transforms imagination's "free play" into teleological acts of judgment.

Every aspect of the postmodernist temper reveals the discontent that arises from the difficulty of overcoming Kant's intertranscendental, ultimately, moral displacements of imagination in the *Critique of Judgment*. Hence postmodernism sometimes emerges as a restless resident in the metaphysical house of modernity. As a new guest, who is weary of looking at the same old objects, postmodernism desires to write a short letter of gratitude to philosophy in view of "the necessity of a certain point of departure," notably, of subjectivity. In its technological twilight, subjectivity is not, as Habermas suggests, dead like modernism, but is, instead, admitted by postmodernism to the subversive destiny of thinking language as *differance*. *Écriture*, as thinking, is a new writing that weaves and interlaces the continuous and discontinuous motifs of philosophy's farewell. The radical trembling that can only come from the *outside* is now inscribed into the forgotten terrain of another *inside* "where" a nonconceptual reflection of the subject discloses a self-consciousness that is overshadowed by the *image-movement*[4] of thinking's playful itinerary.

As Heidegger's *Lichtung* makes possible Derrida's deconstructive critique of binary thinking, so *écriture* initiates the late postmodernist cultural current[5] of the self as *filming*. From the perspectives of *filming*, the self is revealed as a process of images that gathers the "structural" image-movements of *inside* and *outside*, the political, social, economic, and cultural changes of production without manipulating these changes ontotheologically. The postmodern condition of *filming* points to human apperception as imagination infinitely at work in the discontinuous process of relating understanding to reason within postindustrial discursive practices.

The technological destiny of being, which reflects contemporary Western culture, is challenged by imagination's freedom from the *mythos* of philosophy's idiom, the white mythology of Reason. The task of thinking is to measure this new freedom and to avoid the possible hazards of imagination's "free play" with time. Thinking must confront the egocentric continuity disclosed in certain modes of technological developments, in particular, the effects of the military imagination. The power structures of late capitalism and diverse socialism exploit the creative freedom of imagination by subjecting the play of signifiers to the futural signified of nuclear dissemination. These immoderate political games of imagination my result in negative possibilities when imagination is released from the custody of the transcendental signified. However, these military escapades should not prevent us from affirming imagination in a Dionysian sense; nor, should they lead us to disregard the *vigil* of thinking in relation to the nuclear shadow of the metaphysical network.

I turn now more concretely to the postmodern transgression of the thinking self. How may imagination be diverted from the transcendental direction of the subjective *Verstand/Vernunft* interplay? I have already alluded to the invagination of *ego cogitans* into the image-movements of imagination and into the play of being that gathers, inevitably, in a constellation of word and music, the profuse images of temporality. Thus, *filming* may appropriately characterize the diffuse movements of the self within the artistic postmodern destiny of imagination.

Filming, in our strategic naming, does not primarily belong to the technical-functional structures of cinematography, nor to the more conspicuous ontic practices of producing, acting, and directing. A postontological reading of the postmodern mood suggests that *filming* may be related to imagination's perverse elegance of delightfully reaching *out* to the *outside* of the ecstasies of time. Thus, I briefly search for some traces of the subject fading into image-movements of past, present, and future in the luminous process of *filming*. These reflections are merely preliminary.

The historical actuality of photography and film is culturally more "enlightening" when it is viewed in the proximity of postmodern transformations of epistemology. A traditional epistemic dominance of master narratives (*grand récit*), if it were continued, would only distort the production and reproduction of images. The postmodern mode of thinking, however, rejects philosophy's protracted contempt for the priority of images over *Begriff.* And it fails to acclaim a self whose being is readily present and defined in modern theories of society, religion, and science; instead, it accentuates a self that may not even know its "being."

Filming, which should not be confined to instrumental, ideological, profitable functions or any other ontic interests, projects a schizophrenic constellation of images. While "inscribing" the self and image-movements in the *aletheia* of imagination, it affirms a Dionysian breakdown of the relationship between signifiers. *Filming shows a signifier that has lost its signified and has thereby been transformed into an image.* The self *was* such a signifier; now, the self *is* such an image. Thus, the scene of the self has moved away from it-self. Ob-scenity emerges.[6]

Filming may put an end to metaphysical representations. Its "ob-scenity" reveals the *glissement* of the self in imagination's "free play" wherein the self is not thought to be losing time so much as being-lost-in-time. The self as a rapidly fading concept "exists" as a collage of images that does not proceed from past to present into future, nor simply in a circle, unless this circle reveals an eclipse of the self alongside the inside/outside image-movements of difference within repetition. Neither as appearance nor as noumenon will a self be found in the perceptions, actions, and emotions of image-movements; neither as theoretical nor as practical will a self emerge in the late capitalist flow of images; neither as fetish nor as commodity of the postindustrial age will the self appear.

Nevertheless, a self may still be there: Conceivably, in *filming* in which Dasein enables viewer, director, producer, writer, actor, and critic to see, make, write, and reflect upon a montage of images. More than a self, however, it is *filming* that exists. To amplify Godard's statement: "*Je pense, donc le cinéma existe.*"[7] The postmodern impulse to participate in imagination's play of philosophy's farewell discloses a unique mode of *filming* that conceptual directors of metaphysics have failed to consider even in the critical moments of high modernity. A "filmic" dissemination of the self may provide fruitful metonymic modes of reflection on contemporary culture. Such modes may suggest that *filming* "reinstate" the "being" of postmodern *Dasein.*

In formulating the process of *filming,* it is important not to epistemologize the "releasing of imagination's own intrinsic (traditional) reflexivity."[8] As Derrida notes: "The continuous process of making (a subject matter; in this case, the *matter* of the *subject*) explicit, moving toward an opening, risks sinking into the autism of closure."[9] I hope that the transgression from *ego cogitans* to *filming* is not interpreted as a "false exit" from philosophy but rather what Derrida calls "a question of anonymous necessity."[10] The effects of a radical trembling do not lie in another hermeneutic relation of *filming* and *Lichtung*. This relation does not impute to postmodernism an epistemology or social theory with renewed metaphysical traps. Unlike representational thinking, *filming* offers an understanding of *Dasein* that sees the traces of past and future in a present that is no longer present to representation, yet "present" to the absence of transcendental limitations of imagination.

In the absence-presence of imagination, *filming* lets a fleeting self emerge that "sustains" the identity and difference of images. Lyotard gives a concise description of this process: "A self does not amount to much, but no self is an island; each exists in a fabric of relations that is now more complex and mobile than ever before."[11] Heidegger also examines the identity-difference problem of the self in his delimiting ontology without specifically relating the question of imagination to a nondialectic mode of thinking. Derrida develops this mode of thought through the openness of *écriture*, which invites a narrative reading of the vanishing self that may be thought in terms of a "filming" occlusion of imagination. Such an occlusion replaces "Kant's turn toward (aesthetic) subjectivity with a (postmodern) turn toward the play of images."[12] Hence, a "filmic" self is revealed as attending to past and future images amidst the fleeting moments of the present and as yielding to fading moments of past and future in the absence of radical self-presence. The texture of relations between the outside/inside image-movements of the self is, indeed, what one American philosopher calls, "a play of occlusion," if by occlusion we understand "the absorption of the intelligible to the sensible and the collapse of metaphysical distinctions."[13]

In dismantling subjectivity, postmodernism transcends the subject-object polarity and projects a filming of the self which displaces the logocentric images of understanding within imagination's play of absence and presence. In this essay we have only begun to think the *outside* from the infinite image-movements of imagination's "free play," "thereby inhabiting more naïvely and more strictly than ever the *inside* one declares one has deserted."[14]

The irony of the eros of *filming* does not issue in a new determination of the intelligible. On the contrary, the possibilities of *filming* reveal that "images in their play are also turned toward something they image, and in turning toward images, one inevitably passes through them in such fashion as in the end to be turned away from them."[15] John Sallis briefly alludes to the obstruction of postmodernism in general and *filming* in particular when he writes:

> The metaphysical distinction between intelligible and sensible is radically displaced, decisively unsettled, by the turn to the play of imaging, for in that play there is incessant opening and closing of the distance between the tradition, since its beginning in the Platonic dialogues, and what has been thematized as intelligible and sensible. The play of imaging is nothing but the play of occlusion itself.[16]

Nothing seems to escape this play – a play that must still be articulated within the space of thinking and *filming*. Within this space, one may question postmodernism's dissolution of the subject primarily because postmodernism shows that "we are both too much within and too much without metaphysics."[17]

Notes

1. Jacques Derrida, "The Ends of Man," in *Margins of Philosophy*, trans. Alan Bass (Chicago: University of Chicago Press, 1982), p. 134. (Henceforth cited as *Margins*.)

2. F. R. Dallmayr, *Twilight of Subjectivity* (Amherst: Massachusetts Institute of Technology Press, 1983), p. 134.

3. Jacques Derrida, *Margins*, p. 135.

4. See Gilles Deleuze, *Cinema 1, L'Image-Mouvement* (Paris: Minuit, 1983). Despite Deleuze's unique clarification of film's images and signs, he does not examine the postmodern relation of the self and *filming*.

5. Jürgen Habermas, "Modernity – An Incomplete Project," in *The Anti-Aesthetic: Essays on Postmodern Culture*, ed. Hal Foster (Port Townsend, WA: Bay Press, 1983).

6. See Jean Baudrillard, "Ecstasy of Communication," in *The Anti-Aesthetic*, p. 130.

7. See Timothy Corrigan, *The Displaced Image* (Austin: University of Texas Press, 1983).

8. John Sallis, *The Gathering of Reason* (Athens: Ohio University Press, 1980).

9. Jacques Derrida, *Margins*, p. 135.

10. *Ibid.*, p. 134.

11. Jean-François Lyotard, *The Postmodern Condition: A Report on Knowledge* (Minneapolis: University of Minnesota Press, 1984) p. 15: "Le soi est peu, mais il n'est pas isolé, il est pris dans une texture de relations plus complexe et plus mobile que jamais."

12. John Sallis, "Immateriality and the Play of Imagination," in American Catholic Philosophic Association Proceedings, L11, p. 74.

13. *Ibid.*, p. 65.

14. Jacques Derrida, *Margins*, p. 135.

15. John Sallis, "Immateriality and the Play of Imagination," in ACPA Proceedings, L11 p. 74.

16. *Ibid.*, p. 75.

17. *Ibid.*, p. 65.

Contributors

DEBORAH CHAFFIN is Assistant Professor of Philosophy at San Diego State University. Her publications include "Edmund Husserl's *The Apodicticity of Recollection*: An Introduction and Translation," *Husserl Studies* (1985), "Passion and the Ethic of Empowerment," *Cardozo Law Review* (1985), "Hegel, Derrida and the Sign," *Continental Philosophy-II* (forthcoming 1988) and a translation of Ludwig Landgrebe's "The Life-World and Historicity of Human Existence," *Research in Phenomenology* (1981).

MARTIN DILLON is Associate Professor of Philosophy at the State University of New York at Binghamton. He is author of *Merleau-Ponty's Ontology* (Indiana University Press, forthcoming) and more than two dozen articles on Merleau-Ponty, Sartre, Nietzsche, and phenomenological accounts of love and sexuality. Among the more well-known are "Toward a Phenomenology of Love and Sexuality," *Soundings* (1980), "Love, Death and Creation," *Research in Phenomenology* (1981), "Merleau-Ponty and the Reversibility Thesis," *Man and World* (1983), and "Sex, Time, and Love: Erotic Temporality," *Journal of Phenomenological Psychology* (1987).

BARBARA FREEMAN is Lecturer in Western Culture and Feminist Studies at Stanford University. She is completing a doctorate in the History of Consciousness Program at the University of California, Santa Cruz with a thesis on Anglo-American and French Feminist Theory.

GARTH GILLAN is Professor of Philosophy at Southern Illinois University at Carbondale. He is author of *From Sign to Symbol* (Humanities/Harvester, 1982), co-author of *Michel Foucault: Social Theory as Transgression* (Columbia University Press, 1982), and editor of *The Horizons of the Flesh: Critical Perspectives on the Thought of Merleau-Ponty* (Southern Illinois University, 1973).

DALIA JUDOVITZ is Assistant Professor of French at the University of California at Berkeley. She has taught at the University of Pennsylvania and Duke University and is author of *Subjectivity and Representation: The Origins of Modern Thought in Descartes* (Cambridge University Press, 1987). Her many articles include topics such as "The Question of Interpretation in Freud," *Sub-Stance* (1979), "Descartes and Autobiography," *Philosophy and Literature* (1982), "Figure and Writing in J-L Schefer," *Sub-Stance* (1983), and "Philosophy and Literature in Plato and Descartes" in *Literature and the Question of Philosophy* (Johns Hopkins, 1987).

DAVID FARRELL KRELL is Senior Lecturer and Chairman of the Department of Philosophy at the University of Essex in England. He is author of *Intimations of Mortality: Time, Truth, and Finitude in Heidegger's Thinking of Being* (Pennsylvania State University Press, 1986) and *Postponements: Woman, Sensuality, and Death in Nietzsche* (Indiana University Press, 1986). He is also translator of a number of Heidegger's writings.

JULIA KRISTEVA is Professor of Linguistics in the Department of Texts and Documents at the University of Paris-VII (Jussieu). She has been a regular Visiting Professor at Columbia University and serves on the Editorial Board of *Tel Quel* and *Semiotica*. Of her many books, those translated into English include *On Chinese Women* (1977), *Desire in Language* (1980), *Revolution in Poetic Language* (1984), *Powers of Horror* (1984), and *Tales of Love* (1987).

ALPHONSO LINGIS is Professor of Philosophy at the Pennsylvania State University. He is author of *Excesses: Eros and Culture* (1983), *Phenomenological Explanations* (1986), and translator of Merleau-Ponty's *The Visible and the Invisible* (1968), and Levinas' *Totality and Infinity* (1979) and *Otherwise than Being or Beyond Essence* (1981).

CHRISTIE MCDONALD is Professor of French at the Université de Montréal, Quebec, Canada. She has also taught in and chaired the Department of Modern Languages at Emory University. She is author of *The Extravagant Shepherd, The Dialogue of Writing* (1984), and *Dispositions* (1986) as well as editor of *The Ear of the Other: Otobiography, Transference, Translation* (Texts and Discussions with Jacques Derrida) (Schocken, 1985).

ANDREW J. MCKENNA is Professor of French at Loyola University of Chicago. He is author of numerous articles including "History of the Ear: Ideology and Poetic Deconstruction," *Centrum* (1975), "Mass Media: Flaubert and the Art of Nihilism," *Enclitic* (1977), "Biblioclasm: Joycing Jesus and Borges," *Diacritics* (1978), and "Bibliocalsm: Derrida and his Precursors," *Visible Language* (1979). He is also guest editor of *Semeia*, no. 33 on "Rene Girard and Biblical Criticism" (1985).

JOHN O'NEILL is Distinguished Research Professor of Sociology at York University in Downsview, Ontario, Canada. He is author of many books and articles, among them are *Perception, Expression and History* (Northwestern, 1970), *Sociology as a Skin Trade* (Harper and Row, 1972), *Making Sense Together* (Harper and Row, 1974), *Essaying Montaigne* (Routledge and Kegan Paul, 1982), *Five Bodies: The Human Shape of Modern Society* (Cornell, 1985). He has also translated Merleau-Ponty's *The Prose of the World* and *Themes from the Lectures*.

DOROTHEA OLKOWSKI is Assistant Professor of Philosophy at the College of Charleston (South Carolina). She has taught at the University of Nevada, Reno and the University of San Diego and is author of "Merleau-Ponty's Freudianism," *Review of Existential Psychology and Psychiatry* (1985), "If the Shoe Fits: Heidegger and Derrida" in *Hermeneutics and Deconstruction* (SUNY, 1985), and "Art and the Orientation of Thought," *Research in Phenomenology* (1987).

ALAN D. SCHRIFT is Assistant Professor of Philosophy at Grinnell College. He is author of various articles on Nietzsche, Heidegger, Sartre, and Derrida including "Reading, Writing, Text: Nietzsche's Deconstruction of Author-ity," *International Studies in Philosophy* (1985), "Language, Metaphor, Rhetoric: Nietzsche's Deconstruction of Epistemology," *Journal of the History of Philosophy* (1985), and "Reading Derrida Reading Heidegger Reading Nietzsche," *Research in Phenomenology* (1984).

RICHARD TAFT is Research Fellow in the Department of Philosophy, Trinity College, Hartford, CT. He has taught at Loyola University in Chicago and published articles such as "Art and Philosophy in the Early Development of Hegel's System" in the *Owl of Minerva* and "Style and the Post-Metaphysical Project," (1985) "Transgressions," (1984) and "Various Tunings of Thinking" (1983) in *Research in Phenomenology*.

CRAIG VASEY is Assistant Professor in the Department of Classics, Philosophy and Religion at Mary Washington College in Fredericksburg, Virginia. He has also taught at the University of Maryland at Baltimore and Purdue University. He has published "Le probleme de l'intentionalité dans la phénoménologie de Emmanuel Lévinas," *Revue de Métaphysique et de Morale* (1980), "Le corps et l'autre," *Exercises de la Patience* (1980), and "Emmanuel Lévinas: From Intentionality to Proximity," *Philosophy Today* (1981).

DICK WHITE teaches Philosophy at both the University of San Diego and San Diego State University in California. He studied at the University of Warwick and received his doctorate from SUNY at Stony Brook. His forthcoming articles include "The Individual and *The Birth of Tragedy*," *The British Journal of Aesthetics*, "Hume's *Dialogues* and the Comedy of Religion," *Hume Studies*, and "Nietzsche contra Kant and the Problem of Autonomy," *International Studies in Philosophy.*

WILHELM S. WURZER is Associate Professor of Philosophy at Duquesne University. He is author of *Spinoza und Nietzsche* (Hain Verlag, 1975) and several articles including "Nietzsche's Dialectic of Intellectual Integrity," *The Southern Journal of Philosophy* (1975), "Nietzsche's Return to an Aesthetic Beginning," *Man and World* (1978), "Heidegger's Problem of the 'Hermeneutic Who'," *Dialogos* (1980), "Nietzsche's Theory of Hermeneutic *Redlichkeit*," *J.B.S.P.* (1983), and "Heidegger and Lacan: On the Occlusion of the Subject" in *Horizons of Continental Philosophy* (Nijhoff, 1987).

IRIS MARION YOUNG is Associate Professor of Philosophy at Worcester Polytechnic Institute in Worcester, MA. Her articles include "Throwing Like a Girl: A Phenomenology of Feminine Body Comportment, Motility and Spatiality," *Human Studies* (1980), "Pregnant Subjectivity and Alienation," *The Journal of Medicine and Philosophy* (1984), "Humanism, Gynocentrism, and Feminist Politics," *Hypatia* (1985), and "Pregnant Subjectivity and the Limits of Existential Phenomenology" in *Descriptions* (SUNY Press, 1985).

About the Editors

HUGH J. SILVERMAN is Professor of Philosophy and Comparative Literature at the State University of New York at Stony Brook. Author of *Inscriptions: Between Phenomenology and Structuralism* (Routledge and Kegan Paul, 1987), editor of *Piaget, Philosophy and the Human Sciences* (Humanities, 1980), coeditor of *Jean-Paul Sartre: Contemporary Approaches to his Philosophy* (Duquesne, 1980), *Continental Philosophy in America* (Duquesne, 1983), *Descriptions* (SUNY, 1985), *Hermeneutics and Deconstruction* (SUNY, 1985), general editor of *Horizons of Continental Philosophy* (Nijhoff, 1987) and translator of various works by Merleau-Ponty, he is editor of a new series published by Routledge and Kegan Paul entitled *Continental Philosophy.* He has taught at Stanford University, has been visiting professor at New York University and Duquesne University, and visiting senior lecturer at the University of Warwick (England) and the University of Nice (France). He served as Executive Co-Director of the Society for Phenomenology and Existential Philosophy for six years (1980–86) and is currently Executive Director of the International Association for Philosophy and Literature.

DONN WELTON is Associate Professor of Philosophy and Departmental Chair at the State University of New York at Stony Brook. He received his Ph.D. from Southern Illinois University at Carbondale. He is author of *The Origins of Meaning: A Critical Study of the Thresholds of Husserlian Phenomenology* (Nijhoff Publishers, 1983) and editor of a collection of essays by Ludwig Landgrebe entitled *The Phenomenology of Edmund Husserl* (Cornell University Press, 1981). He was Executive Co-Director of the Society for Phenomenology and Existential Philosophy for three years (1983–86).

Index